THE COLOR OF
ABOLITION

THE COLOR OF
ABOLITION

— ◆ —

How a Printer, a Prophet, and a
Contessa Moved a Nation

Linda Hirshman

MARINER BOOKS
Boston   New York

marinerbooks.com

Library of Congress Cataloging-in-Publication Data has been applied for.
ISBN 978-1-328-90024-1

Book design by Helene Berinsky

Printed in the United States of America
1 2021
4500845210

This book is dedicated to friends Elie Mystal and Keli Goff.
For sharing.

And to the legions of historians, amateur and academic.
For the shoulders to stand on.

CONTENTS

PART III: THE GRAND ALLIANCE AT WORK

PART IV: DOUGLASS TO THE POLITICAL SIDE

PART V: DOUGLASS AND GARRISON DIVIDE

AUTHOR'S NOTE

I WRITE ABOUT SOCIAL MOVEMENTS: THOSE MOMENTS when people act collectively to change their shared world. No social movement in American history matters more than abolition. Slavery was the mortal sin of the American republic. Abolition was the movement to end slavery. It was, like all movements, incomplete. But as my teacher the legendary historian David Brion Davis taught me along with generations of American students, abolition was an astonishing historical achievement, and a crucial landmark of moral progress.

Since the first slave ship landed in Virginia in 1619, there have been movements to resist. Quaker antislavery protest goes back to 1688. Major slave rebellions marked the 1700s. Throughout the early years of the republic, Black activists, fugitive and free, agitated for abolition in the slave states and equality in the free. The social forces reached an inflection point in 1830, when the Black writer David Walker's incendiary *Appeal to the Coloured Citizens of the World, but in Particular, and Very Expressly, to Those of the United States of America* crossed the desk of white printer William Lloyd Garrison. The modern abolition movement lasted from that point roughly until Juneteenth in 1865.

As the historian David Blight said in the introduction to his magisterial *Frederick Douglass: Prophet of Freedom*, "Context and timing are often all." When I finally gathered the courage to take on this most important social movement, a lively and painful conversation about the possibility and conditions of an interracial alliance was taking place all around me in the here and now. From 1841 to 1853, the movement benefited immeasurably from the alliance of Garrison and the fugitive slave, then free man, Frederick Douglass. Until it didn't. Although abolition, like the Civil War, is the subject of an abundance of study, vision, revision, and re-revision, there was not a lot of writing about the Garrison–Douglass alliance so central to the movement.

This story seemed to me worthy of a telling in itself, and also as a window into the larger contemporary question of interracial alliance. Ultimately, the story reflects the focus of all of my work: How did the movement, the abolitionist movement in this case, succeed? The social movement of abolition went from publisher Garrison, who could not pay his newsprint bill when he opened the modern era with the first issue of *The Liberator* in 1831, to the Emancipation Proclamation little more than three decades later, a mere moment in the timetable of social change. Historian Eric Foner set the table for the inquiry into abolition's success for more than a generation of scholars with his study of the cultural and economic forces that pulled the North away from the slave empire. But in seeking the how, I was looking for the mechanics of activism—the meetings, the speeches, the broadsides, the litigation—for my analysis. And Garrison and Douglass were both central to the mechanics of activism. Their alliance fueled critical years of the movement, and their breakup affected the direction of the movement profoundly. This was the project I started.

And then the history gods gave me the ultimate gift: a key player who had never been the subject of a full biography and an archive full of her letters. Meet Maria Weston Chapman, the power beside the throne of Garrison's abolition organization, variously "the Contessa" and "Lady Macbeth." (A woman after my own heart.) Weston Chapman (along with her five sisters) wrote so many letters it's a miracle she had the time to run major portions of the abolitionist movement. Other activists, recognizing her epistolary inclination and the fact that she was really running the show much of the time, also wrote to Maria. The hundreds of letters are online, thanks Clio, as the libraries were mostly closed for this history in the Plague Years. Locked down during the plague, I was able to spend endless hours scrutinizing the illegible handwritten missives, often overwritten at right angles, to squeeze in more text and save on postage.

When I first spotted Maria Weston Chapman, I thought I had hit feminist research gold, a female hero whose gender had obscured her importance. And that is definitely part of the story. At some social sacrifice, she had run the bazaars that funded Garrison's operation for many years, organized the petitions that were the first wave of mass public engagement, and ghosted his newspaper when Garrison was AWOL.

But a closer examination of her letters revealed an ugly downside to her story: she was a prime mover in driving Frederick Douglass out. In a perfect storm of intersectionality, the wealthy, fashionable Contessa added the issue of class to the already fraught alliance across the line of race. Unsurprisingly, she and her Brahmin friends and relatives brought with them — *into the abolitionist movement* — the casual racism of the privileged class. What started out as an analysis of the interracial duo turned into a threesome, as the forces of race and class combined to catapult Frederick Douglass out. The letters were then and are now shocking.

The shameful history that led to the breakup is the bitter story. The sweet story is how the breakup of the interracial cross-class alliance put Frederick Douglass right where the action was. In an opposite response to the Boston branch's behavior, the New York factions of abolition, which had long since separated from Garrison's shop, extended open arms. "Welcome to New York," white upstate abolition leader Gerrit Smith wrote when Douglass transferred his base from Massachusetts to Rochester. He promptly gave Douglass a piece of land, part of his crafty initiative to help Black voters meet the racist property requirements for voting. Smith's unreserved outreach to Douglass is the very model of successful interracial cooperation. The Smith–Douglass alliance also allowed me to tell the story of how new legal thinking and overt political organizing — the hallmarks of New York abolition — came to the forefront of the movement and powered its last, successful decade to the election of 1860.

Douglass's support for those novel and contested initiatives meant the world to the new movement. In 1865 he went to Washington and helped the Chief Justice put on his robes for the second inauguration of Abraham Lincoln.

INTRODUCTION: MEETING ON NANTUCKET
August 11, 1841

ON A HOT NIGHT IN AUGUST 1841, fugitive slave Frederick Douglass stood before a thousand white people inside a rickety wooden building in Nantucket, Massachusetts. A handful of Black people appeared in the crowd, but the group looked like a sea of white to Douglass. "Accustomed to consider white men as my bitterest enemies," he later recalled, he trembled as he prepared to address them.

Not three years had passed since he had escaped from enslavement in Maryland. "There is no spot on the vast domains over which waves the star-spangled banner where the slave is secure," Douglass would later explain. "Go east, go west, go north, go south, he is still exposed to the blood-

Nantucket Atheneum, where Douglass first spoke. *Original illustration on paper by Mr. Samuel Haynes Jenks, ca. 1844. Courtesy of The Nantucket Atheneum.*

hounds that may be let loose against him." No fugitive slave was safe in the United States—not even at an abolitionist convention.

And yet Douglass felt he had no choice about speaking up. He was already part of the movement that ran on words. His host, Quaker William Coffin, had brought him to this meeting of the Massachusetts Anti-Slavery Society after hearing Douglass speak at a Black church in New Bedford. "Tell your story, Frederick," Coffin urged Douglass now, as the abolitionists waited. The strikingly handsome man—strong chin, chiseled mouth, and wide-set eyes—usually dressed in a waistcoat, formal jacket, and high-collared white shirt, rose reluctantly to his feet.

Douglass never could remember what it was he said that evening.

Only the need for adjournment ended his debut appearance. The next day he was immediately invited to resume and spoke at even greater length. Although journalists from various antislavery publications attended the conference, there is no record of Douglass's remarks. But the reporters in the room agreed on one thing: Douglass brought down the house. "Flinty hearts were pierced," Lydia Maria Child reported for the abolitionist newspaper *National Anti-Slavery Standard,* "and cold ones melted by his eloquence. Our best pleaders for the slave held their breath for fear of interrupting him." Later, after Douglass had made countless speeches for the antislavery movement, some speculated that he might have performed one of his signature darkly humorous riffs that night in Nantucket, perhaps imitating a southern clergyman giving a self-righteous sermon about the virtues of slavery. He might even have resorted to song, warbling, "Come saints and sinners, hear me tell,/How pious priests whip Jack and Nell,/And women buy and children sell,/Then preach all sinners down to hell,/And sing of heavenly union."

There is no scarcity of reportage about what came after Douglass's speech. William Lloyd Garrison, white editor and printer of the antislavery paper *The Liberator* and, at age thirty-five, the most prominent leader of the ten-year-old abolitionist movement, stood up to respond. As an orator, Garrison would certainly not equal Douglass, but at the time he was renowned in the antislavery movement. Never again would he rouse a crowd as he did after hearing Frederick Douglass for the first time that night.

"Have we been listening to a thing?" Garrison asked the crowd gathered in the Nantucket Atheneum. "A piece of property, or to a man?"

"A man! A man!" hundreds of voices replied.

"And should such a man be held as a slave in a republican and Christian land?" Garrison continued, his voice rising.

"No, no! Never, never!"

But it was 1841. Abolition seemed a distant prospect at best. So Garrison asked the only question his audience could actually do something about immediately.

"Shall such a man ever be sent back to slavery from the old soil of Massachusetts?"

"No, no!"

As the crowd shouted its refusal to send men back to slavery, Garrison reminded them of why they amplified their cry.

"No! A thousand times no! Sooner the lightnings of heaven blast Bunker Hill monument till not one stone shall be left standing on another."

Garrison's reference to Bunker Hill was no accident. The battle, fought in the hills outside Boston in 1775, was one of the first engagements of the American Revolution. The rebellious colonists at Bunker Hill lost but inflicted unexpected losses on the superior forces of empire. An improbable and outnumbered ragtag army fighting for human freedom, the Americans of 1775 provide a poignant metaphor for the abolitionists. Birthed in freedom and enforcing slavery, America was cracked at the root. The abolitionists would argue countless times: if all men are created equal, then in the land of Bunker Hill, the man Frederick Douglass should never have been enslaved.

As soon as the meeting ended, John A. Collins, theology school dropout and now vice president and general agent for Garrison's Massachusetts Anti-Slavery Society, invited the newcomer to become an antislavery agent. Douglass would travel to the gatherings throughout eastern Massachusetts — a lifeline in the small and beleaguered abolition movement in 1841 — and tell his story.

Although she was not present at Douglass's maiden appearance on Nantucket, Maria Weston Chapman, the beautiful, wealthy Bostonian from a prominent abolitionist family who de facto ran the Society office, would manage much of his new career. Weston Chapman—nicknamed "the Contessa" by one of her admirers—was perhaps Garrison's closest comrade. Since the gorgeously dressed socialite had shocked people in the modest abolition world by walking into a meeting in 1834, her fashionable Boston town house had become the beating heart of the Society that fueled the movement.

The meeting on that remote Massachusetts island in August 1841 was a snapshot of the movement for the abolition of slavery. At the center of the picture was the fugitive, with his indelible story of life in the slave South —the inexcusable wrongdoing at the heart of the American republic. The historian Manisha Sinha would later call these stories "the movement literature of abolition." Then, the audience of white northerners, who had been gathering for over a decade to argue for the immediate, unambiguous abolition of slavery. Here and there, an embarrassingly few, but crucial, Black abolitionists, who had formed the backbone of the movement from the beginning. The action centered on Douglass's "heart-piercing" speech, reflecting the outsized power of rhetoric. The scene opened up the possibility of an alliance interracial and sex-integrated at the very top—the first such major public movement in the history of the nation. For twelve years this alliance worked to change the nation.

But as with all alliances, sooner or later the question would arise: Who gets what from the deal?

This is what breaks up alliances, however fruitful the collaboration. By 1853, the partnership of Garrison, Douglass, and Weston Chapman was done. The creation, duration, and impact of their alliance to abolish slavery is the subject of this book.

The strains on the interracial aspect of the enterprise of Douglass and the mostly white New England abolitionists were visible already in Nantucket. Later, when Douglass was the most popular and renowned speaker in a movement that lived on words, his appearance that night in 1841 became a legend. At the time, however, Garrison took only passing notice of the slave's debut in *The Liberator,* not even giving Douglass the dignity of using his proper name. "Messrs. Bradburn, Collins, Quincy, Pillsbury, Whiting, and other speakers were present, (among them several talented colored young men from New-Bedford, one of them formerly a slave),"

Garrison reported, "whose addresses were listened to by large and attentive audiences with deep interest."

Garrison's foundational abolitionist newspaper survived only because of the support of free Black subscribers in the early 1830s. His original Massachusetts Anti-Slavery Society took shape in 1832 in the basement of a Black meetinghouse. The national American Anti-Slavery Society which he helped found in 1833 also started in the meeting hall of a Black society, this time in Philadelphia. Less than a decade later, his patronizing report of his first meeting with Douglass—and the other nameless "colored young men"—serves as a warning that there was already weakness in the foundation.

Douglass had subscribed to *The Liberator* since arriving in New Bedford two years earlier, in 1839. Like many of the abolitionist paper's supporters, he came into the fold through a network of free Black people, subscription agents who sold the paper, and the promise of liberation, all over the North. Douglass's weekly editions of *The Liberator* were the living signs that he was not alone in his resistance. There is no record of his reaction to Garrison's slight in the August 20 edition, but there is also little chance that Douglass failed to notice it. Douglass was always clear on how he should be treated.

As a subscriber to *The Liberator*, Douglass also had to know he was signing on not to abolition in general but to the radical Boston faction of the abolitionist movement. Until 1840, the united movement had had a robust presence in both Boston and New York City as well as upstate. Unlike the Boston group, both New York branches were led by wealthy churchgoing merchants who came to abolition through their religious and charitable commitments. A year before the Nantucket meeting, the movement had split after the Garrisonians squared off against all institutions that tolerated slavery: churches, the government. The last straw for the conservative New York factions was that the Garrisonians had insisted on including women like Maria Weston Chapman and Quaker abolitionist Abby Kelley to help lead the movement.

By 1841, the clergy and more socially conservative New Yorkers had seceded fully and established the breakaway American and Foreign Anti-Slavery Society. The conservatives stood by the churches, excluding

women from their efforts. In what turned out to be a radical stance, however, they also stood by the government, organizing a political movement
and a legal strategy for taking over the government for abolition rather
than withdrawing from it. They started a nascent political operation, the
Liberty Party. *The Liberator* was consumed with the fracas; by 1844, Garrison added the phrase "No Union with Slaveholders"—aimed directly at
the political activists—to the masthead.

In the summer of 1841, then, Douglass joined Garrison and Weston
Chapman in the sex-integrated, anti-government Massachusetts Anti-Slavery Society faction. Their relationship raises all the questions of
whether an alliance across race, sex, and class can survive. The answer is
unsurprisingly yes. And no. Their paths to abolition reflected the rise of
the movement. Their alliance fueled a crucial decade. And their breakup,
sending Douglass to the politicos, perversely led to its triumph.

PART I

---◆---

ALLIES ARISE

1

(1805–1828)

Printer Garrison Learns His Trade

Orphaned by Poverty

WILLIAM LLOYD GARRISON TURNED THREE IN 1808, the year his father, Abijah, left. At the time, Newburyport, Massachusetts, where Abijah had moved the family from Nova Scotia, was in an economic depression caused by the American boycott of European trade during the Napoleonic Wars. Abijah, who had worked his way up to sailing master before the embargo, could find no employment in the struggling sea trade. His four children were so hungry his little daughter ate a spring shrub that turned out to be poisonous and died in agony. The remaining three were all still under seven, and the Garrison family was living in a few rooms in a boardinghouse of exemplary piety. Abijah turned to drink and then, in a cloud of alcohol fumes, disappeared.

The embargo also ruined Massachusetts sea captain Warren Weston, living in Weymouth with his wife and oldest child, William Lloyd Garrison's contemporary Maria, then two. Unlike Abijah Garrison, Weston, also a drinker, stuck around.

It is hard to know which woman was worse off. On the one hand, Maria Weston's mother, Ann Bates Weston, with her husband still around, kept having babies. Frances Maria Lloyd Garrison (most often called Maria), on the other hand, was left alone and nearly destitute. The Garrison family lived off the charity of church and soup kitchens, of Maria Garrison's occasional employers, and of the maritime associations in that stricken shipping town.

The female-headed Garrison family was lucky in one way: years before,

Maria had converted to become a Baptist. Their landlady in Newburyport, Martha Farnham, was one of the most important Baptists in the little town, and she extended to her unlucky boarders charitable Baptist principles.

The nameless itinerant Baptist preacher who, sometime in the 1790s, had attracted the passionate attention of young Frances Maria Lloyd in her childhood home in maritime Canada could not have known the effect he would have on American history. He was part of a wave of ministers outside formal church buildings who brought a renewed Christian message to North Americans hungry for some Good News. Standing in a tent on the Canadian 'Quoddy Islands, young Maria heard that she could make a conscious choice to repent and embrace Christ. She felt that her soul was transformed. The new religion taught her that she was free to change her life, to embark on a new life, to transform the world into a better place fit for the Second Coming.

Maria Lloyd had certainly never had a similar religious experience at her parents' Anglican church in the area, where establishment religions preached that people had little say about their own salvation or the state of the world. But the new religions made the converted the lead actor in the drama of his or her own redemption and the redemption of the world. Maria converted, defying her parents, who then sent her away to live with her grandparents. But Maria Lloyd was born again—a Baptist for life. When she met co-religionist Abijah Garrison a couple of years later, she was speaking in the meeting tents and teaching Sunday school. In 1798 she married him.

The Second Great Awakening, White and Black

Maria Lloyd was in good company. As Sidney Ahlstrom lays out in his magisterial *Religious History of the American People*, from approximately 1790 to 1830, millions of Americans living all across New England, into the mid-Atlantic states, upstate New York, the new territories of the Western Reserve, later Ohio, and most of all in Kentucky, experienced the religious revival that came to be known as the Second Great Awakening. Baptists joined Methodists, the other burgeoning denomination, to reinvent Christianity in America.

It was time for reinvention. The population was growing and moving. Baptists and Methodists had a long tradition of traveling preachers with no established building, often meeting in tents. The tradition worked to their advantage when it came to converting the West, where there were no established church buildings. Baptists and Methodists also shared a creed of individual responsibility, disputing the old Calvinist idea that you were predestined for heaven or hell no matter what you did. Soon, denominational lines stopped mattering in the tents. People, like Maria Lloyd, came from all religions—or no religion—and gathered by the tens of thousands in the Baptist and Methodist tents. They heard inspired preachers who roused them to a moment of truth so potent they fainted, they shouted, they felt redeemed. They promised in turn to redeem the world. In the years from 1800 to 1820, the number of Baptist churches in Kentucky grew from 106 to 491.

Preachers rose to meet the needs. The denominations most threatened by the uncontrollable and ecstatic new forms of worship were mainstream Protestants, like the Calvinist Congregationalists and Presbyterians. Although, at the height of the tent revival fashion, many of the most prominent mainline clergymen were not particularly happy about the changes in their world, a remarkable number of them adapted to the new order. Congregationalists, Presbyterians, even the upper-crust Episcopalians modified their dogma. They incorporated Great Awakening belief in human perfectibility and in the role of a benevolent concern for others as part of their message.

Congregationalist superstar Reverend Lyman Beecher, famed for his defense of Calvinism at his prestigious Hanover Church pulpit in Boston, changed his mind and dragged his conventional church into the new world of values. The alternative, he saw clearly, was a massive bleed-out to the competitive Methodists and Baptists. In the 1820s and 1830s, Beecher's rival, former Presbyterian minister Charles Grandison Finney, widely acknowledged to be one of the most charismatic preachers in America, reached his height of popularity in upstate New York, attracting huge crowds to his revival meetings. Unlike the wavering Beecher, Finney was firmly antislavery.

Although Finney was explicit about the wrong of slavery, slavery was only one among many causes—temperance, Bible reading, missions to the heathens—for the newly awakened. As men of means joined their more modest brethren in the new awakening, the ministers and the merchants established a network of philanthropic institutions to carry out their new responsibilities, a movement so powerful it came to be known as an empire: the Benevolent Empire. The outreach from the pulpit to the laypeople, which drove the new societies, was unquestionably a response to the destabilizing effect of the evangelical Second Great Awakening.

The benevolent societies, an alliance of the newly thriving Baptists and Methodists, as well as of the Presbyterian and Congregationalist ministers whose flocks often consisted of the relatively wealthy, were inspired by similar initiatives in England. The early successes followed the British societies organized to distribute copies of the Bible. The American movement took off when, during the War of 1812 between the United States and Great Britain, a privateer seized a British ship carrying a load of Bibles to Canada and auctioned them off with the rest of the captured cargo. The nascent Bible Society of Massachusetts indignantly bought the contraband books and sent them to their planned destination. Free to will their futures, responsible for the fate of the world, and backed by an empire, the revivalists were on a collision course with the sin of slavery.

The revival that would ultimately give birth to slavery's demise found fertile ground even in the slave South. In 1801, a camp meeting in Cane Ridge, Kentucky—a slave state—turned into a cultural moment defining a movement. Tens of thousands of people—Presbyterian, Baptist, Methodist—gathered for a week of preaching and communion. Preachers were sermonizing all over the campground, often at the same time. Some estimate the attendance was ten percent of Kentucky's population.

Through preachers riding circuit in the new lands, the breakout religions also reached the people whose oppression meant they needed good news most—African Americans, particularly the enslaved. Eighteenth-century British Methodist founder John Wesley had been an early and influential opponent of slavery, and his Methodist Church licensed Black preachers. Even in the South, Methodism had spread during the colonial period. Black laymen became effective preachers, called "exhorters." For many years in the early Great Awakening, around 1800, the meetings included Black worshippers along with the Black preachers and "exhorters." White Methodist and Baptist preachers addressed meetings including "colored" people, as they called them. Although the clergy never directly assaulted

Cane Ridge revival meeting, 1801. *Watercolor by J. Maze Burbank, ca. 1839. Courtesy of Old Dartmouth Historical Society–New Bedford Whaling Museum. Gift of William F. Havemeyer.*

the institution of slavery, the enthusiastic and informal new religions, with their moral messages and straightforward style, penetrated the South, including its enslaved population.

In some places the new religions even involved the mixing of Black and white worshippers in the pews. But integration was not the norm. The great Kentucky revival meetings, for instance, included a main gathering with rows of plank pews for whites and separate tents at the rear for the participants of color. The legendary 1801 populist meeting at Cane Ridge put the worshippers of color in gatherings 150 yards from the whites. Circuit-riding preachers found separate Black churches and religious schools in the communities they visited.

The born-again white worshippers in the slave states were right to intuit the disruptive potential of the new awakening. Methodism temporarily made peace with its slaveholding followers by agreeing to say nothing about the issue of slavery, but it could not entirely shed its ties to John

Wesley, whose 1774 antislavery tract "Thoughts upon Slavery" is often considered the beginning of Western abolitionism. Only the Quakers had an older claim in acknowledging the wrongness of slavery. The pressure of abolitionism pulled the American Methodist Church apart, and, in 1844, it divided along sectional lines.

Even while evading the issue, Methodism was disruptive. In a 1777 Delaware clearing, an enslaved field hand, later named Richard Allen, heard an itinerant Methodist preach the gospel and brought the pastor home to shame his master into eventually allowing Allen to buy his freedom. Now a newly free Black man, Allen became a Methodist minister himself. He moved to Philadelphia in 1786 and preached to largely Black gatherings, while raising himself up economically by founding a successful business as a chimney sweep. When Allen arrived in Philadelphia, the town, with its long Quaker heritage, was the rare haven for free Blacks in America. They flocked there, escaping their enslavers and seeking refuge with the abolitionists concentrated in that place. With fellow Methodist Absalom Jones, Allen started the first Black benevolent society, the nonsectarian Free African Society.

Once in Philadelphia, newly arrived Black Methodists gathered around St. George's United Methodist Church. As Black members joined, the white worshippers at St. George's squirmed. First they segregated the benches in the church proper. Then they built a balcony and announced that their Black brethren would be confined there. When the segregated balcony was ready, the Black worshippers started praying in the usual place, and the angry white Methodists interrupted their worship to shoo the Black members up to the balcony. The Black worshippers walked out to start their own church. Richard Allen founded the Bethel Church for Negro Methodists in 1793; two years later he was ordained as the first Black deacon in the Methodist denomination.

Thus was born the original formal Black church in America, the African Methodist Episcopal Church, thereafter Mother Bethel Church. The first building appeared at Sixth and Lombard Streets in Philadelphia in 1794, more than a decade before white abolitionist William Lloyd Garrison was born. In 1814 a separate Black Methodist Conference was organized, and in 1816 it made Allen its bishop. With the Black church and Black African society, the foundation for the Black Benevolent Empire was laid.

Original Bethel A.M.E. Building. *Stipple engraving by John Boyd, after the oil painting by Rembrandt Peale, ca. 1823. Courtesy of the Library Company.*

Although it governed no territory, the "Empire" of Black churches and societies laid a critical foundation for resistance to slavery.

The same Second Great Awakening laid the foundation for the predominantly white Garrisonian antislavery movement. Baptist Maria Lloyd Garrison raised her children, including William Lloyd, on the Baptist belief in community and the capacity to redeem the world. Family lore has it that Maria passed her gift for music along to her son, as they sang the Baptist hymns together. Garrison's own children would later remember him sitting at the piano and accompanying himself as he sang his childhood hymns. Throughout her peripatetic life, Garrison's mother always belonged to the local Baptist church wherever she lived. For many years, so did her son.

In Garrison's Beginning Was the Word

As Garrison's biographer Henry Mayer relates, the family would need all the fortitude it could get. In 1811 a devastating fire swept through Newburyport, all but wiping out what remained of the town's economic life, and the family lost its precarious hold on survival. Maria's landlady and mainstay began pressing her for more of a contribution to sustaining the family of four. Maria decided to take her oldest son, James, intractable but also supposedly her favorite, thirty miles to Lynn, Massachusetts, where he secured an apprenticeship.

William, at nine, was essentially orphaned and left with his baby sister and the landlady. Even then, what little money Maria had did not suffice, and she soon had to separate William from his sister, sending him to another poor family in their Baptist circle. William enjoyed a good stretch, though, because his temporary family sent him to the local public school.

When his new family pulled William out of school to put him to work, Maria decided the Garrisons might as well be poor together in Lynn. Even that didn't last a year. James followed his father into drink and lost his apprenticeship. Finally, Maria packed up the whole sorry bunch and moved them hundreds of miles away to Baltimore, where she had, at last, found decent work. In Baltimore the restless William grew homesick for Newburyport and went back there to live with his foster family. His childhood took on a pattern of lousy jobs, separation, and episodes of running away from his own home and others'.

And then in 1818 his Newburyport family learned of a printer's apprentice position at the semi-weekly *Newburyport Herald*. The die was cast. At thirteen, Garrison moved into the house of Ephraim W. Allen, one of the rising class of American printers who were making good money off the spread of literacy and commerce in the North. Newburyport had been a beacon of the printing trade in earlier years.

The same year, 1818, that future printer William Lloyd Garrison took up his life's calling, the man who would become his great ally, Frederick Douglass, began life on this earth. Sometime in 1818 (slaves don't usually know their birthdays) on the Eastern Shore of the slave state of Maryland, enslaved Harriet Bailey gave birth to a son, possibly the product of a rape by her white master.

At the *Herald*, the young apprentice William Lloyd Garrison learned the hard, stinking physical labor of printing, including wringing out the urine-soaked fabric used to apply ink to the metal type. Painstakingly, aided by his phenomenal memory for words, William gained the skill of selecting type and setting it in the type boxes. He had found his calling.

By 1819, when the adolescent Garrison first put on his leather apron, printing was in the throes of an industrial revolution. While Allen ran an old-fashioned lever-driven wooden press operation (Garrison had to stand on a stack of material to reach it), the technology was moving in a radical new direction. Decades earlier, a Frenchman had figured out how to lay out entire pages onto hardened plates made of ceramic or metal. These plates, called "stereotypes," could print as many copies as the publisher wanted: rather than resetting the type with each copy, a printer could make thousands of copies from a single plate. Stereotypes became a way to print books, and writers took to traveling with the plates for their books along with them.

The first adopters of the stereotype technology were the publishers of the most widely circulated of books. In England, both Oxford and Cambridge universities started mass-producing the Bible. Then, in the United States, the American Bible Society, founded in 1816 as part of the Benevolent Empire, began churning out "stereotyped" Bibles. The Society bought the new steam-powered press. By 1829 it had sixteen presses working.

Detail, printing press, William Lloyd Garrison Monument, Bennington, Vermont.
Bennington Museum, Bennington, Vermont.

Improvements proceeded apace. In conventional typeset printing for items like newspapers that changed every day or week, the lever that pressed the inked type onto the paper was replaced by rollers, and then, inevitably, the human force required to roll the paper over the inked type was replaced by steam. Typesetters at London newspapers who got word of the steam development threatened to destroy the machines if they appeared at the factory. But of course they lost that fight. In 1814 the first copy of *The Times* of London was produced by steam in a secret facility the owners set up to keep their workers in the dark. The new machine ran at more than four times the speed of the old.

Garrison learned his trade at Allen's shop on the old-fashioned hand-powered press, turning out two hundred sheets of print an hour. In London, the steam press was already running a thousand an hour. By 1826, when Garrison left his apprenticeship, the automated tally was approaching several thousand pages an hour. When argument and news mattered, the printers were ready to print them.

Although the machinery at the *Newburyport Herald* was outdated, Garrison learned a lot about both printing and reading printed matter in his apprenticeship. The printer's shop was a legendary school for bookish boys who could not afford formal education, and the word-besotted young man embarked on a long course of teaching himself what he had missed in school. His fellow apprentices included Tobias Miller, who was working until he could enter a seminary, and William Crocker, who shared Garrison's committed Baptist faith and later died as a missionary in Liberia. The third was Garrison's longtime associate Isaac Knapp, who would be the first printer of *The Liberator*. Tall and with a head of his mother's rich brown hair, the young Garrison was always at the center of some sociable group, usually with Crocker and Knapp. He regularly attended his old Baptist church from his childhood days. As his apprenticeship drew to a close, he joined a newborn debating society, the "Franklin Club," a hotbed of speechmaking and political discussion.

Garrison's, Crocker's, and Knapp's lives were rich with print. They often met in a garret above the nearby bookstore, which another Newburyport publisher, W. & J. Gilman, maintained. Garrison boarded with the boss, Ephraim Allen, who, as a publisher, had a house full of books. Gilman ran a circulating library, and the town also had a library, the Newburyport

Athenaeum. Garrison took a strong interest in dramatic material — Shakespeare, Sir Walter Scott, Lord Byron. Soon, predictably, the romantic, literary printer's apprentice tried his hand at writing. He submitted to Allen under the pseudonym "An Old Bachelor" a curmudgeonly commentary on the frivolity of women who sued for breach of promise, which met with publisher Allen's approval and appeared in print. Garrison's sons' memoir includes a charming description of their father at seventeen holding his breath while his boss opened the unmarked envelope that contained his covert maiden submission.

His choice of pseudonym was fitting. Garrison soon took on the look of an old bachelor. He went bald and wore his signature rimless glasses for poor vision early on. Garrison continued churning out political commentary for the *Herald*. "Liberty" was his byword. In 1823 "An Old Bachelor" wrote a barnburner of a protest against the European monarchies, which, still mopping up after the French Revolution, were trying to restore a king to the throne in Spain. The reactionary Europeans were, according to Garrison, "the grand engine of destruction," "Royal Banditti" trying to "rob . . . the world of its richest treasure," "Liberty," while "shackling the fairest portions of the globe with manacles that ages cannot decay or sever." Garrison didn't have his eye on slavery yet, but he was writing, and the furious rhetoric and the reverence for liberty were in place. He was not yet eighteen years old.

A Newsroom of His Own

On March 22, 1826, readers of the modest Newburyport paper the *Essex Courant* learned that a new publisher had taken the helm. With a private loan from his old boss, Ephraim Allen, Garrison, the former apprentice and now newly minted printer, had bought the paper from his friend Isaac Knapp, who had failed miserably to make a go of it. From now on, Garrison informed his readers, the renamed *Free Press* would be worthy of its title: "Neither the craven fear of loss, nor the threats of the disappointed, nor the influence of power, shall ever awe one single opinion into silence." Garrison's identity as a defiant newspaperman, one who would go on to help spark first riots and then a civil war, was present the moment he took ownership of the press.

His ownership did not last long. Self-righteous and impulsive, in less than a year Garrison managed to offend his creditor by positioning the *Free Press* against Allen's preferred candidate for Congress. Although Garrison put forth the usual "personal" reasons for leaving the paper, clearly Allen exercised the power of the purse and forced the uppity indebted publisher out. Self-righteous, impulsive, and, if not an Old Bachelor, surely a childless bachelor with no responsibilities, Garrison was going to be a tough man to boss.

Garrison did what many fierce young men did. He put the small-town precincts of Newburyport behind him and moved to Boston, a thriving port nearly ten times the size of his hometown. As always, Garrison had the resources of his Baptist society and his circle of friends in the printing trade to draw on. He moved in with a fellow Baptist and former Allen apprentice and began a frantic search for work so he could afford his own rooms.

Shortly after he arrived in Boston, letters from "An Old Bachelor" began to appear in the local *Boston Courier*. Garrison went to a political caucus on the reelection of Boston's mayor Josiah Quincy, where he found "a Mr. Davis . . . flourishing away in a speech, which for stupidity, egotism and emptiness, merited a more general hiss." A man named Mr. Dunlap had had the temerity to speak against Garrison's favored candidate, and his "indignation was roused at [the speaker's] miserable artifice to touch the passions and blind the good sense of the audience." Reports signed "G" also began to appear in his old paper, the *Newburyport Herald*. For the *Herald*, he attended a meeting to select a candidate for Congress where David Lee Child, a lawyer who later became one of Garrison's closest friends and allies, spoke. Although Garrison agreed with Child on the merits, he was unable to resist informing the public that "Mr. Child's delivery is most unhappy—his matter is always better than his manner. His voice is harsh and stubborn, and when exerted, grates painfully upon the ear." Being unemployed did nothing to curb Garrison's inflammatory style.

Garrison Enters the Benevolent Empire

Garrison finally got enough work to move out of his friend's place. He took lodgings at Baptist William Collier's modest boardinghouse on Federal

Street. In that moment, the freedom-loving, critical idealist dropped his rucksack into the heart of the most robust reform movement of the time. Collier, an elderly, stooped, and gentle man, had left the formal ministry for a long stint as minister at large with a special commitment to the City Mission in Boston. His house was a veritable outpost of the Benevolent Empire, the interfaith social movement of the Second Great Awakening, now at its height.

Garrison's landlord was particularly committed to temperance, but the do-gooder societies of the Benevolent Empire also took on the job of educating ministers, establishing Sunday schools, delivering religious tracts, and, predictably, establishing missions, both within and beyond the nation's borders.

The societies thrived in part because they offered the laymen empowered and inspired by their reawakened religious fervor an outlet. Significantly, the social reform movements were open to women at a time when few other social institutions were. The energetic businessmen and lawyers in the Protestant churches expanded their efforts from their home communities of Boston, New York, and Philadelphia into national societies. By 1826, when Garrison arrived in Boston, the dozen or so leading benevolent institutions had revenues just shy of three million dollars. (For comparison, the United States government, from the Founding to 1828, had spent three and a half-million dollars on internal improvements.) In 1829, the wealthy New York merchants Arthur and Lewis Tappan of the American Tract Society underwrote a citywide initiative to distribute a religious tract a month. Aided by the new printing technology, in March the distributors placed 28,383 copies of *The Institution and Observance of the Sabbath* around New York. (April was Temperance Month.)

Garrison, the vaguely well-intentioned, denominationally curious, self-righteous unemployed newspaperman, fit in with the Boston Empire. Both Lyman Beecher and his rival Unitarian minister William Ellery Channing, who was preaching in Boston when Garrison arrived, appealed to the Baptist-raised Garrison. Garrison was always more interested in who had the best message for a meaningful life than in fine points of religious dogma. What cause would ultimately give his life meaning was an open question. Collier offered Garrison a job running his temperance newspaper, the *National Philanthropist*. Garrison believed in temperance—after all, his father drank and his older brother fell into the same trap.

On March 2, 1828, the *National Philanthropist* informed its readers that a new editor had been chosen: William Lloyd Garrison. The *National Philanthropist* thought its readers would be well satisfied with the results. Quarrelsome, moralistic, vivid, and imaginative, Garrison gave voice to the temperance forces that wanted prohibition and wanted it now. Political representatives must be chosen for their moral character, he asserted, and opponents of temperance were morally reprehensible. By May 2, a reader wrote the paper that "the editor of the Philanthropist complains most intemperately."

In a little-noticed excerpt reprinted from the *New York Observer,* Garrison sent up a tiny flare signaling what would be his ultimate, intemperate commitment. A reporter for the *Observer* had attended a slave auction and was horrified by the sale of human subjects. He was particularly incensed by the inclusion of a "yellow boy" whose own "father was probably there."

In what would become a pattern, without much explanation, in May 1828, after only six months, Garrison departed the *National Philanthropist.*

John the Baptist

While Garrison was edging into the Benevolent Empire at William Collier's boardinghouse, a little-known Quaker, Benjamin Lundy, was laying the groundwork for Garrison's life's work.

The Quakers were the first committed abolitionists. Their belief in the equality of all souls produced the first American antislavery statement, the Germantown Quaker Petition Against Slavery, in 1688. After a boomlet in voluntary emancipation following the American Revolution, by 1804 the northern states had all passed laws to abolish slavery, at once or gradually. By the time Lundy came of age, however, opponents of slavery had their work cut out for them. In 1793 Eli Whitney invented the cotton gin, making American cotton immensely profitable, and the southern enslavers buckled down to running a slave empire built on cotton.

When the penniless, frail Lundy took up saddle making in Wheeling, Virginia, in 1809, he encountered for the first time the "coffle"—the chained and handcuffed gang of slaves force-marched from the worn-out

The slave "coffle." *From A Popular History of the United States (Scribner, Armstrong, and Company, 1876). Courtesy of Library of Congress.*

lands of the coast to the rising cotton plantations of the inland South. Lundy was horrified and made a vow "to break at least one link of that ponderous chain of oppression." He found support in the odd handful of antislavery preachers; in 1816 one of them, George Bourne, wrote a tract called *The Book and Slavery Irreconcilable.* Slavery must be abolished immediately, Bourne argued.

In these early years of resistance, the doctrine of "immediatism," the immediate, rather than gradual, abolition of slavery, emerged from many sources—from the obligation to one's own moral self and to the healing of society, with its roots in the Second Great Awakening; from the experience of the reality of southern slavery by visitors like the author of *The Book* and Lundy himself; and from a growing perception of southern intransigence. The historian Kate Masur has recently published the underreported history of legal and political skirmishes over northern states' laws limiting the rights of free Black Americans, emigrants from former slave states, to settle in their territory during these seemingly placid years. This conflict at the margins, mostly waged by free Black activists and Quakers in places like Ohio and Illinois, unavoidably presented the fundamental arguments

against racial slavery in the nation of Bunker Hill: Who exactly was entitled to claim the honor of being an American "citizen"? Was citizenship a
function of skin color? And what were, in the language of the Constitution, the "privileges and immunities" of such "citizens"?

Lundy began to neglect his saddle making—and his family—and
to travel around the upper South and lower Midwest on foot, preaching
against slavery. He started a society of antislavery activists and then figured
out the only way he was going to change anything was by publishing a
newspaper. He taught himself how to print, although he lacked Garrison's
natural talent.

The debate over the future of slavery was not going to stay at a simmer
for much longer. In 1819, a decade after Lundy saw his first slave coffle,
Missouri, the third prospective state to emerge from the Louisiana Territory, which President Thomas Jefferson had bought from the French in
1803, applied for statehood. After two slave states had been added from
the Territory without much controversy, New York congressman James
Tallmadge Jr. fired the first loud political shot at the slave empire since
the Constitution was ratified in 1788. He proposed that Missouri could
become a state only on condition that no new slaves be introduced there.

The Tallmadge Amendment garnered a surprising amount of support.
Masur speculates that the breakdown of the old Federalist Party, which
eventually disappeared completely, had left a political vacuum. In a brief
moment of one-party politics, proponents of a new party alignment based
on a sectional alliance against slavery, previously unthinkable, filled the
partisan void. The possibility of a sectional alignment would, from 1820
on, always be a factor in the calculations of the two national parties that
emerged after this moment of weakness.

The parties being in flux, northern Federalists, former Federalists, and
northern Republicans found themselves in unlikely concert. Tallmadge was
joined almost immediately by radical Massachusetts representative Timothy Fuller, who suggested that Congress should stop slavery in Missouri
because the Constitution explicitly guarantees to the states a "republican
form of government." Adding insult to injury, Fuller reminded the South
that the founding document of the republic, the Declaration of Independence, is a paean to equality. So, he asserted, slavery is unconstitutional,
full stop. Southern congressmen immediately saw the threat to every slave

state in existence. They first started disavowing the Declaration of Independence, but shortly moved to the marginally more politically defensible position that slaves were not people but property. Slaveowners' property interest was protected by the constitutional guarantees against deprivation of property without due process of law, they argued. Their right to travel with their property was protected by the guarantee that citizens of each state had the same privileges and immunities as citizens of any other state.

The House of Representatives voted for Tallmadge; the more southern-dominated Senate refused. Ultimately, Congress allowed Missouri to come in as a slave state, with Maine as free, and a compromise limiting slavery to the southern half of the rest of the Louisiana Territory. Witnessing the eruption of organized resistance to the spread of slavery almost a half century after his words launched the nation in 1776, Thomas Jefferson, near his end, called the Missouri confrontation the "death knell of the Union."

Lundy went to Missouri in the run-up to the Compromise to work for the antislavery faction. He quickly came to the realization that he had a hard fight ahead of him. He started a newspaper devoted entirely to, as he called it, the *Genius of Universal Emancipation*. In 1825 he left the West and moved east to Baltimore, where the resources for the fight and where Congress—which he realized would be the site of the battle—were to be found. Lundy's crusade had all the elements of the ultimate movement. He pressured churches, proposing that people leave their congregations if the churches refused to renounce slavery. "Come-outerism," as it came to be called more than a decade later, grew out of Lundy's call to "come out from among them," in the *Genius*. He began going anywhere that would have him to start new antislavery societies. When he finally settled in Baltimore, he founded a society there that put up an abolition candidate for the General Assembly. The abolitionists lost horribly, but the slave interests took note. Maryland was, after all, a slave state.

The more he realized what an uphill battle he faced, the more Lundy heated up the rhetoric in the *Genius*. A particular target was Austin Woolfolk, dean of the Baltimore slave traders. In 1826, slaves mutinied on one of Woolfolk's ships and tried to set sail for Haiti. Although the revolt was unsuccessful, most of the rebels got away. The one victim who was caught and hanged said he forgave Woolfolk, in one of the first gallows speeches that would in time become a major weapon in the rhetorical battle over slavery. In a scathing article about Woolfolk, "a monster in human shape," Lundy reported that the slave trader had responded to this speech by cursing his former property. In response, Woolfolk attacked the frail Quaker on the street in Baltimore and beat him almost to death. At his trial for criminal assault, Woolfolk pleaded in his defense that Lundy's article had provoked him into assaulting the editor. The judge punished Woolfolk with a fine of one dollar, and Woolfolk accused Lundy of libel. The grand jury refused to indict. But a pattern emerged: a slave rebellion, a speech at the gallows, abolitionist publicity, and the South's defensive use of the law of libel to shut it down.

As 1827 dawned, Lundy turned his attention to reviving an old technique: petitioning Congress. Banish the slave trade in the nation's capital, where the slavers sold their human goods in the shadow of the Capitol, the small but angry abolitionist movement petitioned the legislature. Congress received the petition and moved immediately to refuse to print it.

Baptism

New England, Lundy thought, was not doing enough to resist slavery. In 1828 he left the *Genius* in the hands of an intern and traveled north to found antislavery societies, start petition drives, and solicit subscriptions to the paper. Nothing worked. Lundy realized that Quakers alone were not enough to end slavery. He turned to William Collier, famed preacher of the Benevolent Empire—and Garrison's landlord—to sponsor a lecture. He hoped Collier would bring the cause to Baptist preachers and others the Great Awakening had produced. There were eight ministers at Collier's that night. They could not have been less helpful. Antislavery, the famed Unitarian William Ellery Channing worried, might lead to civil war. But on March 17, 1828, in William Collier's living room, Lundy did make one convert—William Lloyd Garrison. Garrison had always been a rebel. Now he had a cause.

2

(1806–1828)

Manager Weston Chapman Comes of Age

LESS THAN A YEAR AFTER GARRISON'S BIRTH in 1805, Warren
Weston started his family south of Boston in Weymouth, Massachusetts.
At first glance, Warren, a ship captain and the descendant of a line of ship-
pers, looked to be a more promising prospect than the impecunious sailing
master Abijah Garrison. But when the embargo and then the War of 1812
ruined Weston's maritime business, he, like Abijah Garrison, turned to
drink. Maria Weston's childhood was shaped by a competent, dominant
mother and a close acquaintanceship with need.

The Westons, unlike the Garrisons, had a safety net in their prosperous
extended families. Father Warren's uncle and cousins owned the largest
shipbuilding company in America, E. Weston and Son. After his shipping enterprise failed, Weston got a loan from his widowed mother and
in 1813 bought a small plot in Weymouth, supposedly for farming. He
drank, raged, and begat seven more children, including two erratic and
alcohol-inclined sons.

His wife, Ann Bates Weston, and their daughters, as they came of age,
managed and supported the family. The Weymouth farmhouse would be
home to the family of eight Weston children off and on for the rest of the
century.

While the family lived on the farm they had been given by the Westons,
mother Ann's brother Joshua Bates was the real salvation of the family. In
their youth, while Ann began married life with the unpromising Warren Weston, her brother joined a Boston countinghouse. Sent to London
in 1816 as a shipping agent, he partnered with John Baring in 1826 to
found the great investment bank Baring Brothers & Company. As Ann
was trying to wrest a living from a ten-acre farm for her eight children and

alcoholic husband, her brother became one of the richest men in London. From the beginning, Uncle Joshua took care of the bills of the family too proud to ask for much. He sent his sister an annuity and paid for the children's school.

In New England, school mattered. By the time Maria, the oldest, was ready for school, she, like most New England girls, already knew how to read and write. Although the inclusion of girls was far from universal, by the early nineteenth century, girls like the Weston sisters were riding a wave of support. For years, girls had increasingly appeared in the boys' winter schools (winter being when boys weren't needed for harvest), receiving wider curriculums than they had before, and staying for more years. There does not appear to have been an actual formal battle to integrate the girls, although resistance surfaced occasionally. Thanks to Uncle Joshua, Maria went to private school in Weymouth, studying with legendary teachers.

In 1821 Boston opened a public boys' high school, the English High School of Boston (to distinguish it from the exclusive private Latin schools). Almost immediately, the boys' headmaster at Boston English, George B. Emerson, decided to open a public high school for girls as well. It's a familiar story: upon receiving the news of a free high school, girls all over Boston deluged the place with applications, sending three times the number the new school could accept. Younger girls, allowed in grammar schools until sixteen, prepared instead at twelve to decamp to the new high school. Within a year, autocratic Boston mayor Josiah Quincy proposed to shut the school down. It was expensive, and the girls he was hoping would displace paid teachers in the lower schools in a kind of tutorial system were instead aspiring to higher education for themselves. Worse for the Brahmin Quincy, the school was attracting girls who were Irish. Higher education for the poorer classes would cause them to rise above their station, the mayor's side argued. The headmaster of the girls' school, Ebenezer Bailey, a New England reformer who had led a private girls' school before his public service, fought Mayor Quincy fiercely. The girls were performing well, he argued. He offered to cut expenses and even the years of education offered, but the mayor was unyielding. He would close the public girls' school.

Despite the lack of opportunities for young women like the oldest Weston daughter, she was fortunate, because in 1825, the Bates family invited her to London. For the first time, Maria left her tight sisterly country life for the giant, bustling metropolis. Time hurried by in London, she noted, while the whole city lived in a state of "feverish anticipation."

Uncle Joshua and his high-society Boston wife had two children, a boy, twelve, and a daughter, ten. After Maria spent some time in the family, they came to seem like a brother and sister to her. Early in her stay she fretted that her younger siblings at home would forget her, and she implored them to think of her often. She reassured her sisters, however, that she was not "homesick or unhappy" but was "enjoy[ing] [everything] very much. Although "if I could see you I should be quite happy."

While in London, she enrolled in Mrs. Elwell's school, a pleasant place with a large walled garden. Maria reports mostly about her art lessons — painting, chalk — the parties, and the amateur theatricals, including one in which she played William Shakespeare. There was a French teacher on the faculty, so she also must have been doing the hard work of learning a second language. Her schooling, Maria speculated, would make her "bright as the Methodists," however far behind she had been before moving to London. If Maria, a poor girl from the provinces, encountered any social resistance at Mrs. Elwell's school, she writes nothing of it. The closest she came to revealing emotional stress was when she repeatedly begged her sisters to remember her.

In 1828 Uncle Joshua Bates came back to Boston, bringing Maria with him. The twenty-two-year-old, trailing an ineffably European air, easily secured a job as a principal in Ebenezer Bailey's new private Boston girls' high school, joining the rising social trend of women educating women. The Weston sisters began to enroll in the new school, Caroline following Maria and, in turn, teaching the next sister, Anne.

Meeting Maria on a visit to Boston shortly after her return from London, the British literary lioness Harriet Martineau described the new sensation: "I still see the exquisite beauty which took me by surprise that day — the slender, graceful form — the golden hair ... the brilliant complexion, noble profile and deep blue eyes." Within a year Weston had met Henry Grafton Chapman, the wealthy son of a Boston shipping merchant. Chapman dreamed of being a minister but returned to his father's business when he married the beautiful young educator in 1830.

Unusually for his class, Chapman came from an abolitionist family. His father, Henry Chapman, was an adherent to the movement from its ear-

Portrait of Maria Weston Chapman. *Courtesy of Boston Public Library.*

liest days. It was hard to be a shipper and an abolitionist in antebellum America, as cotton was one of the most lucrative commodities shipping out of the new nation. By the Civil War, raw cotton constituted sixty-one percent of the value of all American exports. A chain of causation ran from European and North American financiers, who provided credit for the planters to produce and the merchants to consume cotton. The system ran on an army of factors, or brokers, who ran the supply chain, taking cotton first to the southern ports and then selling it to the merchants, who shipped it out of the growing network. Before he saw the light, Chapman senior's company, too, was running those lucrative southern routes. In 1831, in service to the abolitionist cause, he ended his southern shipping, and Maria's uncle Joshua again came to the rescue, arranging for rich commissions to the Chapman shipping company for copper and other goods not tainted by slavery.

But good Uncle Joshua Bates was up to his eyeballs in . . . cotton. By

1839, Baring Brothers & Company, Bates's bank, was the largest importer of cotton in the world. The Barings had been investing in cotton since 1812 and had an agent in Boston to watch over their cotton investments. From 1839 to 1840, Baring imported over one hundred thousand bales of cotton—the product of at least seventy thousand slaves. In a diary, Bates routinely tracked the market in cotton just like all the other commodities he traded—indigo, iron, coffee—noting the ups and downs without a syllable about the massive system of enslavement supporting his increasingly massive riches.

Like many people in the North, Bates could live with a little abolitionism while drinking deeply from the poisoned well of the cotton trade. His abolitionist relatives lived on the surplus of his hypocrisy. Maria left no known trace of her thinking on the slave origins of her privileged life.

3

(1828–1830)

Garrison Will Be Heard

Unbeknownst to Joshua Bates when he brought his niece home to Boston in 1828, the corrupt bargain between slave cotton and the supposedly free North was about to become harder to sustain. Just as Maria married into the abolitionist Chapman family in 1830, abolitionist newspaperman Benjamin Lundy recruited William Lloyd Garrison to the cause.

When Lundy came to Boston, Garrison had already seen issues of Lundy's *Genius of Universal Emancipation* and was prepared to meet a crusading editor. Lundy's brew of moral indignation at the slaves' suffering and his political agenda for a northern movement was ideally made to seduce Garrison, the self-confident political moralist. That all the ministers at William Collier's boardinghouse had turned their backs only added spice to the mix. The abandoned child of a moralistic mother, Garrison had already developed the lifelong habit of defying whoever was in authority and relying on his unremitting powers of argument to advance his cause. That's what made him so impossible to employ as the editor of anyone else's newspaper. Abolition was perfect for him. Once he saw the extent of the wrongdoing, he was relentless.

Lundy brought Garrison critical news. There was a skeleton, a faint outline of the structure that would, within four momentous years, burst open into the ultimate antislavery movement. Lundy had a newspaper: there were newspapers. The Quakers had generated a network of antislavery societies in the West and the upper South. There were local boomlets of manumission—enslavers setting their slaves free—where remnants of free white labor recognized the threat of the slave system to the value of their toil. There were antislavery gatherings. And there were people in the Benevolent Empire who could be converted. William Goodell, a temperance reformer from New York; the Tappan brothers, wool and silk fabric merchants who were bankrolling the blanketing of New York City with religious tracts; lawyers; sympathetic clergymen. There were Black churches and Black benevolent societies, like Richard Allen's network in Philadelphia. There was a Black newspaper in New York, *Freedom's Journal.* The Black activists and the Quakers had already generated a resistance movement to the banning of free black emigrants to the new states of the Northwest, like Ohio and Illinois, and an unlikely opportunity had nearly brought Congress to a halt when Missouri came in.

Garrison was riveted. Where could he sign up? Within a year, Lundy brought his avid young follower to Baltimore to help run the *Genius.* The paper became better typeset and longer. And it also became more combative. Garrison restarted Lundy's catalogue of slavery atrocities, the "Black List." In Garrison's later organ, *The Liberator,* the compilation would become the "Refuge of Oppression," one of the most effective propaganda devices in American history.

Antislavery as Libel: The First Political Trial

If the mild-mannered Lundy generated a small storm, Garrison attracted litigation like a tornado sucking up dust. In his first months at the *Genius* in 1829, he published an attack on a New England shipping magnate, Francis Todd. Todd's ship, the *Francis,* sailed out of Baltimore, bound for New Orleans with a cargo of seventy-five slaves. Todd's transportation of slaves between the states was in no way illegal. The Founding Fathers had agreed to ban only the foreign slave trade; after 1808, Americans were forbidden to bring slaves into the country. But, especially by 1829, the slave owners of the Old South, including Maryland, were actively engaged in the horrific business of using their enslaved humans for breeding more slaves and then shipping the human cargo to the developing cotton areas of the New South. New Orleans was ground zero in that trade in human beings, and Francis Todd's self-named ship was engaged in that trade.

Garrison knew what his task was: he had learned from Lundy that the key to success was to transform the way slavery was seen in the North. Todd was a New Englander, and Garrison planned to shame him. He wrote:

> I have stated that the ship Francis hails from my native place, New-buryport (Massachusetts) is commanded by a Yankee captain, and owned by a townsman name
>   FRANCIS TODD.
>   I am resolved to cover with thick infamy all who were concerned in this nefarious business.

Using his signature symbol for statements of particular seriousness, the manicule, or pointing hand, he continued, "The men who have the wickedness to participate therein, for the purpose of heaping up wealth, should be ☞SENTENCED TO SOLITARY CONFINEMENT FOR LIFE;☜ *they are the enemies of their own species — highway robbers and murderers.*"

Todd brought a criminal complaint against Garrison and Lundy for libel and, unlike Lundy's prior close call, this time the charge was successful. Lundy was ultimately let go, but Garrison was indicted and tried for the crime. Todd also sued Garrison civilly for damages.

Garrison's libel trial was the first big legal battle in a movement marked and shaped by lawsuits. There is a straight line from the libel suit against Garrison by the State of Maryland in 1830 to *Dred Scott v. Sandford,* the 1857 decision of the Supreme Court that stated no Black person could be a citizen of the United States. From *State v. Garrison* to *Dred Scott,* the slave power tried to use the courts to shut down abolition. For their part, the abolitionists tried to use the legal system to expand the realm of freedom. The pull and tug of litigation fueled the abolitionist movement until, after the decision in *Dred Scott,* the Civil War seemed inevitable.

The story of abolition litigation even has a central villain: Roger B. Taney, who in 1857 was chief justice of the United States and author of the dominant opinion in *Dred Scott.* Twenty-seven years earlier, in 1830, Taney, a Maryland lawyer and politician, was state attorney general. Taney's law partner from when he was in private practice, Jonathan Meredith, represented ship owner Francis Todd in the civil suit against Garrison and actively participated in the criminal prosecution. Not only did Roger Taney's partner control the litigation, civil and criminal, but also Chief Judge Nicholas Brice of the Baltimore court, who had earlier unsuccessfully sent Lundy to the grand jury for libel, assigned Garrison's case to himself.

At trial, the judge radically misstated the libel law, which was actually on Garrison's side. As Garrison biographer Henry Mayer lays out, before a wave of reform in Maryland and elsewhere, criminal libel originally did not depend on whether the troublemaker was telling the truth or not. The law existed simply to give angry victims of a publisher a lawful way of hurting the writer back, decreasing the likelihood of violence, like dueling, for example. Since 1804, however, Maryland defamation law had explicitly included the defense of truth. In adopting the defense of truth, Maryland was one of several American jurisdictions to move away from the repressive old English model of libel as a deterrent to violence to one more favorable to free speech.

The state had based its indictment on statements by Garrison that were indisputably true. Todd had shipped slaves. Nonetheless, Judge Brice allowed the state to introduce the whole disputed article, way beyond the allegations of the indictment. The entire article, including Garrison's description of the slaves' suffering on board, contained statements whose truth could at least be disputed. The ship's pilot then testified about the wonderful conditions on the slave ship: good food and plenty of comfortable room to rest. The prosecutor argued that Garrison had to be convicted in the interest of public order, an explicit appeal to the old, discarded model of defamation law. It took the jury fifteen minutes to convict. Judge Brice levied a sentence of fifty dollars plus costs, much more than the young editor could possibly pay.

No harm; he didn't want to pay anyway. Less than a year into his conversion to the cause of abolition, William Lloyd Garrison was ready to play the long game of martyrdom. For the next three months, all his letters were sent with transparent boastfulness from the "Baltimore Jail." Two months into his sentence, Garrison wrote one of his many letters to the editor, this time to his old employer the *Newburyport Herald:* "A few days since, Judge Brice observed to the Warden of the Jail, that 'Mr. Garrison was ambitious of becoming a martyr.' 'Tell his Honor,' I responded, 'that if his assertion be true, he is equally ambitious of gathering the faggots and applying the torch.'" And so the battle was joined.

Garrison thought he was akin to another nineteenth-century freedom fighter, Lord Byron. Like Byron's "prisoner of Chillon," Garrison, a patriot in a dungeon, wrote poetry attesting to the eternal freedom of his thoughts and scratched it on the walls of his cell. Garrison also wrote the story of his trial, which Lundy made into a small pamphlet and immediately sent out.

Never jail a newspaperman. "Up to that period," Garrison wrote in the preface to the second edition of his screed, "no single incident connected with the subject of slavery had ever excited so much attention, or elicited such a spontaneous burst of general indignation." One copy of the trial story caught the attention of Arthur Tappan, the millionaire sponsor of the Benevolent Empire and the head of a clique of white reformist business-men in New York, the "Association of Gentlemen." Most of the gentleman reformers favored sending Blacks back to Africa, an ill-conceived proj-ect called "colonization." Yet through involvement in a proposal to start a school for free Blacks, Tappan had learned of Black leaders' overwhelming opposition to moving away to a place many of them had never known. In 1830, after Garrison had been seven weeks in prison, Tappan bailed him out.

Garrison's time in jail made a difference. While he was there, slave traders like Austin Woolfolk, who had so tormented Lundy, stopped their practice of going to the jail to find prospects to buy and sell into the new cotton states. There would be no slave hunting where Garrison could see it. When Garrison was released from prison, he realized that his mentor Benjamin Lundy was not the man for the fight. Lundy left Baltimore and so did not have to answer for either the criminal libel or Todd's ensuing civil suit against the abolitionist publishers. He was not interested in Gar-rison's big plans for reviving the fighting newspaper.

But by 1830 it was clear the time had come for a fight. Unbeknownst to Garrison, as he made his plans for print, the privileged and energetic Maria Weston had just married into an old abolitionist family in Boston, and a young Black slave named Frederick living a few blocks away from Garrison's new home in Baltimore had just learned to read and write. He avidly pursued the skill, he later reported, because he had overheard his enslaver forbidding it. Slaves who read, Frederick learned from him, are slaves who run away.

4

(1798–1845)

The Enslaved Write Their History

You remember the old fable of "The Man and the Lion," where the
lion complained that he should not be so misrepresented "when the
lions wrote history."

—*Wendell Phillips,*
introduction to Narrative of the Life of Frederick Douglass,
an American Slave

WHAT WE KNOW ABOUT FREDERICK DOUGLASS'S EARLY life we
know mostly from his own words. Douglass wrote three versions of his
memoirs: *Narrative of the Life of Frederick Douglass, an American Slave,* in
1845; *My Bondage and My Freedom,* in 1855; and *The Life and Times of*
Frederick Douglass, in 1881 (revised in 1892).

Douglass's first memoir, *Narrative of the Life of Frederick Douglass, an*
American Slave, was the most important entry in a long and rich tradition
of slave narratives. In 1798, a generation before Douglass was born, the
freed slave Venture Smith set down the first narrative of enslavement after
the American Founding: *A Narrative of the Life and Adventures of Venture,*
a Native of Africa: But Resident Above Sixty Years in the United States of
America, Related by Himself. In the next half century, dozens of slave stories were published, often by the abolitionist societies, to raise money and
awareness. Once their popularity was established, the form attracted entrepreneurs of varying degrees of reliability and motivation, including white
authors trying to make the case against—and occasionally for—slavery.

The tales follow a consistent pattern. There is a recollection of the idyllic time before the fall into slavery. Often, as in Venture Smith's story,

NARRATIVE

OF THE

LIFE

OF

FREDERICK DOUGLASS,

AN

AMERICAN SLAVE.

WRITTEN BY HIMSELF.

BOSTON:
PUBLISHED AT THE ANTI-SLAVERY OFFICE,
No. 25 CORNHILL
1845.

Title page of *Narrative of the Life of Frederick Douglass, an American Slave. Courtesy of Documenting the American South.*

the paradise is in Africa before the slave hunters come. "Before I dismiss this country," he writes of Guinea, "I must just inform my reader what I remember concerning this place . . . It scarce ever rains there, yet the land is fertile." If the storyteller is not himself from Africa, an ancestral story remembered by the narrator brings the tale of the paradise lost.

Then the narrator is introduced into the world of the enslaved, usually by an episode of terrible violence. A warlike tribe, armed and "instigated by some white nation," attacks Smith's people. "The very first salute I had from them," he writes, "was a violent blow on the head with the fore part of a gun, and at the same time a grasp round the neck." The narrator is beaten by his master, or worse, and at some point tries to fight back and escape. Smith resists almost immediately.

Third, somehow—or, of course, he would not be telling the tale— he gets away. Venture Smith was not, in the 1780s, serving in the cotton empire, which had yet to be established; in New York he performed or- dinary agricultural tasks and had access to a market economy. Eventually,

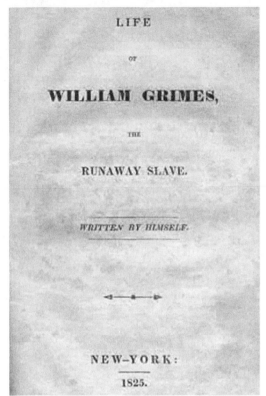

LIFE

OF

WILLIAM GRIMES,

THE

RUNAWAY SLAVE.

WRITTEN BY HIMSELF.

◄—▪—►

NEW-YORK:

1825.

Title page of *Life of William Grimes, the Runaway Slave. Courtesy of Documenting the American South.*

by moonlighting and overtime, he managed to buy himself out of slavery. Through heroic hard labor he did the same for his wife and children. In this, Smith's pathway is not typical; most of the later slave narratives involve actual physical escape.

In 1825, twenty-seven years after Smith's tale, the fugitive slave William Grimes wrote a book-length slave narrative, *Life of William Grimes, the Runaway Slave.* Grimes has little of the Edenic past in his story, and remembers only that his childhood master was kind. He plunges the reader into slavery almost immediately with the announcement that his mistress was jealous of him and beat him. His matter-of-fact recitation of the beatings and separations of slavery has a disproportionate impact on the reader:

Gabriel, one of the servants ... was ordered to strip my shirt up and whip me; (the word severely, has been so many times used it needs no repetition) my master stood by to see the thing well executed: and as he thought he did not be severe enough, he ordered me to strip him and perform the same ceremony, which I did. He then ordered Gabriel to try to whip me harder than he did before. Then Gabriel knew what the old man meant, to wit, to whip me as severe as lay in his power, which he affected on the second trial, exerting all his strength and agility to the utmost to make me suffer, only to please his master.

Young Grimes goes from one overseer to another, experiencing various degrees of flogging and abuse, until one such individual, "whipping us all the time most unmercifully," drives him to run away. As was the case with most escapes attempted by slaves, Grimes failed. Many years and many beatings later, Grimes's master left him alone in Savannah while the family vacationed in Bermuda. Instructed to hire himself out on the docks during their absence, Grimes befriended the sailors loading a boat with cotton to ship to New York, and they made a space for him to hide in one of the bales.

Douglass's account of life before the fall, which appears only in the second of his three memoirs, *My Bondage and My Freedom,* takes place in his grandmother's cabin, which he later realizes was a shed that did not belong to her.

To my child's eye, however, it was a noble structure, admirably adapted to promote the comforts and conveniences of its inmates. A few rough, Virginia fence-rails, flung loosely over the rafters above, answered the triple purpose of floors, ceilings, and bedsteads. To be sure, this upper apartment was reached only by a ladder—but what in the world for climbing could be better than a ladder? To me, this ladder was really a high invention, and possessed a sort of charm as I played with delight upon the rounds of it. In this little hut there was a large family of children: I dare not say how many. My grandmother—whether because too old for field service, or because she had so faithfully discharged the duties of her station in early life, I know not—enjoyed the high privilege of living in a cabin, separate from the quarter, with no other burden than her own support, and the necessary care of the little children, imposed.

The structure of the slave narratives enabled the tales to serve their critical political role. The idyllic beginning showed the Black people as well meaning, creative, skilled, and perfectly capable of self-government. Venture Smith's African father was a prosperous man who ruled his lands with a benevolent hand, sacrificing his own riches to try to buy off the invaders who threatened his people. Douglass's "grandmother, especially, was held in high esteem, far higher than is the lot of most colored persons in the slave states. She was a good nurse, and a capital hand at making nets for catching shad and herring; and these nets were in great demand . . . She was not only good at making the nets, but was also somewhat famous for her good fortune in taking the fishes referred to." As a result, "this high reputation was full of advantage to her, and to the children around her. Though Tuckahoe [Maryland] had but few of the good things of life, yet of such as it did possess grandmother got a full share in the way of presents." These stories purposefully portrayed Black people not as inferior or incapable of ruling themselves or others, not as creatures, as the ignorant anthropology of the time asserted, of a different species.

The narratives follow the pattern of introducing the peculiar institution of slavery with stunning acts of violence. The conquering African tribe tortured Venture's father to death. In Douglass's memoir, the violence appears soon after Douglass is delivered from his grandmother's house to his master. He witnesses the enslaver, Aaron Anthony, whipping his aunt Hester in a savage act of sexual sadism:

> After crossing her hands, he tied them with a strong rope, and led her to a stool under a large hook in the joist, put in for the purpose. He made her get upon the stool, and tied her hands to the hook. She now stood fair for his infernal purpose. Her arms were stretched up at their full length, so that she stood upon the ends of her toes. He then said to her, 'Now, you d— —d b—h, I'll learn you how to disobey my orders!' and after rolling up his sleeves, he commenced to lay on the heavy cowskin, and soon the warm, red blood (amid heart-rending shrieks from her, and horrid oaths from him) came dripping to the floor.

The power of slave narratives is greater than any polemical writing. How could any social arrangement with such a horrific genesis possibly be legitimate? Only in a state that denies the human claim to freedom and equality. Only in a religion that denies that every man has a soul. And here is where the slave writers of the new republic intervene in their narratives to drive the lesson home explicitly. Douglass turns to the hypocrisy of the church: "The overwhelming mass of professed Christians in America . . . strain at a gnat, and swallow a camel. Could any thing be more true of our churches? They would be shocked at the proposition of fellowshipping a *sheep*-stealer; and at the same time they hug to their communion a *man*-stealer."

William Grimes turns to the hypocrisy in the country's founding. He introduces himself as a citizen of the home of the free: "I was born in the year 1784, in J—, County of King George, Virginia; in a land boasting its freedom, and under a government whose motto is Liberty and Equality." After telling the story of his life under slavery and his unusual escape, Grimes drives the point home: "If it were not for the stripes on my back which were made while I was a slave, I would in my will, leave my skin a legacy to the government, desiring that it might be taken off and made into parchment, and then bind the constitution of glorious happy *and free* America. Let the skin of an American slave, bind the charter of American Liberty."

The narratives tell the story of slavery as violation of both ancient Christianity and the new American experiment. The two poles of abolition are set up.

5

(1818–1838)

Frederick Douglass's History in Slavery

"IT IS A COMMON CUSTOM, IN THE part of Maryland from which I ran away," Douglass begins his *Narrative*, "to part children from their mothers at a very early age."

When Douglass's mother was sent twelve miles away to work for another planter in 1819, he couldn't have been much more than a year old. He never knew his father, who he'd heard was "a white man." There was talk that the man was his enslaver, but of this, he says, "I know nothing; the means of knowing was withheld from me." Douglass was lucky enough in his early years to be sent to his mother's mother to be raised until he was old enough to be of use. During his slave years, he was called by his mother's surname, Frederick Bailey; he named himself Douglass later, after he escaped. She did not live long after their parting, but he was "not allowed to be present during her illness, at her death, or burial."

The master's enslaved children were, Douglass astutely notes, "a constant offence to their mistress." The master had to mollify her by treating them worse, beating them more often, and selling them to the "human flesh mongers" who traded in slaves. Indeed, Douglass writes, the masters often acted more kindly in selling their children than in keeping them, because keeping them meant beating their own slave offspring or having their children's white half brothers do the cruel deed to their own siblings.

Douglass had been so completely separated from his mother that he "received the tidings of her death with much the same emotions I should have probably felt at the death of a stranger." In his second telling of his story ten years later, however, Douglass places his mother in a heroic narrative. He remembers what she looked like, he says; she resembled a drawing "in 'Prichard's Natural History of Man.'" Her visits to him "were few in number, brief in duration, and mostly made in the night. The pains she took, and the toil she endured, to see me, tells me that a true mother's heart was hers, and that slavery had difficulty in paralyzing it with unmotherly indifference." In his second version—the 1855 memoir *My Bondage and My Freedom*—Douglass pens a maternal visit worthy of a fairy tale or the novel *Uncle Tom's Cabin*. The cruel plantation slave cook, Katy, had cut off his rations in an attempt, she claims, to starve him into submission. As he tells it, he was suffering the extreme hunger of a day of fasting when his mother appeared for one of her rare visits. Dressing down the abusive servant, she made Douglass a ginger cake and fed him on her lap.

As with so much of Douglass's life, it is the telling rather than the content that matters. How much more powerful than this sweet story is the brief and poignant one-sentence indictment of his separation from his mother, written in the first version, when his memory was freshest: "It is a common custom, in the part of Maryland from which I ran away, to part children from their mothers at a very early age."

Around 1823, when he was still a toddler, Douglass's grandmother brought him from her peaceable kingdom outside the plantation to live in the master's house. Thereafter Douglass was a chattel, little better than a "thing," as Garrison would so defiantly deny in their fateful first meeting

Wye House Plantation. *Photograph by Jack E. Boucher. Courtesy of Library of Congress.*

on Nantucket. He was hungry and terrified by the constant threat of brutal abuse. He was sent from one owner to another like a piece of furniture. With each transfer, his life changed.

Life as a Chattel

Douglass's legal owner, Aaron Anthony, was an administrator for a huge slaveholding plantation owner named Colonel Edward Lloyd. At first, when his grandmother delivered him to Anthony's house on Lloyd's plantation, the young boy was not worked, but he was hungry all the time. Indeed, the slaves on the plantation were so hungry that Colonel Lloyd had to tar every fence around his fabled fruit orchards to stop them from stealing the apples and the oranges. And Frederick was so cold he later remembered that his feet "so cracked with the frost, that the pen with which I am writing might be laid in the gashes."

When Douglass was around seven, Aaron Anthony decided to send the boy to his son-in-law's brother Hugh Auld in Baltimore to care for the Aulds' young son. Frederick was delighted. He was eager to see Baltimore, which had mythic status on the rural Maryland plantation. When he was delivered to the Aulds at their house on Happy Alley off Aliceanna Street, Frederick saw "what I had never seen before," he writes; "it was a white face beaming with the most kindly emotions; it was the face of my new mistress, Sophia Auld." Douglass remembered his transfer to the Aulds in Baltimore as a manifestation of divine providence in his life. The Aulds had not owned slaves, and Sophia in particular treated Frederick like the person he was.

In the Beginning Was the Word

When Sophia started to teach her son to read, she taught Frederick as well. If ever an act could be attributed to divine providence it was the moment when the slave met the alphabet. Sophia had even progressed to words of several letters when, as Douglass reports, her husband, Hugh, found out what was going on. "'Now,' said he, 'if you teach that nigger (speaking of myself) how to read, there would be no keeping him.'" And so Frederick determined to learn two things: how to read and therefore "the pathway from slavery to freedom." The harder his formerly sympathetic masters tried to stop him from learning, the more determined he was to learn how to read. Frederick would not merely be a person; he would be a man of letters.

"The plan . . . I adopted," he writes,

> [and] the one by which I was the most successful, was that of making friends of all the little white boys whom I met in the street. As many of these as I could, I converted into teachers. With their kindly aid, obtained at different times and in different places, I finally succeeded in learning to read. When I was sent on errands, I always took my book with me, and by going one part of my errand quickly, I found time to get a lesson before my return. I used also to carry bread with me, enough of which was always in the house, and to which I was always welcome; for I was much better off in this regard than many of the poor white children in our neighborhood. This bread I used to bestow upon the hungry little urchins, who, in return, would give me that more valuable bread of knowledge.

Douglass knew their bread was worth more than his. As the young Douglass would say to the hungry boys: "I wished I could be as free as they would be when they got to be men. 'You will be free as soon as you are twenty-one, *but I am a slave for life!*'" This is the second place in the memoir where Douglass speaks of the occasional kindness of a white person who came across his path. He would thank these people specifically, he continues, but he is afraid he would get them in trouble for teaching a Black slave to read.

Because he was treated as mere chattel, when his formal owner died, the Aulds were compelled to send Frederick back to the plantation to be evaluated as part of the "inventory." Douglass was relieved when his dead master's son-in-law Thomas Auld sent him back to the Baltimore Aulds. Douglass had no way of knowing, but right after he arrived back in Baltimore, enslaved, William Lloyd Garrison moved a mile away, to edit the abolitionist paper the *Genius of Universal Emancipation.* There would be no universal emancipation in 1830, nor even the particular emancipation of Frederick Douglass. His respite was brief: a few years later, in 1832, Douglass was sent back to the country estate to work on the farm. Formally, at that point he belonged to Thomas Auld. But Frederick was then fourteen or fifteen and had tasted freedom. And he knew how to read. Auld could not break him to rural slavery. He sent his ungovernable chattel for a year of torment to Edward Covey, a man renowned for breaking slaves.

Slave Breaker

At first Covey seemed to succeed in breaking Douglass. Daily beatings, relentless labor, unstinting surveillance all combined to strip him of his will. Douglass even stopped reading. Six months into his time with Covey, he fell ill. Covey kicked and beat him with a plank and left him bleeding on the ground. Douglass ran away seven miles to his legal master, Thomas Auld, to beg for release from Covey's service, but Auld ordered him back.

When at last Frederick revealed his presence back at Covey's, the slave breaker walked toward him with a rope to tie him up for another beating. In "the turning-point in [Douglass's] career as a slave," instead of submitting, he took hold of his tormentor. He resisted for two hours: "My long-crushed spirit rose, cowardice departed, bold defiance took its place; and I now resolved that, however long I might remain a slave in form, the day had passed forever when I could be a slave in fact."

Covey could have called the authorities and had his recalcitrant charge chained to the public whipping post and beaten without restraint. He did nothing, and he never touched Frederick again. Douglass later speculated that Covey was afraid of losing his reputation, and hence his income, as a slave breaker.

When his year was up (on Christmas Day, 1833), Frederick, unbroken, was sent to another master, one William Freeland, who was not as abusive as Covey. But as Douglass later punned, he "began to want to live upon free land, as well as with Freeland." He made his first real attempt at escape. Gathering four other enslaved men, he plotted to steal a canoe and paddle up Chesapeake Bay to its northern end and then "follow the guidance of the North Star." Then he proved Hugh Auld's point: because he could write, he forged passes for the five to "go to Baltimore and spend the Easter holidays." Betrayed before they could even set out, Frederick and his band were arrested. The only thing he could think to do was toss his forged pass into the fire. Eat your pass, he counseled his co-conspirators as they were hustled off to jail.

Alone behind bars, Frederick contemplated his prospects, fearing he might be sold deep into the slave empire: "We had been in jail scarcely twenty minutes, when a swarm of slave traders, and agents for slave traders, flocked into jail to look at us, and to ascertain if we were for sale. Such a set of beings I never saw before! I felt myself surrounded by so many fiends from perdition. A band of pirates never looked more like their father, the devil. They laughed and grinned over us, saying, 'Ah, my boys! We have got you, haven't we?'" (There was no William Lloyd Garrison there to chase away the fiends from Douglass's prison, as he had chased away slaver Austin Woolfolk from the Baltimore jail when imprisoned there.)

Douglass was not sold down the river. Instead, in 1836, Thomas Auld sent the ungovernable slave back to his brother Hugh in Baltimore, who, having no need for a slave, hired Douglass out to a local shipbuilder. Douglass took to shipbuilding well, and soon Hugh Auld was hiring Douglass out to several shipbuilders, bringing in up to nine dollars a week. The slave earned all the money, and the master took it all, sometimes tossing him a few coins as a "reward of this toil." After some months, Douglass managed to persuade Auld to let him function as an independent contractor, making his own deals and living on his own, not an uncommon arrangement in Baltimore. All Douglass had to do was pay Auld three dollars a week. It was a big step for the enslaved worker; he lived among the free Blacks and bondsmen in Baltimore, and he met his future wife, a free Black woman named Anna Murray. When Douglass was late bringing his weekly payment to Auld one time, and his enslaver revoked his privilege by bringing him back into the slave household, Douglass made up his mind to escape.

Not until long after the Emancipation Proclamation would Douglass tell the whole story of his escape. Even then, he did not say how he knew to organize such a sophisticated strategy or how he knew where to go once he got out. He thought it was unforgivable of escaped fugitives to reveal those things, since by doing so they would educate the slaveholder and contribute to his "facilities for capturing the slave." Even the fabled Henry "Box" Brown, the slave who escaped by boxing himself in a crate being shipped to the North and living without food or water while en route, talked too much, according to Douglass. We might have had more boxed escapes, he asserted accusatorily in his first memoir, had Brown kept the lid on it. Finally, in *The Life and Times of Frederick Douglass,* the 1881 version of his memoir, Douglass described the details of his escape.

6

(1792–1841)

Frederick Douglass's Escape

AFTER HE PUBLISHED THE STORY IN HIS 1881 third memoir, revised in 1892, Douglass wrote to Wilbur H. Siebert, a white man who was writing a history of the Underground Railroad, revealing that he had had a "connection" with the Underground Railroad long before he left the South. R. C. Smedley, another early white historian of fugitive slavery, records that the Philadelphia Black abolitionists had recruited two "market women," one black and one white, in Baltimore as agents as early as 1838.

The Black network of support and escape that helped Frederick from the moment in 1838 when he could wait no longer until he settled in New Bedford in 1839 was in fact well established before he was born. Richard Allen's Mother Bethel Church in Philadelphia was, if any place was, the center. After Allen and the Philadelphia Methodists founded the separate Black Methodist diocese and made Allen their first bishop, the new churches and their benevolent societies quickly turned their efforts to abolition. Indeed, long before Lundy, Allen's Free African Society was lobbying Congress as early as the late 1790s with petitions to end the abuse of slavery—to abolish slavery and to stop enforcing the first Fugitive Slave Act, passed in 1793. The Philadelphians were not just early adopters of abolition; they ultimately included some of the most important players, including the wealthy Black sailmaker James Forten, who often bankrolled the efforts.

In Baltimore, the Black Methodist movement soon established a separate congregation, and in 1815, before Douglass was born, one Daniel Coker broke with white Methodism and became a powerful founder of Allen's group. Coker's 1810 pamphlet *A Dialogue Between a Virginian and an African Minister* set out the basic arguments for abolition. The "Virginian" makes the South's case that abolition would be nothing more than stealing the slave owners' property. Given a choice between two wrongs, the minister astutely argues, can anyone doubt that the suffering of the Black slaves is vastly worse than the white owners' pain at the loss of their human property? Coker did not remain long in Baltimore, but his church and those who followed him had established a robust free Black abolitionist movement there by the time Douglass arrived.

A Way Out: Africa

As the historian Manisha Sinha relates in her encyclopedic volume *The Slave's Cause,* early Black abolitionists, some of whom had been brought from Africa or were but a generation or two removed from abduction and enslavement, not unreasonably thought of going back to Africa. They made common cause with the white opponents of slavery who organized to send Black Americans back to Africa as well. In 1816 a Presbyterian pastor from New Jersey, Robert Finley, along with some well-meaning Quakers and other opponents of slavery, founded the American Colonization Society, which, in 1822, established the colony of Liberia to receive the freed slaves who would be expelled. The American Colonization Society was a weird alliance of well-meaning clergymen like Finley and other prominent activists of the Benevolent Empire and southerners, including slaveholders. The colonization movement became the first outpost of the Benevolent Empire to address the issue of abolition. It fit perfectly with the religious, reformist, ambivalently racist social milieu that produced the other benevolent movements, like the segregated camp meetings and little schools to "elevate the Blacks."

Within months after the American Colonization Society was founded, a standing-room-only crowd of Black Americans gathered in the Mother Bethel Church to decide whether Black Americans should go back to Africa. Black abolitionist pioneers including Richard Allen, his early comrade Episcopal pastor Absalom Jones, and the wealthy sailmaker James Forten —many big players in Black abolition—were on the podium, and some spoke in favor. But when Forten asked the crowd, "How many here favor colonization?" not a single voice was raised. "Nay?" Forten reports the nays were fit to bring the building down. The Philadelphia resisters met with a delegate from the American Colonization Society, with neither party changing its mind. They turned to making sure that no person of color in any position within the community would support the scheme, and they spoke out and wrote against it every chance they got. Slave owners were eager to ship ex-slaves to the west coast of Africa, certain that if the free Blacks were going to stay in the United States, it was because they wanted to help their enslaved brethren to freedom.

In 1827, the same year slavery was finally totally abolished in New York, two Black activists, the minister Samuel E. Cornish and the first Black Bowdoin College graduate, John B. Russwurm, decided the moment had come. *Freedom's Journal,* the first African American–owned and –operated newspaper in America, would roll off the press. By 1838, when Frederick made his break for it, the commingled free and slave Black community in places like Baltimore had become good at moving their enslaved brethren to the North.

Douglass's Way Out

The key element in escape was the fugitive's papers. In an effort to keep control of its enslaved population, Maryland, with its large community of free Blacks, had devised a system of identification papers Blacks had to show at a moment's notice. Brave and unselfish free Black volunteers, Douglass reported in his 1881 memoir, when emancipation was no longer a crime, would share their papers with enslaved people whom they resembled. The fugitives then would use the papers to ride the train to Philadelphia. But Douglass, a light-skinned man with a light-skinned father, could find no one who looked enough like him. Instead, he got from a sailor friend a different document, one that Black sailors used to avoid enslavement if their ships got stopped. Douglass's sailor's papers, whether authentic or not, had an impressive-looking eagle at the top. Someone (family lore had it that it was Anna, his free Black fiancée) made him a nautical-looking outfit.

His only problem was that he didn't resemble the description of the sailor in the papers he carried. To minimize the scrutiny at the ticket window, a Black cabman took him right to the train, and Douglass hopped

Underground Railroad conductor David Ruggles. *Courtesy of The David Ruggles Center for History and Education.*

on board just as it started. When the conductor came to the "negro car," his manner toward Douglass was markedly friendly. "He took my fare and went on about his business," he reported, but "this moment of time was one of the most anxious I ever experienced." And then there was still the ferry ride through slave Delaware and the train to Philadelphia and then another train to New York. In free New York, Douglass wrote, "I felt as one might feel upon escape from a den of hungry lions."

Frederick had a tough day or two wandering around New York, afraid to ask anyone for help or directions for fear of being betrayed back into slavery. "Free" soil in 1838 was anything but free, with slave catchers hunting around the border and transit places, looking for their prey. As Douglass writes in his second and third memoirs, he chanced upon a Black sailor and decided to trust him. The stranger took Douglass to David Ruggles, Black activist and famed conductor on the real Underground Railroad in New York. A few days later Anna arrived from Baltimore, and the two

Anna Murray Douglass. *Courtesy of Library of Congress.*

were married in Ruggles's living room. Learning Douglass was skilled at
caulking ships, Ruggles determined that he and his new wife should settle
in New Bedford, Massachusetts, a shipping town known for its hostility
to itinerant slave catchers from the South. This is when the former slave
named Frederick Bailey gave himself a new name, Douglass, and left for
New Bedford. He met a white man who was not a hungry lion, Quaker
William Coffin. After hearing his story, in 1841 Coffin decided Douglass
should go to Nantucket.

PART II

—— • ◆ • ——

ABOLITION TAKES ROOT

7

(1826–1841)

David Walker Appeals and Garrison Hears

ON NANTUCKET, DOUGLASS WOULD MEET GARRISON, WHO had lived so close to him in Baltimore in the earliest days of abolition in 1830. Things had changed a lot by 1841. While Douglass schemed and struggled to escape slavery himself during the 1830s, Garrison and the others on Nantucket had been building the movement to end slavery completely.

David Walker Appeals

As the unexpected conflict over Missouri in 1819 revealed, resistance to slavery had been brewing for a while when Garrison signed on in 1830. But if anything can be said to mark the formal beginning of the modern abolition movement that greeted Frederick Douglass, it was the publication of Black activist David Walker's *Appeal to the Coloured Citizens of the World* in September of 1829. Walker, the son of a slave father and a free Black mother, traced the path of Black abolition in his own life. Born free but in slave North Carolina, he settled in Boston just in time to join the Massachusetts General Colored Association, a very early, unambiguously abolitionist Black society. By then around thirty and married, he made a good living selling used clothes.

When Walker arrived in Boston, all three elements of a radical social movement were in place: a network, proximity, and oppression. The foundational Black church was firmly established all over the Northeast, and the Black communal leaders had founded a web of mutual aid societies in the wake of the church movement. Hostility to free Blacks in northern cities forced them to live in close proximity to one another. They faced growing vocal hostility from white workingmen as Black competitors began flowing north into an increasingly competitive economy.

Black people were grouped together, oppressed, and organized. What could they do? The only white antislavery movement of any consequence kept suggesting they move to Africa. Since a month after the American Colonization Society was founded in 1817, Black spokesmen had been telling their white "benefactors" that they would not be moved.

In 1826, three men from the Revolutionary War–era Black Masonic Lodge founded the Massachusetts General Colored Association, explicitly to fight slavery in the South and discrimination in the North. In 1827 they finally got their mouthpiece, *Freedom's Journal.* At its height the Black newspaper had roughly a thousand subscribers. Although *Freedom's Journal* ultimately faltered in its opposition to colonization, for a crucial year, every week, Black Americans could gather around the latest issue of their newspaper for news on the topics of slavery and discrimination.

Walker was vocal: in an address to the Massachusetts General Colored Association, he movingly vowed that he would do anything "to meliorate our miserable condition." When speeches and orations no longer did the job, Walker, who had been a subscription agent for *Freedom's Journal,* turned to the press. Like Lundy and Garrison, he knew precisely the value of print.

Boston was full of printers. Printers who were able to buy a printing press, even the printers who were publishers of regular newspapers, made the business work by contracting odd printing jobs in addition to their main business. This practice made marginal enterprises like Walker's pamphlet possible and is probably how *Freedom's Journal* stayed afloat even for its brief lifespan. Walker, however, accurately presented the seventy-five-page pamphlet as being *published* by himself. The emotional appeal is visually startling, with multiple exclamation points, capital letters, and the pointing finger, the "manicule," which, as we have seen, appears in much of Garrison's writing as well.

Walker wrote the *Appeal* in explicit imitation of the Declaration of Independence. Article I explains the "wretchedness in consequence of slavery." Walker saw that the condition of Black people is the consequence of human decisions by their oppressors, not nature. He focused particularly on the insulting suggestion from, of all people, Thomas Jefferson that his

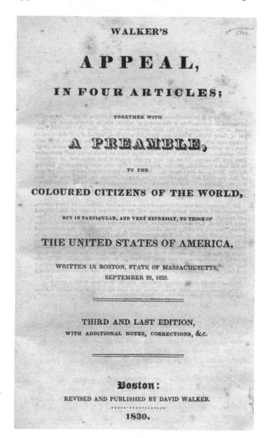

David Walker's *Appeal. Courtesy of Documenting the American South.*

race was naturally suited for servitude. Walker stressed that oppression is man-made—a critical moment in any movement. Article II turns to "Our Wretchedness in Consequence of Ignorance." Much of it is a call to "education" and "enlightenment," through school, thrift, and the like, but the worst ignorance Walker described is "if any thing is whispered by one, which has any allusion to the melioration of their dreadful condition, they run and tell tyrants, that they may be enabled to keep them the longer in wretchedness and miseries." Walker offered his readers an explanation for this self-destructive behavior: "Natural observations have taught me these things; there is a solemn awe in the hearts of the blacks, as it respects *murdering* men.*"

And then he elaborated, with agonizing clarity, "*Which is the reason the whites take the advantage of us."

Article III blames the wretchedness on Christian Americans, who, in

defiance of the explicit teachings of the Bible, abuse their Black fellow
humans at every turn, beating them even for the effrontery of practicing
Christianity. Finally, Article IV turns to the proposal to send Black people
to Africa, where Walker simply invokes the colonizationists' own words
about their motives: America must rid itself of free Blacks, the colonizationists wrote with alarming candor, or they would teach the slaves that
the slaves were men.

Throughout the *Appeal*, Walker described what he thought lay in wait
for white citizens:

> The whites have had us under them for more than three centuries,
> murdering, and treating us like brutes; and, as Mr. Jefferson wisely said,
> they have never *found us out*—they do not know, indeed, that there is
> an unconquerable disposition in the breasts of the blacks, which, when
> it is fully awakened and put in motion, will be subdued, only with the
> destruction of the animal existence. Get the blacks started, and if you
> do not have a gang of tigers and lions to deal with, I am a deceiver of
> the blacks and of the whites.

If that wasn't scary enough, Walker turned again to Jefferson. "Now, I
ask you," he inquired of his "Dearly Beloved Brethren," invoking the core
meaning of the Declaration of Independence, "had you not rather be killed
than to be a slave to a tyrant?"

Walker ended his *Appeal* with a recitation of "A declaration made July
4, 1776." Within a few weeks, a white sailor delivered a packet containing
copies of Walker's *Appeal* to a free Black Baptist minister in Savannah,
who turned the papers in to the white masters. The Georgia authorities,
predictably, had fits. Jefferson's fellow white citizens were afraid. And they
were right to be afraid.

Garrison Hears Walker's *Appeal*

David Walker's *Appeal* reached Garrison at his desk in Baltimore in 1829
at the abolitionist *Genius of Universal Emancipation*. The paper, then still in
the hands of pacifist Quaker Benjamin Lundy, was silent for some weeks.
Walker's *Appeal*, with its call to arms, posed the dilemma Garrison would

wrestle with until Fort Sumter: his pacifism versus his hatred of slavery. But Garrison covered Walker's tract nonetheless. Starting in January of 1830, in the months before his libel trial, Garrison ran a series of articles praising the passionate denunciation of slavery.

Tuberculosis plagued Boston in 1830, and less than a year after the *Appeal,* David Walker was dead. Had Walker lived, he might well have occupied some of the space Frederick Douglass filled ten years later, but with more and earlier militancy. In arguing from Christian and secular American ideals, the *Appeal* bears more than a passing resemblance to Douglass's second memoir, *My Bondage and My Freedom.*

Walker's *Appeal to the Coloured Citizens of the World* reached Garrison at a crucial moment. (Walker's son, born posthumously, was named Edwin Garrison Walker.) Cast out by the cautious Lundy in the spring of 1830, Garrison left Baltimore determined to start his own abolitionist newspaper.

Garrison's travels over the next seven months are a map of the social organization he would put together: Benevolent Emperors, the Black community, idealistic clergymen, and liberal intellectuals of both sexes.

Garrison follower Samuel May.
Courtesy of Massachusetts Historical Society.

First he went to New York for funding from Benevolent Emperor Arthur Tappan, the silk merchant who had bailed him out of jail. Tappan gave Garrison a hundred dollars. Using what little money he'd gleaned, he went to Philadelphia, where he met with Lundy's Quaker circle and, most importantly, with Lundy's Black abolitionist friend James Forten. Garrison spoke three times in Quaker Philadelphia, and each time the only white people in the audience were ... Quakers. As Lundy had said when he came to Boston looking for Presbyterians, a few Quakers don't make a movement. But Garrison also attracted Forten and the Philadelphia Black benevolent leaders. In New Haven, where a white Tappan ally, Simeon Jocelyn, was temporarily running the United African Society, Garrison spoke to a Black audience.

Then he came back to Boston. None of the established church leaders would let him in to speak—certainly not the famed Lyman Beecher, who had spurred the adoption of the Great Awakening into the conventional Congregational Church. The most marginal player in the Boston circuit, the minister of a freethinking Universalist Society, offered his shabby quarters, and Garrison went there. In his lecture at the Universalists' in 1830, Garrison assembled the last two pieces of his coalition, the clergy and the idealists. One man, Samuel J. May, was both. Son of a wealthy old Boston merchant family, the Harvard-educated May had become a Unitarian minister and New Awakening reformer. Like many of Garrison's early contacts, May was also an acquaintance of Lundy; he came to the lecture to hear Lundy's protégé Garrison speak. Transformed by the experience, May offered himself to Garrison as an apostle and remained until the end of his life. We know of the prominence of the May family because the wealthy and well-connected Samuel May's sister Abigail was Louisa May Alcott's mother and the model for "Marmee," the kind, socially conscious mother from *Little Women*. Samuel May pulled the strings to get Garrison into the Boston Athenaeum in 1830 to repeat his lecture. Slowly, in Samuel May's wake, the followers surfaced: May's brother-in-law (Louisa's father) A. Bronson Alcott; May's cousin Samuel Sewall, the son of an old Revolutionary War–era abolitionist; May's Harvard classmate David L. Child, editor of the newspaper the *Massachusetts Journal;* and the first white female activist, Lydia Maria Child, successful writer and David Child's wife.

The Liberator

It would be Boston, then. Garrison reconnected with his pal from apprenticeship days, Isaac Knapp, a true worker bee. They finagled space in the Merchants' Hall building on Water Street. In the same building, Stephen Foster, in past years a printer on David Child's *Massachusetts Journal,* had become the foreman of the Unitarian paper *Christian Examiner.* Foster bargained for time on the *Examiner's* press to run three issues of Garrison's newspaper.

On December 10, 1830, as Garrison was putting together the inaugural issue, he took time to address a meeting of the "colored people" of Boston. One of the most prominent, James G. Barbadoes, later wrote a note to Garrison: "I would acknowledge the debt of gratitude under which we labor, for your Address before us ... We cannot sufficiently express our feelings; for nothing was ever uttered more important and beneficial to our color."

But the gratitude ran both ways. Barbadoes was to become one of three core Black Garrison associates at every step of the establishment of the modern abolitionist movement. Barbadoes, a founding father of two of the most important Black Boston institutions—the African Masonic Lodge 459 and David Walker's Massachusetts General Colored Association —was the grandson of free Blacks. His uncle Isaac Barbadoes, Fifteenth Massachusetts Regiment, died fighting for American independence in the Revolutionary War. Barbadoes's brother Robert was kidnapped off an American ship in the Port of New Orleans, where he was held in chains for more than five months and flogged for claiming that he was freeborn. By chance, a cellmate was released after proving his own free status and, when he got out, found Robert's parents, who petitioned everyone up to the governor of Massachusetts to demand Robert's release. He was successfully returned to Boston. James told his brother's story to Garrisonian David Lee Child, who made it part of his 1833 compilation of slavery outrages, *The Despotism of Freedom.*

The 1830 address to a Black audience was the first of many as Garrison gathered the critical Black support that got *The Liberator* going. James Barbadoes led the Black Boston abolition group into union with the white abolitionists and was one of the three Black founders of the mostly white

American Anti-Slavery Society in Philadelphia in 1833. Right after he met with Barbadoes's group, Garrison again wrote to wealthy Black Philadelphian James Forten, begging for money. He had bought a little newsprint on credit to get the first issue of *The Liberator* printed, and the bill was due in days. Just in time, a check came. It was a payment for twenty-seven subscriptions, Forten wrote, in a typically generous move, saving face for Garrison.

He Would Be Heard

First issue of *The Liberator. Courtesy of Massachusetts Historical Society.*

On January 1, 1831, the first issue of *The Liberator* came off the (borrowed) press. There are many important pronouncements in American history— *when in the course of human events, in order to form a more perfect union, fourscore and seven years ago.* But surely one of the most important, though lesser known, is Garrison's announcement of his stance on abolition in the first issue of *The Liberator:* "I do not wish to think, or speak, or write, with moderation . . . I am in earnest—I will not equivocate—I will not excuse —I will not retreat a single inch—AND I WILL BE HEARD."

Who heard him? Black people and white. First, a few hundred subscribers, most of them free and Black. Garrison was clear about the importance of his Black audience. In the early months, while single-handedly writing most of *The Liberator*'s content and, with Knapp's help, printing it on a cobbled-together mess of used type and a ridiculously outmoded press, he kept speaking to groups of Black Americans, in cities up and down the East Coast. In his speeches, he promised to devote himself to them. "I NEVER," he began, "rise to address a colored audience, without feeling ashamed of my own color, ashamed of being identified with a race of men who have done you so much injustice, and who yet retain so large a portion of your brethren in servile chains. To make atonement, in part, for this conduct, I have solemnly dedicated my health, and strength, and life, to your service. I love to plan and to work for your social, intellectual, political and spiritual advancement. My happiness is augmented with yours: in your sufferings I participate."

It wasn't just slavery. From the first year, Garrison also took on the Massachusetts law against interracial marriage (the law was abolished in 1843). The race/sex laws were an artifact of the early eighteenth century but were nonetheless ground zero in the long battle for equality for free Black Americans.

As Garrison circulated among his Black supporters, he also came to realize that he had to do something about the competition, the American Colonization Society. Starting in 1830, the leaders of the growing Black activist community had begun holding annual conventions. Garrison did not attend the legendary first meeting, hosted by Bishop Richard Allen in Philadelphia months before Allen's death. But he did go to the second meeting — the first formally named convention — in 1831. This meeting was composed of more than a dozen elected delegates from at least seven states; the convention elected as president the Philadelphia used-clothes merchant John C. Bowers and as vice presidents Abraham Shadd, already active in the Underground Railroad from his strategic location in Delaware, and William Duncan. The white cohort from *The Liberator* came too: Garrison, his predecessor William Lundy, and their benefactor Arthur Tappan. The white guests listened while the Black delegates resolved that the American Colonization Society was a major cause of their suffering. "Not doubting the benevolent feelings" of "some individuals engaged in the [colonization] cause," they nevertheless called on "Christians of every denomination firmly to resist it." And to be faithful to his brethren of color, as he promised, Garrison would have to take up the fight against colonization too.

Colonization had more white supporters than Garrison's lonely immediatist *Liberator* had. For many years, the American Colonization Society had occupied the abolitionist energies of the Benevolent Empire. Since many of the Emperors were big city northern businessmen with interests in the cotton trade, the racist and unthreatening colonization strategy appealed mightily to them.

The majority of Black abolitionists detested colonization. They felt, as the second convention expressed so graphically in 1831, that colonization, with its assumption that nonwhite Americans would never be able to assume citizenship, was the cause of abuse of Blacks, even those who were free from slavery. Garrison took on the job of harrowing the powerful, well-connected banishment society in the paper, using his sharpest weapon against the colonizers and highlighting their hypocrisy. Would you send the Englishman back to England? *The Liberator* asked. Colonization, Garrison later wrote, was a "CONSPIRACY AGAINST HUMAN RIGHTS," printing the phrase in his characteristic all caps.

Within a year, Garrison had figured out that his project of immediate abolition could gain no traction while his best prospects for white allies remained drugged with the unjust and unattainable project of sending their countrymen to Africa. His first salvo in the pamphlet campaigns that would do so much to abolish slavery was a broadside against colonization.

With his belated support of David Walker—author of the militant *Appeal*—his fierce antagonism toward colonization, and his farsighted opposition to the racial marriage laws, Garrison launched *The Liberator* on a sea of Black subscribers. John Hilton, Grand Master of Prince Hall African Masonic Lodge, and a committee of his peers assured the new editor that "the descendants of Africa ... are now convinced of the sincerity of your intentions, and are proud to claim you as their advocate."

The Gallows Confession of Nat Turner

In August 1831, eight months after the first issue of *The Liberator*, enslaved Nat Turner led an uprising in Virginia. Sixty or so slaves followed Turner's call to revolt, and fifty some white Virginians were killed before the armed whites captured the leader. A Virginia lawyer, Thomas Ruffin Gray, published *The Confessions of Nat Turner*, supposedly a rendition of Gray's interview with Turner on the eve of his execution. Turner's gallows speech in the *Confessions* is one of the first of many such scenes in the slave narrative literature. These unrepentant deathbed scenes of slave rebels and, later, their would-be emancipators like John Brown greatly multiplied the political impact of what would otherwise have been garden-variety criminal trials. When Gray asked Turner if he now understood how wrong he was, Turner supposedly responded, "Was not Christ crucified?"

The Slave Empire Takes on *The Liberator*

It didn't take the enslavers long to make a connection. Nat Turner was literate and claimed to be divinely inspired. Whether he read *The Liberator* or not, Turner's rebellion triggered a region-wide campaign against Garrison, who was in fact revolted by the violence although sympathetic to the cause, and the publisher's tiny band. In the wake of Nat Turner's rebellion, the slave empire launched its thirty-year campaign against *The Liberator* and thus unwittingly recruited to the cause of abolition defenders of the press, who otherwise would have remained uninterested in defending the enslaved. Southern postmasters confiscated copies of *The Liberator*. A grand jury in Raleigh, North Carolina, indicted Garrison for distributing incendiary matter. A South Carolina senator asked his old friend the mayor of Boston to suppress *The Liberator*. The state of Georgia offered a five-thousand-dollar reward for its editor's rendition.

Outside the slave states, the leading Washington, D.C., political newspaper, the *National Intelligencer*, published an article comparing *The Liberator* to poison in the public water. The editors demanded that the mayor of Boston and the Massachusetts legislature suppress its publication. The attack from this powerful quarter showed how deep and wide the opposition to abolition ran. Although the publishers of the *National Intelligencer* had ties to North Carolina, their families, including a family member active in the American Colonization Society, were not slave-owning families. The official position of the *National Intelligencer* was that slavery, while bad, should not be allowed to tear the union apart. Garrison thought the attack on him was a great opportunity to give his obscure paper coverage, and wrote a scathing response for the pages of the *National Intelligencer*. The professionals at the Washington paper refused to give Garrison the exposure.

The politicians and journalists in the slave South exercised no such strategic restraint. Garrison's movement and the Nat Turner rebellion were on everyone's lips. Serving in the Aulds' house at the time, "every little

while" enslaved teenager Douglass would hear someone talk of "the abolitionists." "If a slave ran away and succeeded in getting clear, or if a slave
killed his master, set fire to a barn, or did any thing very wrong in the mind
of a slaveholder, it was spoken of as the fruit of *abolition*. Hearing the word
in this connection very often, I set about learning what it meant," he would
write in the *Narrative* of his life, years later.

The enslaved teen was not the only one to notice that "the abolitionists" were on to something crucial. Every act the South took to silence the
abolitionists only created allies for the otherwise marginal and powerless
Garrison and his mostly Black readers. Garrison continued to provoke the
southerners. Eight months after starting his own journal, he adopted a
new tool for provocation. He put an engraving of a slave auction in front
of the national Capitol in Washington at the top of the front page of *The
Liberator*. If words from his tiny publication had attracted the attention of
senators and governors, Garrison thought, think what pictures would do.

8

(1830–1833)

Starting the Black and White Antislavery Societies

GARRISON WAS A NATURAL NEWSPAPERMAN. BUT HIS mission did not stop at the printshop. Garrison had learned from Lundy and from the British antislavery movement, which was about to accomplish complete abolition in the British West Indies, that any effective movement had to have boots on the ground. Even with no constituents other than a handful of Quakers, Lundy had started modest manumission societies in the upper South and the West, where slavery was not so well entrenched as in the cotton empire. Garrison had to turn from journalism to activism.

Band of White Brothers

Unlike Lundy, by 1831 Garrison had a starting place: the Black abolition societies like the Massachusetts General Colored Association in Boston. But Garrison always acted on the assumption that an effective antislavery society needed to include prominent and well-connected white supporters. He started efforts to establish such a society with, as usual, an appeal to the wealthy Tappan brothers of New York.

The New York merchants' "association of gentlemen" had become the New York Committee. Inspired by the progress the gentlemen in Great Britain had been making against slavery in the British Empire, the New York reformers were increasingly looking at the abolition movement. Nonetheless, Arthur Tappan turned Garrison away with a pat on the back and a pittance. Reflecting the deep ties between the powerful economic engine that was the slave economy and the commercial institutions of the eastern seaboard, a few months later Tappan rebuked Garrison for discussing him in *The Liberator,* reminding Garrison that the Tappan enterprises relied on southern customers for the money he was using to support Garrison's cause. Tappan was to become such a hero of abolition that he was later hanged in effigy by the enslavers. Yet Arthur Tappan was, like Maria Weston Chapman's uncle Joshua, dependent for his largesse on profits from slavery.

Tappan's refusal led Garrison back to the idealists of the Samuel May circle, who had gathered around him since his first Boston lecture. Garrison's Boston social circle was expanding. For a man with his reputation as an obsessive, uncompromising do-gooder, Garrison was in fact charismatic and charming. From his days in the printshop at the *Newburyport Herald,* he had the gift of gathering people around him and crafting passionate, articulate conversation. The *Liberator* office soon became a kind of seminar room. Oliver Johnson, a young printer and early supporter from the print

CONSTITUTION

OF THE

NEW-ENGLAND ANTI-SLAVERY SOCIETY:

WITH AN

ADDRESS TO THE PUBLIC.

———

BOSTON:
PRINTED BY GARRISON AND KNAPP.

1832.

Constitution of the New England Anti-Slavery Society. *Courtesy of the University of Minnesota.*

house seminars, now turning out a Christian paper on Garrison's modest press, had the good sense to keep a journal recording those founding days.

On November 13, 1831, Johnson, Samuel May, and a dozen more supporters met in the law offices of Samuel Sewall, one of Garrison's toniest followers, to discuss forming an organization. Garrison had hoped for twelve "apostles" among the all-white group, but that night only nine of the attendees agreed that immediate abolition should be specified in the founding documents. Still, they appointed a drafting committee to report at a follow-up meeting, this time scheduled in a schoolroom under the African Baptist Church on Joy Street. On January 6, 1832, a fierce storm was raging, and the streets were full of slush. It was dark, light not being lavished by the City of Boston upon what locals called "N—r Hill." In the presence of a half-dozen or more luminaries of the Boston Black community, the requisite twelve white men steeled themselves to sign off on immediate abolition. The first significant white immediatist abolition organization, the New England Anti-Slavery Society, was born. On February 18, Garrison published its constitution and bylaws in *The Liberator:* emancipation must be immediate, the state of free colored citizens eased and elevated, and all talk of colonization banished.

Historians dispute the role of Black people at the creation of the New England Anti-Slavery Society. Below the signatures of the white twelve, the Society's constitution contains a parallel list of Black names, including James Barbadoes. Later joiners, Black and white, signed off on integrated lists. Historian Henry Mayer concluded that the Black signatures were auxiliary at the beginning, and no one has uncovered contrary evidence. This arrangement did not last. In January 1833, a little over a year after the Society's founding, the Massachusetts General Colored Association voted to affiliate as an auxiliary to the New England Anti-Slavery Society. By 1835, two Black men—Barbadoes and Hosea Easton—were members of the Board of Counsellors of Garrison's antislavery group.

The Antislavery Empire

Within weeks of the founding, New England Anti-Slavery Society board member the poet and publisher Alonzo Lewis, also known as the "Bard of Lynn," established an antislavery society in Lynn, Massachusetts. The humble Quaker hatmaker Arnold Buffum took the role of first "agent" for the new group. For a tiny fee he wandered across New England, seeking followers who would contribute something. He wasn't a dynamic speaker, and often could not even get the Quakers to open their meetinghouses to his radical ideas. He spoke to small crowds in small halls. Occasionally he lucked into a denunciation from a conventional pulpit, which swelled his turnout. Women came, and Black supporters. In 1832, "black women of Salem, Massachusetts" started the first Female Anti-Slavery Society.

The New England Anti-Slavery Society apostles, worthy of their name, fanned out from Boston and started preaching immediate emancipation. They leaned on the liberal preachers they knew; many of the people associated with the early chapters were the rare abolitionist Presbyterian and Methodist ministers.

The ministry is a through line in the survival of Garrison's movement. One of the two lions of the Great Awakening, American preacher Charles Grandison Finney, was antislavery. He never gave abolition priority over his primary religious commitment, saving souls, but his support lent the movement legitimacy as it sought the backing of other, more worldly preachers. Whenever a minister signed on, he could usually find a few others in his small town — often among the local lawyers — who agreed on the evils of slavery. The New Englanders hired three or four agents to go into the field. Within two years after the Society's founding, the group of twelve "apostles" reported they had established forty-seven societies from Maine to Ohio. The turbulence that surfaced in the debates over admitting slave Missouri in 1820 had been a prophetic, not a passing, warning.

The establishment American Colonization Society began to feel the hot breath of the insurgents. At first the well-funded and well-connected colonizers ignored the low-class upstarts. A snobbish American Constitution Society spokesman called Buffum, derisively, the "Quaker hatter." Big mistake. Most of the antislavery activists in the small New England towns were to come from the middling ranks of society — craftsmen, skilled laborers, shoemakers, cordwainers. Garrison took the insult and ran with it.

Like the hapless southerners who had attacked *The Liberator*, the American Colonization Society leaders decided to debate the newcomers. All that did was raise attendance at their appearances. Garrison carefully assembled the damning things the opposition had said about the real, racist intention of colonization, added an introduction, and published the assemblage in his only book-length production, *Thoughts on African Colonization*, in 1832.

Thoughts on African Colonization was a hit. The Tappan brothers bought hundreds of copies and distributed them around the Benevolent Empire. The colonizationists couldn't win: If they ignored Garrison's troops, the antislavery activists had a clear shot at the potential supporters. If they debated the Garrisonians, they turned out audiences for Garrison's newborn movement and were routinely humiliated. Colonization was impractical, incoherent, and racist. The movement had transported a few thousand mostly free Blacks, while two and a half million souls remained enslaved. The book spurred debates, and in small New England towns, one dissenting minister could always be found to take the anti-colonization position. Debates were the bread and butter of the dissenting colleges, like Maine's Colby College and Western Reserve College in Ohio. Propelled by the debate, the support for antislavery spread.

Theodore D. Weld. *Courtesy of Connecticut Freedom Trail.*

The Dignity of Labor

Abolition found unexpected allies. Garrison's friends from the Benevolent Empire embraced a range of interests, including a movement to elevate the status of manual labor. No more effete seminary study for their sons, the manual labor leaders proclaimed. The manual labor movement founded schools like the Oneida Institute in upstate New York, which required students to labor on farms for part of each school year. The manual labor movement bled right into antislavery. If labor was noble, why would people have to be enslaved to do it? The idea of the Greek model of slavery, much invoked in the South as a necessary evil for liberating the noble citizens to do higher work, lost some of its power. Beriah Green, the president of Oneida, had read Garrison and insisted that his appeal for abolition be made part of the makeup of the manual labor school. In July of 1832, shortly after Garrison founded *The Liberator,* the students at Oneida started a society for immediate abolition.

One of the Oneida Institute's most avid products was the scion of an old New England family of preachers, Theodore D. Weld. A trained Protestant minister deeply embedded in the social movements that emerged from the Second Great Awakening, Weld, like many of the abolitionists, first took up not abolition but the cause of an earlier reform movement — in Weld's case, the dignity of manual labor. While Weld was at Oneida, he met two abolitionist mentors, the Great Awakening preacher Charles Grandison Finney and the British abolitionist Charles Stuart. Stuart became a lifelong friend and is often credited with financing Weld's years at Oneida. Weld and Finney were soon preaching together for revival, abolition, and temperance.

When the Tappans decided to open a seminary to train leaders for the new labor movement, they hired Weld to find a location. Weld and the Tappans landed on Cincinnati, Ohio, deep in the rapidly developing Northwest, for their new school, the Lane Seminary. Boston Congregationalist minister Lyman Beecher was recruited as president. As often was the case with Weld, a band of his fellows followed him, this time from Oneida to Lane. Once Weld settled in at Lane, he looked at the assembled students, from North and South alike, and decided that what the campus needed was a teach-in on abolition. When Weld had finished his lectures in 1834, the participants, including several southerners experiencing pangs of conscience, were born again to the abolition cause. Abandoning all thoughts of colonization, they adopted Garrisonian radical immediatism and started tutoring the free Blacks and fugitive slaves who had settled in Cincinnati.

Correctly fearing that students throughout the North would demand abolitionist courses of their own, a conclave of college presidents, including Lane's president, Lyman Beecher, adopted a set of resolutions to stop the discussion of abolition. By December, the seminary board, laden with businessmen with strong ties to the South, had tossed Weld and his friends out, gifting the renegades with the irresistible title "Lane Rebels." The runaways found refuge at Oberlin College, one of the first interracial and coeducational colleges in America, which had been dying for lack of funds. Predictably, the college presidents' repressive measures set off an explosion of campus activism all across the North. Weld, done with school, and the rebels started lecturing around the region. In Ohio alone, Weld's appearances created dozens of antislavery strongholds with stunning results.

From twelve white men in the basement of a Black church, through the efforts of workingmen and women, Black and white, and of dissenting ministers and argumentative college students, the tendrils of immediate abolitionism began to spread throughout the North.

The British Connection

In the spring of 1833, Garrison had learned that the American Colonization Society was sending an emissary to England to celebrate the abolition of slavery in the British Empire. He promptly cadged enough money to go himself—his first trip abroad—to head off the competition. Money from Black supporters paid much of the freight, and Garrison's joint appearances with fellow American abolitionist and Black Baptist minister Nathaniel Paul may have been the first major public appearance of the new, interracial movement.

The trip served Garrison's purposes beyond his wildest dreams. An editor of a paper always on the edge of bankruptcy with a circulation of a few hundred, now he was meeting all the lions of the legendary British abolition movement as they succeeded in banning slavery in British lands.

Again he used the debate-and-lose or refuse-to-debate-and-lose trap on the colonization representatives in England. Spotting an American Colonization Society representative in the audience at a big Garrison lecture, the radicals challenged the man to debate. "I'll give him two hours to my one," Garrison's English ally boasted. But the Society said no dice, not realizing perhaps that refusing to debate in England is regarded as the clearest manifestation of cowardice. The meeting went wild, with jeering and hooting. By the time Garrison finished with the American Colonization Society, the powerful and successful English abolitionist movement was heavily on the side of the Garrisonian immediatists.

As Garrison slowly built his resistance network, the machinery of slavery ground on without a hiccup. While Garrison was scrounging for twelve white founders for the first Anti-Slavery Society in 1832, Douglass, aged fourteen, was being sent back to rural Maryland in a dispute in the family that owned him. It was a "painful separation," he recalled, from the street boys who had helped him learn to read and encouraged his desire for freedom. But as the ship carried him back, he took note of the steamboats sailing north to Philadelphia. He was "determined to be off."

9

(1833–1834)

A National Movement Emerges

WHEN GARRISON RETURNED FROM ENGLAND IN OCTOBER 1833, he found Tappan ready to take risks. Theodore Weld and the New York faction had organized a national group, the American Anti-Slavery Society. Without Garrison's knowledge, the New Yorkers set a meeting at Clinton Hall for the day he arrived back in New York from Europe. The New York papers had gotten wind of the meeting, and an anti-abolition mob, the Clinton Hall rioters, closed the New York effort down. The 1833 riot reveals how the strains within abolition sometimes outweighed the importance of the cause. Many historians believe it was the Colonization Society people, thinking their new competitor Garrison would be leading the assemblage, who went to the New York papers to incite the mob.

Regardless of the disparate motives, mob violence would mark the rest of the 1830s for the young immediatist movement. The abolitionists were in that dangerous middle ground for a true social change movement: successful enough to be threatening—to the American union, and therefore to the commercial interests of places like New York and Boston—but not successful enough to attract any protectors with real muscle. Volunteers from Boston's Black community took turns covertly following Garrison home from the *Liberator* office when he stayed late. Yet every time a mob gathered, it was the Black residents who suffered. At Clinton Hall, a Black spectator with no apparent connection to the organization was made to play "Arthur Tappan" in a burlesque of the abandoned meeting after the mob drove the abolitionists out. New York City rioters turned on the Black neighborhoods, destroying homes, businesses, and churches. Resi-

Rioting in New York in 1837. *Courtesy of the Metropolitan Museum of Art, New York City.*

dents' lives were spared only because Black New Yorkers had been warned in advance to flee their own homes.

The violence reached its peak in the mid-1830s. In July 1834, a mob infiltrated the celebration of the anniversary of New York State's abolition of slavery and then ransacked Lewis Tappan's home. In Boston on October 21, 1835, a bloodthirsty mob of merchants and a crowd of men and boys coming from the vicinity of the New England Anti-Slavery Society headquarters at 46 Washington Street attacked the meeting of the newly formed Boston Female Anti-Slavery Society. Maria Weston Chapman, who had joined the women's group only the previous year, had to flee the violence. The group came within a hair's breadth of tarring and feathering Garrison himself as he tried to escape the building. Rescued by a couple of quick-thinking teamsters in the area, who hustled him to sanctuary at City Hall, he spent another night in jail, this time for his own protection. Several of Garrison's most important supporters — the patricians Edmund Quincy and Wendell Phillips — dated their conversion to Garrison's cause to their witnessing that event. The anti-abolitionist mob made the fundamental mistake of attacking a man who bought ink by the barrel, once again giving Garrison a martyrdom story he could tell in *The Liberator.*

Two years later, in 1837, a mob attacked the warehouse in Alton, Illinois, where the abolitionist editor Elijah P. Lovejoy had hidden his printing press. In anticipation of trouble. Lovejoy and his allies had armed themselves to defend the press, but when he stepped out of the building, Lovejoy was instantly gunned down. His murder touched the heart of a rising Illinois politician, and Abraham Lincoln, who had previously been silent, gave a moving speech against the rioters: "Let every man remember that to violate the law, is to trample on the blood of his father, and to tear the charter of his own, and his children's liberty . . . Let reverence for the laws be breathed by every American mother . . . in short let it become the political religion of the nation."

The opponents of abolition saw that Garrison and the abolitionists were gaining traction. The purpose of the meeting the Clinton Hall mob dispersed in 1833 had been to plan the first national organization. When Garrison found that the mob had driven off the Tappan crowd, he insisted on holding the meeting immediately anyway. Philadelphia, the original ground zero of antislavery, would be the site of the first national meeting of the American Anti-Slavery Society.

When the Philadelphia meeting opened on December 4, 1833, the founders set a familiar pattern for the movement. Sixty idealistic white men came from all over the North. Although the white men would always be dominant, there would be Black participants, at every level. Three of the delegates were prominent Black abolitionists like Barbadoes, and the governing body included three more. There was at least one woman, Quaker Lucretia Mott, although soon there would be many more. The first meeting, held at the meeting hall of the Black benevolent society, the Adelphi, could exist only because the free Black community enabled it to happen: when the police chief told the organizers he could not be responsible for the delegates' safety after dark, the delegates boarded at their Black allies' homes. Garrison wrote the founding document at the home of Black delegate James McCrummell, a Philadelphia dentist.

The overwhelmingly white gathering sheltered by the overwhelmingly Black community adopted the Declaration of Sentiments Garrison had written for them. As in his speech about Douglass at Nantucket eight years later, Garrison sounded the two perennial themes of abolition: slavery was a sin, and it was a stain upon the holy writ of liberty, the Declaration of Independence. Regarding that compromise with evil, the Constitution, its slave clauses must be broken up.

Sixty white men (mostly ministers of the most marginal beliefs and affiliations, and a couple of New York silk merchants), one Quaker woman, and three Black abolitionists were going to end slavery in America.

Look Around, Look Around

The sixty had their work cut out for them. By 1835, more than two million Americans, or fifteen percent of the population, were held in slavery. As early as 1820, three hundred thousand slaves had been transferred to the western cotton lands from Maryland and Virginia alone, in the largest movement of people in American history. Cotton eclipsed all other southern crops. By the Civil War, raw cotton would constitute more than half the exports from the entire United States.

Cotton was southern. But almost everything surrounding the crop enriched the "free" North, especially the commercial city of New York. Ships from New York's deep harbor carried the cotton to the world. Only the big New York and London banks—like Maria's uncle Joshua's Baring Brothers—had the resources to manage the planters' credit from crop to crop. Even slaves were usually bought on credit. New England supplied the ships, first to bring the slaves, then, after the international slave trade was curtailed in 1808, to ship the slave-produced cotton. Northern insurers insured the whole business, and New England mills wove the cloth. The people who ran the South and the North were, in abolitionist senator Charles Sumner's later immortal phrase, an "unhallowed alliance of the lords of the lash and the lords of the loom." Few shipowners had the moral courage, as Maria Weston Chapman's father-in-law did, to forgo the tainted crop.

Politics, the normal locus for battles over the country's meaning and future, offered no purchase for abolition. A few years before the first antislavery society was formed, after a long period with only one major American political party—the Democratic-Republicans—the backers of upstart

Andrew Jackson broke up the one-party era and formed a separate faction, a more southern-oriented Democratic Party. In 1828 the popular Jackson and the new Democrats took the White House. In response to Jackson's policies, more conservative, more northern business interests formed a second party, the Whigs. Crucially, after the reorientation, each party had supporters in both the North and the South. More conservative, wealthy large plantation owners in the South joined the wealthy, business-friendly northern Whigs. Populist, individualistic northern voters joined Jackson's Democrats.

Although the two parties disagreed vehemently about many crucial public issues — tariffs, the need for a national bank, the relative power of the states versus the federal government — they presented an eerily united front over slavery. Historians dispute almost every aspect of the politics of the antebellum period. Some argue that politicians concentrated on matters like tariffs to avoid the corrosive power of the slavery issue, which had been glaringly visible since the Missouri fracas in 1820. Others contend that the questions dividing the parties were genuinely important to their supporters for decades and only when they declined in importance did slavery emerge as salient. The academic disagreement is central to the core argument about American history — the causes of the Civil War.

Unarguably, however, by 1835, the two national political parties, the Democrats and the Whigs, were poised in mutually assured destruction. The party that took up the issue of slavery first would split along sectional lines and disappear. At every level of politics, both parties tried to maintain the sounds of silence.

The churches, even those the reformers might once have expected to fulfill their Great Awakening commitments, were also unwilling to endure sectional schism. The Congregationalists of New England definitively rejected immediate abolition as "perplexing and agitating" and forbade all Massachusetts churches to allow abolitionists to meet. The Methodists, with their honorable antislavery heritage in Great Britain, were too deeply enmeshed in southern congregations to allow abolition to break up their denomination. Southern Methodists powerfully resisted abolition within the church. As Douglass tells it in his first report, after his new master Thomas Auld converted to Methodism in one of the Great Awakening camp meetings, Douglass entertained a faint hope that his religious awakening would lead Auld to treat his slaves more humanely. Maybe he would stop starving them with scant rations and beating them randomly. But Methodism appeared to have no effect on the enslaver. Indeed, Douglass speculated, it might have made him meaner. Before the conversion there had been only Auld's general depravity to explain his behavior. Now he had religious texts, like the oft-cited injunction to obey your master, to sanction his brutal treatment of the humans in his power.

Even the revivalist most sympathetic to abolition, Charles Grandison Finney, took the position that religious conversion was more important than antislavery. Change men's souls and they would eventually come around, he argued. After their banishment from the Congregational churches of the original home of antislavery, Garrison's abolitionists gathered in secular meeting places, like Philadelphia's Pennsylvania Hall and the lecture space in the Massachusetts State House in Boston.

All this self-interested resistance to abolition, North and South, rested securely on a foundation of almost unquestioning racism. From Founding Father Thomas Jefferson to neutral observer Frenchman Alexis de Tocqueville, sages of the national culture assumed or asserted the incontrovertible fact of Black inferiority. Being classified by the powerful as inferior, northern Blacks, except in a few localities in New England, were not generally allowed the right to vote, to serve on juries, or even to bring suits in courts of law. Oregon, Ohio, Indiana, Michigan, and Illinois either banned Black immigration outright, imposing discriminatory state regulations, or required African Americans to post bonds that could amount to hundreds of dollars to ensure their "good conduct." They could not ride with whites on trains, ferries, or stagecoaches. Or marry them. Or attend the same schools. According to one sage, the joint appearance of Black and white choirs at an antislavery meeting caused the New York race riots in 1834.

There Will Be Ink

After helping to found the national society, Garrison returned from New York to his printshop. Leaving the machinery of antislavery organizing in the hands of the New Yorkers, he would print and he would be read.

It was a fateful decision. From December 1833 until the Civil War, although the American Anti-Slavery Society published newspapers, the Garrisonians would dominate the movement journals. In the New England world of print, Garrison would be the publisher, the prevailing voice on the all-important page. After Douglass emerged in 1841, the printers had a star speaker, and they made the most of it. But even he must have been profoundly affected by Garrison's print-based eminence.

10

(1833–1834)

The Liberator Will Be Read

IN CONTRAST TO GARRISON, WITH HIS EMPHASIS on print, the New York–based national organization seized on the strategy of the spoken word. Organized by the philanthropic Tappan brothers and other converts from the Benevolent Empire, the New York abolitionists adopted the evangelistic techniques of the missionary societies—agents of conversion. After its founding in 1833, the American Anti-Slavery Society immediately gave contracts to anyone who could deliver a speech and live on a pittance, sending people to small towns all over New England, the mid-Atlantic, and the Midwest to lecture about the cause. Theodore Weld, who had already proved himself to be the most effective speaker in the group, led the movement.

Early on, the older New England Anti-Slavery Society hired Garrison to be an agent, really a way of paying him something, as he was, as usual, in precarious straits. He was actually a pretty good speaker, though never as good as Weld. The more conventional New York cliques sometimes winced at Garrison's radicalism. Weld may have been the matinee idol in this political drama, but Garrison was the playwright and *The Liberator* his stage.

He did have an interlude as a romantic lead. Before leaving for Britain in 1833, he met the sister of an abolitionist friend from Connecticut— Helen Eliza Benson, the youngest and, according to Garrison biographer Walter Merrill, most beautiful Benson daughter. Ten months later, in January 1834, Garrison wrote his friend's sister an "epistle," a "strong token of my esteem." His friendship must be very ardent, he informed her upon this first occasion, to motivate him to take up the pen. The epistolary romance that took place over the next several months reveals a charming, vulnerable side of the fiery reformer. At one point he was visiting the Bensons under the pretext of some abolitionist business in the neighborhood, and Helen went on a walk without him. Taking her absence as a deliberate rebuff, he waited until he got back to Massachusetts to declare his love and ask her if she had anything to give him "in the shape of a heart?"

Helen Benson revealed the intensity of her feelings for the activist, and by summer 1834 they were planning their wedding. The terms of their relationship were clear. She (from an abolitionist family of long standing) shared his principles. But she would not be his comrade in the movement. Tellingly, in an early letter, he asked her to start a women's antislavery society, as women's groups were beginning to spring up around New England. She refused. She wasn't important enough for activism, she coyly responded, so her efforts would be "inefficient." Helen Benson's family called her "Peace and Plenty," and from all reports she was the calm and private companion ideally suited to someone in Garrison's activist and exposed position. Helen Benson and William Lloyd Garrison married on September 4, 1834, not long before he would meet the movement women who would be companions in his political passion.

Every Saturday, even in the midst of Garrison and Benson's courtship, copies of *The Liberator* rolled off the press from its cramped quarters in Boston's Merchants' Hall. One week after the founders of the American Anti-Slavery Society signed the mission statement in Philadelphia in 1833, *The Liberator* carried the full text of Garrison's incendiary founding statement. It asserted:

> In view of the civil and religious privileges of this nation . . . no man has a right to enslave or embute his brother . . . The right to enjoy liberty is inalienable.
>
> That every American citizen who retains a human being in involuntary bondage is a MAN-STEALER
>
> That the slaves ought instantly to be set free and brought under the protection of law
>
> That all those laws . . . admitting the right of slavery are before God utterly null and void

All persons of color who possess the qualifications which are demanded of others, ought to be admitted forthwith to the enjoyment of
the same privileges and same prerogatives as others,

No compensation ought to be given to the planters emancipating
their slaves

Any scheme of repatriation is delusional cruel and dangerous.

The new society had a political scheme for abolition. True, it held that
Congress *under the present national compact* had no power to abolish slavery where it existed. But that did not exculpate the North. First, Congress
could abolish the interstate slave trade and slavery in the territories. But
even if it took those steps, that would not be enough. The northerners were
not merely tolerating a minimum of slavery in the South where it existed,
the abolitionists contended; they were up to their elbows in sustaining
the southern system. Under the Constitution, they were obliged to send
armies to the South to suppress slave revolts, send the slaves back if they
ran away, and obey the three-fifths clause in apportionment of the House
of Representatives, which counted each slave as three-fifths of a person for
purposes of a state's representation in Congress, thus making the slaves
unwittingly complicit in their own oppression. The relation to slavery was
criminal and dangerous, the founding document concluded, and it must
be broken up.

The issues of *The Liberator* from the early abolition period in the 1830s
reveal how seriously the little band took their competition from the colonizationists. Every issue included an embattled exchange with some spokesman from, or report or coverage of, the competing movement, often on the
first page. Garrison figured that the so-called reformist colonizationists
were as much a threat as the dug-in southern slaveholders. The prospect
of colonization kept offering the northerners an escape hatch from their
responsibility for enforcing slavery. The immediatists had to assemble and
unify their own constituents before they could take on the enemy.

To this end, Garrison revived a device he had learned from Lundy years
before. On January 11, 1834, *The Liberator* introduced its new column, a
sampling of quotations from abolition's enemies. The aggregation, called
the "Refuge of Oppression," occupied prime space at the upper left of page
one. Later, Garrison took a moment to explain to his readers why the paper

was giving space to the other side: "to show how ridiculous, false and malignant are the doctrines of our opponents, and their representations of anti-slavery men and measures." Again reflecting the seriousness with which the abolitionists took colonizers in these early years, Garrison lumped together without distinction "the choicest specimens of pro-slavery and colonization benevolence and good-will."

The Liberator would not "stoop" to contend with attacks, Garrison notes, but the "Refuge of Oppression" exercise "proves that we are ready to let both sides of the controversy be seen in our columns." In truth, the "Refuge" structure reflected Garrison's greatest strength (and some say his greatest weakness): he could not resist an argument. Looking at the front page of *The Liberator* as it arrived every week, the reader saw the attacks on the left of the front page—Garrison the diabolical renegade, the miscreant Tappan brothers, the deserved threat of tar and feathers. Then the reader saw three or four columns of implicit rebuttal to the right—reports of conversion to immediate abolition, notice of small emerging antislavery societies, speeches on the wrongness of slavery in light of the rights of man, and quotations from Methodist founder John Wesley.

Subscribing to *The Liberator* was the equivalent of attending a debating society every week. As Garrison must have realized early, as argument, slavery didn't stand a chance. A nation of Christians founded by a declaration of man's equality could never defend slavery in argument. But winning in a debate society is a far cry from winning the cultural battle, much less accomplishing the political task of separating two and a half million increasingly valuable slaves from their enslavers. While Garrison marshaled arguments in print, someone had to do more organizing on the ground. The answer came from an unexpected yet predictable quarter.

11
(1832–1838)
Maria Weston Chapman Takes the Reins

"Am I Not a Woman" in *The Liberator*. *Courtesy of The Liberator Files.*

BY JANUARY 7, 1832, *THE LIBERATOR*'S FIRST birthday, and a few months after the founding of the New England Anti-Slavery Society (the American Anti-Slavery Society would follow in a year), Garrison knew his movement needed more support. "Am I Not a Woman and a Sister?" was the caption beneath *The Liberator*'s image of a female slave, in chains and kneeling, her arms modestly positioned to conceal her bare breasts, but a skirt clearly indicating her sex. "The fact that one million of the female sex are reduced, by the slave system, to the most deplorable condition . . . exposed to all the violence of lust and passion—and treated with more indelicacy and cruelty than cattle, ought to excite the sympathy and indignation of American women," Garrison continued, dispatching a cry for help. "We have therefore concluded that a Ladies' Department in the Liberator would add greatly to its interest, and give a new impetus to the cause of emancipation."

As usual, the inspiration came from the community of free Black Americans. Garrison had just been to the founding meeting of a new organization, the Afric-American Female Intelligence Society of Boston. A month later, a group of Black women in Salem founded the first explicitly female antislavery society. When Garrison's message reached his white followers in 1833, Boston women founded a female antislavery society, which was, unbelievably, at first confined to white women. Within a year of its founding, however, the Boston Female Anti-Slavery Society welcomed into membership women, like minister's daughter Susan Paul, from Boston's Black elite.

The Contessa Arrives

The Chapman family was involved from the beginning. Maria's cousins by marriage, Susan and Mary Grew, were early abolitionists. They quickly became officers of the Boston Female Anti-Slavery Society. Maria's sister Anne joined in 1834, and a few months later Maria herself showed up at a meeting. One by one, her other energetic and competent sisters followed.

When the members of the Boston Female Anti-Slavery Society saw the beautiful, wealthy, well-connected Maria Weston Chapman walk into their precincts for the first time, they thought she was a spy. No one that well dressed had ever shown an interest in their movement. Almost from the earliest days of her association with the movement, Weston Chapman's astonishing stream of letters to her sisters and others reflects her elite mindset and her clear confidence in her own judgment and competence in a wide range of activities.

The Merchant Contessa

The Boston Female Anti-Slavery Society did two main things: it proselytized by gathering signatures on antislavery petitions. And it ran a bazaar.

The first Boston women's antislavery bazaar, or "fair," offered the public "useful articles" donated by its handful of rich members and raised little money. Then, in 1835, Maria Weston Chapman took over. Her early letters are full of the most detailed arrangements for the goods she was soliciting to sell for the cause. In a typical letter, she writes about dozens of chemises and a bedspread, which, she boasts, will "sell for a fortune!" She scheduled the bazaar for late December, with an eye to Christmas. When it became clear the antislavery headquarters was vulnerable to the mobs, she moved the fair to the house on exclusive Chauncy Street where her in-laws lived. In a year, Maria's businessman husband, Henry Chapman, crowed that the proceeds from her fair would pay off the antislavery society's debt. Within three years, Weston Chapman had almost tripled the take to eight hundred dollars.

Although her fans in the movement nicknamed her "the Contessa," Weston Chapman's American aristocracy manifested itself in the distinctly bourgeois arena of trade. She was running a bazaar; she wanted the people with the most money to spend to come. She and her sisters let the world know that the antislavery bazaar would be a fashionable event by listing society women as sponsors on the announcement every year.

As early as 1836, the Weston sisters were scrutinizing the house for evidence of their enterprise's social success. "A large body of people assembled in the morning," Anne Warren Weston reported to her sister Debora, but "nobody of special note." Finally "a few worldly people of note" arrived, including "Mrs. Lowell and Mrs. Chief Justice Scott and a few others of that sort."

Watching for big spenders, Weston Chapman scoured the world for delectable items to appeal to upper-class customers, things like fine china, soft shawls, and French jewelry. Anytime any abolitionists traveled anywhere, especially to Europe, she deputized them to scout out merchandise for her. She did not spare herself, either. When the Chapmans went to Haiti in the early 1840s in hopes of ameliorating Henry Chapman's tuberculosis, he wrote glowingly about the medallions they had received from a local clergyman, soon to be for sale at the upcoming antislavery fair. Maria organized ordering in advance, securing items from the artisans for identified clients.

At fair time, the Chapmans' town house in Boston effectively turned into a boardinghouse. Sellers of merchandise from other antislavery societies, relatives and friends arriving to shop, the Weston sisters from Weymouth—all of them came, and historians record the women at West Street sleeping several to a bed. Why, Weston Chapman wrote after a few years of expanding the event, there was no reason the female fair should not equal the big citywide Mechanics Charity Fair in effectiveness.

Soon Chapman's fair was sending over a thousand dollars to sustain the antislavery society and to Garrison personally. Everywhere Garrison's movement spread, the women's societies held fairs to pay the bills. But nothing ever compared to Weston Chapman's—and her sisters'—extravaganzas.

The Movement Contessa

Around late summer of 1835, Weston Chapman took the reins as corresponding secretary of the Female Society.

In October, the Society scheduled a meeting to mark its first anniversary. Word got out that the international hero of the British emancipation movement, George Thompson, who was in the United States for abolitionist recruiting, would address the gathering. The anti-abolitionist forces in Boston were outraged. They were right to be alarmed, as Thompson's tours of the United States, beginning that fall, were stunningly successful in expanding the still youthful American movement.

Weston Chapman gathered her forces to defend her meeting against those who criticized the Society for inviting the foreigner. Thompson had been caught embezzling from his employer several years before, critics charged. He had confessed and paid the sum back. "It's the same thing they said about the apostles!" she wrote indignantly. "I wish the 'poor ignorant godly creatures' who oppose the plans for Thompson 'to give the Acts of the Apostles one faithful reading.'" Who could be a better speaker to warn people of evil, Weston Chapman asked, than someone who has experienced the evil he is trying to cure? Even former slaveholders are allowed to speak if they have repented. If he is now a Christian, what care "you about his prior transgressions?" Then in full Contessa mode, she specifically instructed that "the above is the tone [the antislavery spokesperson] ought to take about Thompson. Confess nothing—but deny crime—admit the possibility of indiscretion and assert his right of preaching and ours of hearing even if he were a murderer." She continued, drilling down to the detail in her usual way, "Better request whoever of your number makes the prayer to remember in it their friends everywhere who may be persecuted for conscience's sake," and finished with a ringing invocation of Jesus's taking the sin on his own head. Apparently realizing belatedly how commanding she sounded, she added a lame postscript asking her correspondent to "make what you please of this letter," as if any of her members might ignore her injunctions.

Just a year or so after her appearance at her first meeting, Maria Weston Chapman was all in. Abolition, she pronounced, was "the symbol of righteousness and truth on the subject of Freedom." Although, looking back decades later, she occasionally castigated herself as "harsh, heretical, moonstruck and unsexed," at the time, she was as confident as this early letter sounds: "We were possessed of great social influence before we were abolitionists. Now let us use it—for we have never lost it."

As we have seen, the Female Anti-Slavery Society had decided to hold its meeting at the Massachusetts Anti-Slavery Society headquarters on Washington Street. Garrison persuaded the women that he should speak in place of Thompson, lest their foreign guest be put in danger. But the mob was undeterred by the substitution. By the time the women opened their meeting that October day, the fists of the anti-abolitionists were pounding on the thin doors. Weston Chapman was calm. "If this is the last bulwark of freedom," she famously said, "we may as well die here as anywhere." Then the mayor, Theodore Lyman, burst in and said, "Ladies, go home," to which Weston Chapman, who was furious, replied: "They're your friends instigating this. Have you asked *them* to leave?" As a member of the Boston elite, Weston Chapman had already reached out to the mayor for protection. Given her social position, she was accustomed to being respected, but instead, she had been told that the abolitionists were causing too much trouble for the mayor. Finally, Mayor Lyman persuaded the women to leave, agreeing to protect them if they went right away. Arm in arm, Black linked with white, the women of the Boston Female Anti-Slavery Society walked through the screaming mob to sanctuary in

Weston Chapman's West Street town house. They did not know Garrison was still in the building and would just barely escape the mob.

That terrible October day, as on most of those early days, all roads led to the Chapman house. When she joined the abolition cause, Weston Chapman's socialite days came to a screeching halt. She could not walk into a shop without being shunned by the clerks. Ministers preached and editors editorialized about her husband's shocking failure to control his wife (and her unruly sisters). At her luxurious house, strategically located near the *Liberator* offices and the homes of the core Boston clique—Wendell Phillips, lawyer Ellis Gray Loring, and Garrison—the abolitionists could confer with their female colleagues without revealing the coed nature of the enterprise. Weston Chapman and her sisters were always about, it was beautiful and quiet, and the study was piled high with the books and other references the abolitionists needed for their growing flood of publications and correspondence. There was tea.

A big part of Weston Chapman's agenda was to integrate the women, who were the backbone of the Massachusetts society (in 1835, the New England Anti-Slavery Society changed its name to the Massachusetts Anti-Slavery Society), into its actual governance. In 1836, a scant two years after signing up, she invited her socially prominent friend Samuel May to bring the Massachusetts Anti-Slavery Society board—at the time, all men—to her living room so the "Ladies," as May called them in his notes, could freely "give their opinion." And he did! The whole gang gathered at Weston Chapman's. A score of "Ladies"—writer Lydia Maria Child, who was Garrison's earliest female associate; lawyer Ellis Loring's wife, Louisa Loring; poet and educator Eliza Lee Cabot Follen of the eminent Boston Cabot family; several Chapmans; and four Weston sisters—sat down with the Society board and the sex-integrated group discussed all the relevant issues, including the very important question of where the Society should hold its next big convention.

By all accounts the happily married, heroic abolitionist activist Maria Weston Chapman had it all. When she was extending her rule over the Boston Female Anti-Slavery Society and rising in the New England/Massachusetts group, she had two toddlers; her third child was born in 1837.

A couple of years later, with three children and the abolitionist movement based in the house, her husband's tuberculosis became undeniable. As the historian Lee Chambers compellingly sets out, Maria's sisters were her secret weapon. Anne, Caroline, Debora, Lucia, Emma—all single and all devoted to the movement—functioned like a well-oiled machine. They, particularly the three older sisters, took on the management of Maria's children almost immediately, traveling back and forth between Boston and their family home in Weymouth, depending on the children's needs. Because Maria was the oldest of the six, her children were almost of a generation with her youngest sisters. For much of their youth the Chapman children lived sometimes in Weymouth with their young aunts and grandmother, and sometimes one or more aunts lived with them in Boston. Things got a lot harder in the late 1830s as Henry got sicker. Still, when Maria and Henry went to Haiti in 1842 in the vain hope of saving his life with a milder climate, it was the Weston sisters who took over the children. Caroline, the next down from Maria, was the most devoted helper. Of the older three, she and Debora were the more caregiving, Anne the more political.

Having whipped the bazaar into shape and set up a center for abolition in her town house, and with all-important sisterly support, Weston Chapman turned her attention to the remaining female initiative—petitions. Garrison had been pushing the petition initiative since early *Liberator* days. Take note of your English sisters, he urged abolition's women in 1833. "A petition, containing the names of 179,000 ladies, was presented on the 14th of May in the House of Lords . . . Why cannot a hundred and seventy-nine thousand ladies be found in New England, during the present year who will sign a petition for the abolition of slavery in the District of Columbia?"

The Weston sisters set about running a petition campaign in their usual well-organized way. The Boston branch set up a committee and assigned a town or two to each member. Weston sisters—Anne in Bristol, Fall River, Taunton, and New Bedford and Maria in Boston, plus sister-in-law Ann Greene Chapman in Worcester—began knocking on people's doors. All over New England and New York and everywhere there was an abolitionist presence, women started doing retail politics.

At first the petitioners spent most of their time justifying women talking at all. After all, women had no civic standing, and their petitions traditionally were limited to asking for private favors, like pensions. They acknowledged that they normally had no place in party or political strife.

Despite their deferential tone, when the 175 petitions (almost half from women) reached the House of Representatives in December 1835, Representative Henry Hammond of South Carolina proposed a rule—the "gag rule"—to reject such petitions out of hand. Six months of uninterrupted controversy later, the House resolved that "all petitions on the subject of slavery . . . be laid upon the table," unread, not printed or referred to, and subject to no further action. The abolitionists, including the women, would be, as it came to be known, "gagged." (By 1837, the women had far exceeded Garrison's call for 179,000 signatures, filing petitions with almost twice that number.)

Maybe gagged in Congress, but the abolitionists would not be silenced elsewhere. Nearby in slave Maryland, teenaged enslaved Douglass, who knew how to read, got hold of a local paper and read of the petitions to abolish the slave trade in the nation's capital and between the states. Now he knew what his enslavers meant when they spoke so angrily about "abolition" at dinner.

The fiery representatives of the slave South once again set their own house ablaze. A movement—abolition—with at best 100,000 active members, produced, in the next few years, petitions bearing more than two million signatures. The abolitionists made their first major political ally, former president John Quincy Adams, now representing Massachusetts in the House of Representatives. Adams made the brilliant move of defending not abolition but the rights of Americans to petition their government. In 1837 he asked for permission to present Congress with a petition ostensibly sent by slaves, provoking the southerners into trying to censure him for even suggesting such a thing. But the ex-president's sterling reputation in the North and his long service to the country prevailed, and the censure motion failed. It was not a victory exactly, but it was abolition's first positive outcome in the United States Congress in a very long time.

The Lawyer Contessa

As corresponding secretary of the Boston Female Anti-Slavery Society, Maria Weston Chapman continued to organize her women. One day in 1836, the Boston women found out that a young Black girl was residing at the home of the white merchant Thomas Aves. Posing as representatives of a Sunday school society, a delegation of the most elite abolitionist women got themselves invited to tea at Aves's Beacon Hill house. There they confirmed that Aves's daughter Mary Aves Slater, who had married into a slave-owning family in Louisiana, had brought the enslaved girl, six-year-old "Little Med," as she came to be called, to Boston. Failing to persuade Med's mistress or the enslaver's father to free Little Med, the women turned to an abolitionist lawyer friend, Ellis Gray Loring, for help. He ran to the state courthouse to get a writ of habeas corpus, ordering Aves to produce Med in court. One of the leading jurists of the age, chief justice of Massachusetts Lemuel Shaw, was sitting as a trial judge that day.

And so the women of the Boston Female Anti-Slavery Society brought the first major slave "transit" case. The abolitionists had a powerful tool: in 1772, shortly before the American colonies separated from Great Britain, the highest English court had ruled that a slave, James Somerset, brought to England from America by his enslaver, Charles Stewart, could not be forced to return to the land of slavery. Slavery, the court ruled, is unnatural. If legal bondage exists at all, it is only in law positively made by governments in their territories. If the colonies want to make slavery legal, fine. But once the slave Somerset came to the free soil of the British Isles, he could not be sent back. The principle of *Somerset v. Stewart* is often called the "municipal theory or freedom principle, confining the institution to its local boundaries." Four years later, the slave-ridden American colonies revolted against the British.

For decades the issue mostly lay dormant. The northern states were not free soil, like England. Slavery existed, explicitly or implicitly, in all the former colonies. (Before the Constitution was written, the new nation had forbidden slavery in the Northwest Territory, which would become states such as Ohio and Illinois.) The Constitution, which specifically addressed runaways, did not speak explicitly to transient or resident slaves brought out of slave states. Without free soil states comparable to the English homeland nearby, there was nothing to argue about.

Slowly, however, after the Revolution, emancipation spread through the North. When abolishing slavery for their residents, some states, including Pennsylvania and New York, put a generous limit on how long slaveholders could stay in the state with their slaves as guests. Others, like New Jersey, Connecticut, and Ohio, explicitly or implicitly exempted transient enslavers from their freedom laws altogether. The northern tolerance for what was arguably a local southern legal doctrine (the "municipal theory") was generally cloaked in the language of "comity," or tolerance, for the peculiar institutions of southern jurisdictions.

Only Pennsylvania, with its old and active abolitionist community, tried robustly to enforce even the generous six-month limit on the transient slaveholders in its midst. But as travelers from the South traversed the "free" states with their human chattels, antislavery activists and lawyers continued to push the lesson of the long-ago *Somerset v. Stewart* decision: slavery was unnatural, and free jurisdictions should push it out.

Then, after all those years of going along and getting along, the Boston women found a slave girl living on Beacon Hill and went to court to contest her status. The women's lawyer, Ellis Loring, claimed, as the English court had ruled a half century before, that slaveholders could not bring their peculiar institution onto free soil and expect Massachusetts to enforce their regime of bondage. Slavery was protected in the slave states, which came into the constitutional bargain with their slave laws; everywhere else was open to regulation. The states could regulate the procedures governing claims for transient slaves or even fugitive slaves on their own soil, Loring argued. Aves's lawyer Benjamin Curtis disputed Loring's claim. The free states agreed to the legitimacy of slavery when they signed off on the Constitution, he argued. Deference to the Louisiana slave law was not just good manners; it was a matter of being part of the union. Free states owed the slave states "comity" for staying in the same nation with them.

The ramifications of this argument were clear: if Massachusetts let Mary Slater settle for an indefinite period with her slave, there would be no such thing as a free state. The extreme proslavery forces had started arguing for the comity position as early as the Missouri Compromise. Now they had a chance to see if they could persuade an American court to take their side.

Would Massachusetts enforce Louisiana's slavery regime? The relationship of slavery, from faraway Louisiana, involved a laundry list of behaviors that were, by 1836, repugnant to the free state of Massachusetts. "A slave has no civil rights," Med's lawyer reminded the court. "Even to maim or murder him, is only an offense against Government: and is punished on the same principle that we forbid cruelty to brutes,—not for their sakes, but for our own."

Furthermore, "if the slave refuse to leave the State, how shall he be compelled," Loring asked. "Will you justify an assault and battery upon him?—Suppose he kill his master in self-defense; is his crime murder? How far will this Court go, in giving validity to contracts for the hiring or sale of slaves here? Will you enforce specific performance of a contract for the sale of a fellow creature, thus making the Supreme Court an instrument in the domestic slave-trade?

"These consequences seem indeed revolting," the abolitionist advocate concluded, "but they are in character with the system to which they belong." Revolting legal doctrines—or, in legal terms, human laws contrary to the law of nature—are an exception to the respect states owe to one another's laws. Even to preserve the union, he argued. The abolitionists had a potent ally. Just before they sighted Little Med, the leading American legal scholar on the matter of conflict of laws, constitutional commentator Joseph Story, had published his opinion that comity was a matter of discretion in the enforcing court, not an obligation.

Chief Justice Shaw followed Story and held that slaves brought into the free state of Massachusetts would immediately be free. He didn't give the abolitionists everything they asked for. Still, he ruled, slavery in Louisiana cannot mean slavery everywhere in the United States. Med was free, he ruled, because there was no Massachusetts state law that warranted the forcible detention of human "property." There were, however, Massachusetts laws, like those against kidnapping, which prohibited the detention of human beings, and these laws forbade involuntary servitude.

Shaw was careful to exclude from the ruling the case of a fugitive slave, who, unlike the transient slave, was the subject of affirmative language in the Constitution itself. He simply rejected the extreme southern position that the Constitution protected southerners' interest in their slaves as property even if they traveled to free soil. He did not say what a state should do if a slaveholder was passing through very briefly.

Shaw would wrestle with the legal status of inhumane and unjust slavery for much of the rest of his career. Fourteen years later, when he finally had to address the fugitive slave—subject of explicit provisions of the Constitution—he blinked and ruled in favor of the enslavers. (Shaw was the father-in-law of the renowned writer Herman Melville, and many critics see him as the tormented Captain Vere, who condemns the Christlike Billy Budd to death in Melville's famous novella.)

Commentator Joseph Story picked Shaw's opinion right up, and it essentially became the law of the North. The change in the law in turn fueled the movement. When Ellis Loring stood up in the case of Little Med, abolitionists were so despised that he hastened to assure the judge that Med was not a member of the Boston Anti-Slavery Society. A year later, in 1837, Connecticut emulated Massachusetts's example, followed by New York, under antislavery governor William Seward, in 1839. By 1843, when the Illinois Supreme Court opted to enforce slavery for comity, the decision was attacked in newspapers all over the state. Was Illinois to be a slave state? the editorialists asked, correctly seeing the implication of unlimited slave migration to their state. Time to amend the state constitution. After a half century of accommodating slaveholders, 1843 was the last year when a northern court rejected a petition from a transient slave — that is, until the U.S. Supreme Court decided the case of the transient slave Dred Scott in 1857.

Southern newspapers did not miss the opportunity to threaten disunion in the wake of Justice Shaw's opinion. "Are you willing to sustain forever a confederation with States into which you dare not travel with your property, lest that property becomes by law actually confiscated?" asked the *Augusta Sentinel,* in an editorial cannily reprinted by William Lloyd Garrison in the "Refuge of Oppression."

The Boston women took Little Med to the newly opened Black orphan asylum in Boston. In honor of the forces that freed her, they named her Maria Somerset — Maria after Maria Weston Chapman and Somerset after the long-ago slave who had claimed his emancipation upon touching British free soil in 1772.

Abolition Women

The women did not pause. Weston Chapman cooked up a printed form for their petition campaign, so all the troops had to do was gather signatures and paste them on. No more drafting new pleas each time. Then she reached out to her cousin and counterpart in Philadelphia, Mary Grew, suggesting they create a more national women's petition committee. Grew wrote back that the Philadelphians would prefer a seat at the table at the American Anti-Slavery Society; why should only men be members of the national organization? Weston Chapman responded by suggesting the women all

Sarah Mapps Douglass integrated
the first women's convention.
Courtesy of the African American Registry.

meet in Philadelphia at the same time as the national society. Finally, the
two cousins resolved to hold a women's antislavery convention in New York.

And so, in 1837, American women in abolition held their first national
public political meeting. Around seventy attended as delegates, mostly from
Philadelphia and Boston, as well as host city New York, but there was a
smattering from other societies. Weston Chapman, who had had her third
child, Anne, that year, could not come. Notably, the gathering was not completely white. This was not an accident. When Black Philadelphia wom-
en's group member Sarah Mapps Douglass found out about the planned
meeting, she wrote to a white colleague, the famed abolitionist speaker
Angelina Grimké, that she would not travel to New York for a meeting
where Black women were not welcome. Grimké immediately pressured
New York to welcome Black delegates and then wrote to implore Mapps
Douglass (and her mother) to come and help fight the "wicked" racism.
Somewhere around seven Black women attended, representing ten percent
of the women's meeting at the first national, and interracial, gathering.

Angelina Grimké proposed a motion asserting women's right and duty
to advocate for the cause of the slave. Although not unanimous, the convention passed Grimké's resolution. Garrison's female troops were getting
some big ideas.

12

(1835–1840)

Antislavery on the March

GARRISON HIMSELF, HOWEVER, WAS MISSING IN ACTION. After the close call with the Boston rioters in October 1835, Garrison closed up his house there, stored his furniture, and moved in with his in-laws in Brooklyn, Connecticut, to await the birth of his first child. Other than brief visits, he was not to return until the following spring. This was the first, but it would not be the last time Garrison disappeared from the activist scene. He had a big family, he was a hypochondriac, and in his expanding family, the children were sometimes frail.

Each time Garrison left *The Liberator,* Maria Weston Chapman, with printer Isaac Knapp and Boston abolitionist Edmund Quincy, would take up the burden of keeping it alive—writing, editing, and even performing some mechanical tasks like layout. Weston Chapman also began to write her own pieces. First she published a collection of antislavery hymns, including some of her creations. Then she transformed the seemingly unimportant bureaucratic job of recording secretary of the Boston Female Anti-Slavery Society into the role of reporter on the state of the abolitionist movement. Her first annual report, titled, ambitiously, "Right and Wrong in Boston," took on the clergy for their lack of support for abolition and women's rights. Without fanfare, she was added to the business committee of the mostly male Massachusetts Anti-Slavery Society.

As after the 1835 attack on the women's meeting, the movement leaders were often at her table. With her sisters, Weston Chapman created a kind of news service for the activists gathered in her parlor by collecting newspapers and letters from the nearby headquarters. Hearing all the gossip, Weston Chapman, her sisters, and others debriefed the stream of movers and shakers. The Boston players—Garrison, Edmund Quincy, printer and pamphleteer Stephen Foster, real estate developer and radical Francis Jackson—created strategy at Weston Chapman's. Strategy became an increasingly fraught business task as the movement began to splinter.

When Garrison began his halting return from his sabbatical in March 1836, his first stop was the Chapman town house. He told his abolitionist family gathered there what he was thinking: he had tried martyrdom—in the Baltimore jail, in the 1835 rioting. Maybe it was time to break with all institutions—churches, political parties—that didn't reject slavery. For years, Garrison had been steering the abolitionist movement toward nonresistance—the rejection of any use of violence, even in self-defense. Now he took it one step further to argue for the rejection of institutions of coercion, which by definition included government.

Antislavery Spreads Across the Land

Gerrit Smith mansion at Peterboro, New York. *From* Gerrit Smith: A Biography *by Octavius Brooks Frothingham (G. P. Putnam's Sons, 1878).*

In the same years Garrison was coming to his break with all authority, the solons of the church-driven, political New York movement, who were essentially running the national American Anti-Slavery Society, started to taste real power. Unlike Garrison's New England group, surviving on the proceeds of Weston Chapman's bazaars and the like, the New York City branch had the wealthy Tappan brothers at its head. Shortly after the rioting started in 1835, the upstate New York real estate speculator Gerrit Smith, one of the richest men in America, signed on with the immediatist movement. As a result, a third center of antislavery activism sprang up around him in the growing towns of New York State.

In the spring of 1835, the American Anti-Slavery Society's Elizur Wright had a brainstorm. The new printing technology made it possible to produce tens of thousands of copies of the four Society publications — its newspaper, its heartrending tales of slave life, a children's publication, and its fundraiser. The national society could imitate the great print-driven campaigns of the Bible Society from times past.

It was too dangerous for antislavery agents to venture south to give speeches or hand out literature, but they could make use of the United States Postal Service. The Society raised an impressive thirty thousand dollars and gathered a list of thousands of names from existing newspaper subscribers, church members, and city directories. Thick packets of antislavery publications arrived at post offices all over the country, including the South. When the mail sacks appeared in Charleston, South Carolina, the local postmaster placed the incendiary material aside. That night a mob broke into the post office and set abolitionist literature on fire. The mob burned effigies of Arthur Tappan, who was behind the campaign, and also, as an homage to his status, Garrison. Then the Charleston postmaster and activists in the South asked President Andrew Jackson's postmaster general to put an end to abolitionist mailings, and he did. The United States Post Office conceded the right of censorship to local southern communities. Soon, even New York City was refusing to take delivery of abolitionist mailings.

The churches were turning their backs, postmasters were banning their pamphlets, and in the cities, protesters were mobbing the antislavery meetings. This was when the American Anti-Slavery Society made a turn from print to the spoken word. The abolitionists, as we have seen, had founded a corps of lecturers led by the irresistibly handsome and charismatic Theodore Weld. By 1836, two years into the lecture program, the national society saw how Weld's rhetoric was winning the West, planting societies all over Ohio and recruiting new agents to do more recruiting.

At its 1836 meeting, the Society established a formal agency program, later known as "the Seventy" or "Weld's Seventy."

Then they set about teaching the new recruits how to spread the word. In November 1836, the abolitionists gathered scores of handpicked agents who would become the core of the Seventy in New York. From Presbyterian and Baptist ministers, to Lane Rebels from Weld's old confrontation with Lyman Beecher at the Lane Seminary, to manual labor advocates, to lawyers with a reformist bent, the Seventy were a diverse lot. (Notably, two women, Sarah and Angelina Grimké, Quakers and renegade abolitionists from slave South Carolina, were among the apprentice speakers. The organizers treated the legendary Grimké sisters as full members of the crew.)

Their charge was to lecture and debate immediate abolition and to seed the land with local societies. At nine a.m. on November 15, 1836, Theodore Weld stood up at the American Anti-Slavery Society headquarters in New York and began to teach his troops how to deploy the power of the word. Here is what you will need to know, Weld and the other teachers explained. "What is slavery? What is immediate emancipation? Why don't you go South? The slaves, if emancipated, would overrun the North. The consequences of emancipation to the South. Hebrew servitude. Compensation. Colonization. Prejudice. Treatment and condition of our free colored population. Gradualism." Lecturing all day and then staying up all night to prepare, Weld gave everything he had to the cause. The fortnight in New York was the beginning of the laryngitis that would eventually silence his instrument.

William Lloyd Garrison later said that, other than the founding of the original society, the training meetings of 1836 were of greater importance to the antislavery cause than any other event that had ever been held. The trainees became the Seventy and the Seventy became the cadres who led the movement. From that New York meeting, the new lecturers fanned out across the North. First Garrison and then Weld had opened the floodgates, and the river of Seventy began to flow. Forty of the Seventy were ministers, mostly Presbyterians; twenty-one of the youngest, including many clergy, came from the Oneida–Lane–Oberlin hotbed and many more from the spreading network of college teach-ins. Perhaps reflecting the unchallenged social prejudice against racial mingling, there were no Black lecturers against racial slavery at first. New York's Elizur Wright wrote an exigent letter to Weld exhorting him to enlist Black agents. Charles Lenox Remond, from a free Black family of means, became the first recorded Black agent.

In the beginning the agents went to places where there was already a local abolitionist society, however small. Here the movement stood on the shoulders of the few brave pioneers—Quakers, Benjamin Lundy's tiny band of humanitarians, the remnant of the Methodist tradition of antislavery, the small following the Garrisonians had created around New England. Some of the early abolitionist speakers, like Yale's Simeon Jocelyn, came from the evangelical movement, especially the followers of Charles Grandison Finney, the most antislavery of the early evangelical leaders. Others came from the Benevolent Empire. David Thurston graduated from Dartmouth in 1804; he returned to his home state of Maine as an agent of the Massachusetts Missionary Society. After preaching acceptably in the town of Winthrop, Thurston was voted a call to the ministry by the church. On November 21, 1833, he preached his first sermon on the sinfulness of slavery, and when the Maine antislavery society was founded six months later, Thurston was elected its first president. George Storrs of New Hampshire came through the Methodist Church, with its long history of antislavery. Many of the Seventy organized around the breakaway Methodist antislavery movement, formed when the mother church would not take a stand against its southern members.

According to one typical story, Weld opened a service in Frankfort, in slave Kentucky, in the vestry of the Episcopal church after the Presbyterian pastor repeatedly denied him his space. Weld was met with loud and ferocious opposition. At the last lecture, however, he filled the church with a hundred people and "the Lord restrained" his attackers, leaving him at the end, he reported, with "not a hair on my head injured." Fervent, enthusiastic, and possessed of remarkable expressiveness, Weld was by all accounts "the best platform orator of his time." A local newspaper on one of his tours gave a revealing account of his technique: he was "not a declaimer," the *Pittsburgh Times* began, "but a logician of great tact and power." Weld's wealth of anecdotes, many pathetic and wrenching, which later fueled the best-selling collection he wrote with the Grimkés, *American Slavery as It*

Is, bridged the gap from his generalizations into "clear, striking and famil-iar illustrations." Slavery was sin, Weld never forgot, and also, as he framed it, a habit of oppression that soon became unbreakable.

The lecturers were strategic: more than half of them being trained clergymen, they often started with the pastor in each place they visited. Proceeding from his Frankfort triumph to nearby Circleville, when the Presbyterian church closed its doors to him, Weld appealed successfully to the Episcopalians. Sometimes the speakers went down the food chain of venues—from churches, to meetinghouses, to living rooms, to open air, whatever the weather. They separated from their families, fell ill, lost their voices, and faced raging mobs, usually riled up by local merchants.

The speakers had to hope that their local contacts had made prepara-tions, securing a church or public meetinghouse, distributing advertise-ments, and urging their friends and family to attend. Often the outreach came from the local college; the Lane rebellion, for example, had found rich soil in the many colleges of the North, and the students were star-struck by Weld. The planning of the events was key: if notice of a visiting speaker had not reached the proper audience, the agent would lose several days obtaining a meetinghouse, speaking with leading townspeople, and making himself visible enough to arouse interest. Sometimes rather odd expedients were required of the speaker: one agent recorded that in order to talk about slavery, "he had to agree to address the audience for an equal time upon the more popular issue of temperance." The antislavery lecturers had learned multiple lessons from the evangelical movement that preceded them, for instance, speaking day after day until they started seeing an im-pact on the community. They would end their long visit in each place with an appeal to their listeners, much like the born-again appeal, to stand if their hearts had been changed. They organized local societies, wrote their constitutions for them, and arranged for the new societies to pay dues to the national organization. When they finished, the area was considered "abolitionized." The abolitionist lecture tours were the secular version of the Second Great Awakening.

Shutting down the post office to northern mail, gagging the citizens who tried to petition Congress, and wrecking the printer's press, the pro-slavery activists gave the unpopular cause of abolition an incomparable gift: they linked the activists' right to speak on abolition to the right to speak on anything at all, the touchstone of American liberty. In 1836 one proslavery mob attacked lecturer James G. Birney, who was publishing an antislavery newspaper in Cincinnati, right across the Ohio River from slave Kentucky. The assault raised the ire of Birney's lawyer, Salmon P. Chase. As he witnessed the rioters closing in on his client's printing press, Chase converted to the cause. A brilliant and ruthless politician, Chase is often regarded as the father of the Republican Party.

In 1833 the American Anti-Slavery Society counted fifty societies. By 1837 the number was one thousand, with a hundred thousand members. By 1840 there were an estimated 150,000. Many historians think membership was twice that.

13

(1837–1841)

Moral Garrison Splits with the Politicos

THE AMERICAN ANTI-SLAVERY SOCIETY AND ITS NEW York cohort was starting to taste real power, and the churches were an important part of their campaign. But founder William Lloyd Garrison was turning to a much different vision.

Garrison changed over the years from his roots in the new religions and his demands for political action, but he never lost sight of his belief that slavery was sin. He said it in his first public speech at the Park Street Church, and he said it to the last. At a time when sin still mattered, this was a powerful accusation. The sinfulness of slavery generated powerful argument among religious scholars. Garrison wasn't interested in their debates over the fine points of Hebrew translation. Servant? Slave? Simply put, slavery originated in manstealing, explicitly proscribed in Exodus. And it violated the later, New Testament ideal of the equality of all souls and the Great Awakening promise of salvation for all. Slavery was sin, and Garrison expected the churches to oppose it. Instead, one by one, churches, even churches with an honorable history of abolition activism, like the Methodists, had adopted resolutions forgoing their moral judgment on slavery and welcomed converts like Frederick's enslaver Thomas Auld.

Garrison Breaks with the Churches

The Garrisonians' battle with the churches was joined in 1836 when Congregationalist Lyman Beecher persuaded a prominent Connecticut Congregationalist minister to lobby church associations in both Connecticut and Massachusetts to banish abolitionist preachers from their pulpits.

After leading the banishment initiative, Beecher then gave a long speech about how important the ties to southern churches were in the battle for observance of the Sabbath.

Each and every time a church resolved that slavery was none of its business, Garrison printed the resolution in the "Refuge of Oppression," but it took most of the exclamation points in his boxes of movable type to punctuate Garrison's 1836 attacks on Beecher. Beecher had written a lengthy essay on the importance of the Sabbath as part of his campaign against Sunday mail service. The slave system, Garrison railed, "annihilates ... THE WHOLE DECALOGUE!" as well as excludes from the Holy Sabbath that Beecher reveres two and a half million of his "fellow countrymen!!" Nowhere in Beecher's catalogue of sins did Garrison find mention of slavery. Beecher pulls up his dainty skirts at the prospect of free love utopianism — the utopian reformers Fanny Wright and Robert Owen are called "ministers of sin," Garrison wrote — but he never mentions the South's "vast system of whoredom and adultery" by which the white masters used their female slaves as brood animals. Issue after issue of *The Liberator* in that summer of 1836 contained Garrison's explosive invective against the national churches ignoring slavery.

Even sympathetic clergymen like Boston Unitarian William Ellery Channing were still hesitant about abolition in 1836. Slavery might be bad, he admitted in a long pamphlet, but Garrison and his followers were moralizing, precipitate, noisy, and worst of all, they were riling up the "mixed and excitable" multitude of "colored people." Garrison pounded the mealy-mouthed Unitarian with almost the same fervor he directed at Beecher. Channing addresses the slaveholders who do not wish their human chattels any harm and are protecting them from the greater harm of emancipation in the present moment. To which Garrison responds, "What a delightful lullaby to ... comfort oppressors." Channing offers the enslavers a clear conscience, "void of offence toward God and toward man!" Worse, Channing offers a laundry list of things the abolitionist movement shouldn't do, and every suggestion he makes — stop meeting, stop publishing, stop associating with Black members — is exactly what the slaveholders suggest. In sum, Garrison charges, the preacher is "calumnious, contradictory and unsound," and "he that is not with us is against us."

Confident in her social authority, Maria Weston Chapman, too, refused to accept that the ministers in Boston wouldn't support the movement. She thought that religious functionaries should (like the secular mayor of Boston in the 1835 riot) do what she requested. When the Weymouth and Boston churches barred abolitionist preachers, she organized a campaign of female abolitionists to deliver notices of abolition meetings to every church in Boston every Sunday. Then she and her sister Anne turned up the temperature under the churches further by taking up the cause of women lecturing. The Grimké sisters, who had been such a central part of the 1837 women's antislavery convention, came to Massachusetts as part of the American Anti-Slavery Society lecture tour, and the Weston sisters escorted them around. The Westons deployed the Boston Female Anti-Slavery Society to organize the tour, and on June 21, the Society turned out five hundred women to listen to the Grimkés.

Pressed by the Weston sisters to announce the abolitionist lectures, and horrified by the sight of women lecturing, the Massachusetts Congregationalist ministers held a meeting and sent out a "Pastoral Letter." Stop pressuring us, Boston Congregationalist preacher Nehemiah Adams wrote to the flock. Abolition might cause dissension in the church. And especially, he continued, women needed to stop. Consider "the dangers which at present seem to threaten the female character with wide-spread and permanent injury." (Adams later made a name for himself with a book, *A South-side View of Slavery*, about how slavery was good for Black people, written just as the union was entering its death throes in 1854.)

Just in case anyone failed to recognize the target of the ministers' ire, Weston Chapman's own Weymouth clergyman followed Adams up a couple of months later with a separate attack on Garrison for defending the female congregants who had been pressing notices of antislavery meetings on Boston churches.

The Westons geared up to mobilize the abolition activists to defend Garrison against the clergy. But the sensitive seismograph that was the Weston Chapman living room registered ominous vibrations from the confrontation. So threatening was Garrison's absolutism to churches that the executive committee of the American Anti-Slavery Society in New York was "all shivering in the wind," Anne Warren Weston wrote to sister Debora Weston.

Thus began Garrison's long, portentous breach with the church and, ultimately, with all sources of public authority. He would follow his inner moral compass, against all opposition. He had always been inclined toward pacifism, resistance to armed service of any kind. He broadened his resistance to any legal stricture, including ultimately the whole structure of American constitutional support for slavery. For a while, the Weston sisters' superior political skills held the rank and file behind him. But it would not be long before his independence would be cast against the American Anti-Slavery Society itself.

Abolition and Women's Rights

In the end, Garrison and his faction were at odds with the rest of the abolitionist movement on a range of issues—timing, tactics, alliances, rhetoric. But when the movement broke wide open, it was seemingly about another matter entirely—the role of women. The equal treatment of women seems like a natural issue to emerge from the movement to free the slaves. The principles of freedom and equality that made American slavery seem so harrowing would also seem to cast doubt on the disenfranchisement and exclusion of women from public life.

But the second prong of antislavery—sinfulness—was a harder fit with the cause of women's equality. The New Testament is full of prescriptions for female subordination, particularly from the Apostle Paul, and most particularly about women's injunction to be silent in church. Conservative clergymen, worried about their denominations' southern membership, or about the diversion of the religious impulse away from observance and toward social reform, were already predisposed against the demanding abolitionists, particularly Garrison, their most exigent member. Products of a religious tradition long tainted by its subordination of women, they opposed a wider role for women anyway, but women as advocates for abolition were a double threat.

The soft-spoken Quaker sisters Sarah and Angelina Grimké were hardly the obvious candidates to trigger a gender war. But perhaps the courage they displayed in abandoning all family ties and riches in their native Charleston and coming north to fight the slave empire they'd left behind was a clue. The Grimké sisters were a draw in part because, being from a slave-owning family in the South, they told the story of slavery firsthand. They had already begun to lecture to small private female gatherings when the American Anti-Slavery Society invited them to be guests at Weld's training camp in 1836. When, along with Weld's other trainees, the sisters emerged onto the circuit, it proved impossible to confine their appearances to female gatherings. First one man slipped in to hear the famed reformed slaveholders, then a few gathered at the back. Soon their audiences grew decidedly mixed.

Defending her organization's campaign for the Grimkés, on June 7, 1837, in her role as corresponding secretary, Maria Weston Chapman wrote a letter from the Boston chapter to all the female antislavery societies in New England. "In all spiritual things, Women," she proclaimed, "are functionally identical with men." The conventional faction in the Boston women's group began to complain loudly about her annual letters, and the new president threatened to censor any further efforts by her outspoken corresponding secretary.

With her usual instinct for the jugular, Weston Chapman responded with a poem. These are, she wrote, "The Times That Try Men's Souls."

> Confusion has seized us, and all things go wrong,
> The women have leaped from "their spheres,"
> And, instead of fixed stars, shoot as comets along,
> And are setting the world by the ears! . . .
> They've taken a notion to speak for themselves,
> And are wielding the tongue and pen;
> They've mounted the rostrum; the termagant elves,
> And—oh horrid!—are talking to men!

But it wasn't funny. The religious divide on the role of women was hard on the women's abolition movement. Female societies like Boston's included both upper-class women such as the Weston Chapman clan and women from the growing population of artisans and entrepreneurs in an up-and-coming Boston, rising on a tide of manufacturing and commerce. As told by the historian Debra Gold Hansen, the upper-class women, mostly Unitarians and Quakers, were largely disinclined to take direction from the Congregationalist and Baptist ministers who were mustering the resistance to Garrison's vision. But the wives of small proprietors, artisans, and clerks who had come to the movement largely through their religious awakening were content to pursue abolition without a public presence and found a flourishing alternative path. The New England conventional faction connected with the conventional women of the New York antislavery precincts. Big donor Julianna Tappan, Lewis Tappan's daughter, wrote to Maria's sister Anne, who had just succeeded Maria as corresponding secretary of the Boston group, counseling female modesty and deference to the ministers. Clerical pressure increased.

Maria Weston Chapman, stunningly self-righteous, had sacrificed all social standing for the cause. She thought the Bible was on her side and thought women were the fuel of abolition. Garrison's position was irresistible to her. She organized everywhere on his behalf. She wrote to the national society in New York, asking founder and corresponding secretary Elizur Wright to embrace Garrison "with a giant grasp." She and her sisters packed the quarterly meeting of the Massachusetts society in Worcester in 1837 with relatives to ensure an ardent reception for Garrison, and she angrily wrote of how much more work the women did for the movement than most of their critics did.

As the 1838 national meetings loomed, the threat of division in the whole organization sharpened. Women's participation and, implicitly, full equality was not the only issue on which the increasingly radical Garrison differed with his conservative brethren. His ally Weston Chapman sent him a copy of a speech by transcendentalist Ralph Waldo Emerson. Real religion comes down to the individual's insight, Emerson proposed. Weston Chapman's and Garrison's radical individualism did not bode well for the unity of the movement, and Garrison's philosophy grew increasingly incoherent. If all government was fatally tainted, the legal theory embodied in the founding document of the American Anti-Slavery Society —that Congress *under the present national compact* has no power to abolish slavery where it exists, but it can abolish the interstate slave trade and slavery in the territories—would be rendered moot. There was no point to voting. Abolitionist campaigns would be useless.

Breaking Up

The movement accelerated toward disunion. In a series of meetings, the New England societies and then the national society fought over women's participation, which was, in a sense, a proxy for the real disagreement. Would abolition be a pure force for equality for all and for the unrestrained governance of each individual's conscience? Or would the movement focus only on slavery, compromise at any price with any supporters who would advance the cause, and recognize the legitimacy of social institutions like political parties, the government, and the church?

While the New York and Boston blocs argued over political theory, a faction of Gerrit Smith's upstate New York group advanced the movement to push the government toward abolition by organizing an actual political party. Starting with two conventions in 1840, one in Albany and one in Cleveland, the new party, named the Liberty Party, nominated candidates for president and vice president. The Party attracted only about seven thousand votes in 1840, but it got the attention of the brilliant Ohio lawyer Salmon P. Chase. He had been thinking about whether the Constitution really protected slavery after all. If it did not, all political avenues to abolition were possible.

At the big convention of the Massachusetts Anti-Slavery Society in May 1838, Garrison and his allies won the first internal battle. The Society admitted scores of women to its ranks and appointed leading female lecturer Abby Kelley to a key committee. As Garrison's philosophy—his separation from institutions—dissolved the ties that bound him to the rest of the movement, it bound Weston Chapman more tightly to Garrison's side. She and her Weston sisters joined Garrison to found a separate Non-Resistance Society for his cherished cause, and Weston Chapman began to edit the journal *The Non-Resistant*. The non-resistants pledged to withhold their votes from any government that used force to support its rule—basically every government.

Voting soon emerged as an issue equal to the seemingly unrelated issue of the role of women. In a dramatic move, a New York faction visitor to the annual meeting of the Massachusetts society in January 1839 raised the question of making voting a litmus test for membership in the local.

Weston Chapman's own former minister Amos Phelps demanded that Garrison own up to thinking it was a sin to vote under the slaveholders' Constitution. "Sin for me," Garrison answered, ducking the question of whether an abolitionist activist could refuse to vote. What good would voting do? he asked. The Constitution protected slavery in the states, and none of the parties seemed interested in taking the issue on. Must "the precious time of a thousand friends of the slave," Weston Chapman wrote indignantly in resistance to the vote-or-leave motion, "be consumed in making every abolitionist a voter?" She and Garrison won the Massachusetts round.

Victorious in Massachusetts, the radical Bostonians now sent women delegates to the May 1839 national meeting and won the motion for votes for women in the national society. But the disagreements in the movement would not go away. In the ensuing months, the woman issue split the local societies all across New England. Dissidents formed a second Massachusetts antislavery society, limited to men and committed to electoral activism. Weston Chapman and her troops even lost control of their beloved Boston Female Anti-Slavery Society as the more conventional women sided with the clergymen. To the Weston sisters' dismay, all over New England, women's auxiliaries moved to take a subordinate role in the all-male breakaway societies.

Both sides dug in for a definitive battle over control of the national abolition movement. By the May 1840 annual meeting, all but one of the New York-based executive board were opposed to Garrison. The battle centered on the two newspapers, Garrison's *Liberator* and the New York society's *Emancipator*, which was edited by clergyman and legal scholar Joshua Leavitt. For a year, angry pronouncements flew back and forth. Pro-politics Cincinnati publisher James G. Birney, newly relocated to New York, proposed that voting be made a condition for participation in the abolitionist movement and accused the Garrisonians of being of no human government. Garrison shot back: "[Abolition] has no authority to determine which is orthodox or which heterodox ... [I]t recognizes only the fact, that slavery is protected both by Church and State, and therefore, must, in the order of events, be overthrown by influencing Church and State." Agents of the New York persuasion were dispatched to organize opposition to Garrison among the local New England chapters, and damning letters were written and leaked. Women, political action, church-going: the movement began to split along every plane of disagreement.

By the 1840 national meeting, everyone was ready for a showdown. Garrisonians had organized a literal boatload of New England support-ers to sail from Boston to New York for the meeting. Before the actual convention could begin, the Society routinely appointed a business com-mittee to manage it—a consciously mixed slate of Boston's own and the representatives of the New York faction. But one of the candidates for the business committee was the female abolitionist lecturer Abby Kelley. As Massachusetts delegate John Greenleaf Whittier put it, "Our friend Abby . . . was the bombshell that exploded the society."

Abby Kelley was a social change bombshell for sure. In that context, she was explosive. A modest New England schoolteacher, in 1832 she heard Garrison speak and was transformed. She was as militant a lecturer as abolition possessed, and she was the face of female abolitionism—as well as a potent fundraiser—for twenty years. After a tumultuous vote at the 1840 meeting, in which Kelley was elected to the business committee, New York leader Lewis Tappan announced that he would not sit on the committee with her. The meeting chair decided it was time to adjourn, thus forestalling a dramatic walkout. This was to be, however, the last of the undivided American Anti-Slavery Society gatherings. That night, the defeated anti-female faction gathered at Tappan's New York apartment to start a new society.

The Vanguard

Garrison became the de facto leader of a national antislavery society, riven almost in half, stripped of its main funders, and in outright rebellion against church and state. He had started the movement on January 1, 1831, with a cry in the wilderness from the front page of the first *Liberator*. Would his movement ever achieve anything more than a cry in the wilderness? He had one potent weapon: in 1841, Weston Chapman officially became a councilor of the Boston group.

He had a weapon, and soon he had a rallying event to engage his com-mitment to perfect equality. In June of 1841, the great Black abolitionist and leader of the New York Committee of Vigilance, David Ruggles, was attacked by the captain on the Nantucket steamer when he protested the transit company's racial segregation policy. Garrison and a big contingent of Boston activists were going to the late summer meeting of the New England society on the island, and they decided to organize against the steamship policies en route. After a triumphant confrontation with the segregationist transit company on the dock, the abolitionists integrated the upper deck of the ship and arrived in Nantucket feeling quite empowered.

Two days later, on August 11, another Black Massachusetts resident, newly named Frederick Douglass, of New Bedford, joined the Massachusetts society members in Nantucket and rose hesitatingly to tell them of *his* journey to Nantucket—from the slave state of Maryland. Garrison's firepower was about to increase exponentially.

PART III

THE GRAND ALLIANCE AT WORK

14

(1835–1842)

Douglass Joins Garrison

DOUGLASS HAD GOTTEN OUT WHEN HE COULD. Like most fugitive slaves, he was a young man from a border state. He arrived just as the role of Black activists in the abolitionist movement was growing explosively in meaning and effectiveness, thanks in large part to Black advocacy for fugitives from slavery.

Of course, there had been a Black movement from the beginning: Garrison's breakthrough to immediate abolitionism was, as we have seen, the direct product of Black activist David Walker's appeal in 1829. The free Blacks who were the backbone of the stirrings among white activists—the first subscribers and lifeblood of the early *Liberator*, the hosts of the first meetings in Philadelphia—also spent much time and effort fighting racial segregation, denial of the vote, Black unemployment in the North. Many of the leading Black activists, like James Barbadoes, were also members of the mostly white groups. Although the predominantly white antislavery societies were somewhat integrated, few white abolitionists turned the full force of their attention on their free Black brethren's plight in freedom.

When the movement splintered around 1840, the Black abolitionists' instinct, especially in Boston, was to stick with Garrison, one of the first and most sincere advocates of equality. It was Garrison who organized boycotts against the Jim Crow Massachusetts railroad lines and, on the eve of the schism, presided over a true interracial party for the wedding of abolitionists Theodore Weld and Angelina Grimké. But almost immediately, the Black movement people in New York, where the breakaway faction was centered, were torn. In the end, the Tappans' new American

DR. JAMES McCUNE SMITH,
First regularly-educated Colored Physician in the United
States. (See page 325.)

James McCune Smith, leading Black abolitionist in the mostly white movement. *From* Recollections of Seventy Years *by Daniel Alexander Payne (A.M.E. Sunday School Union, 1888).*

and Foreign Anti-Slavery Society attracted such Black stalwarts as Samuel E. Cornish and Amos Beman and named three Black abolitionists to its twelve-member executive committee; by 1849, Samuel Cornish, Charles B. Ray, Christopher Rush, George Whipple, and James W. C. Pennington had served. The essayist James McCune Smith, America's first Black physician and one of the leading lights of the movement, tried to keep a foot in both camps. He would be at the first big annual meeting of the Boston faction in 1842, where he met the Garrisonians' new phenom, Frederick Douglass. It was the beginning of a long and important relationship.

As the ten-year-old mostly white movement splintered, critics like the economics professor Gilbert Hobbs Barnes suggest, abolition became weakened and marginalized. In fact, the movement decentralized. State and local societies, often uninterested in the personality-driven quarrels of the national, stopped sending in dues and attending national meetings. But they continued to function. The locals often finessed the debates that split the national, embracing, as in Ohio, both women's rights and political participation.

The Centrality of the Black Movement

In the space left by the weakened central movement, the real action centered on a coalition of free Black activists and fugitive slaves. The Black convention movement, active since 1830, moved in. Although the majority of organized free Blacks always preferred cooperation with the white-run organizations, it was usually the Black movement that looked after fugitives. Days before Weston Chapman and her cohort brought Little Med to court, for example, the abolitionists in Boston had rescued two enslaved women from a slave catcher on a passing ship and gone to court for help. While Justice Lemuel Shaw was considering the women's fate, a mostly Black throng in the courtroom stopped the proceedings and carried the fugitives away to safety.

Starting with Little Med, the legal abolitionists began reshaping the North as an official place of sanctuary. Whether legitimate or not, legal protection for Black people on northern soil sparked the momentum of flight. Fugitives arrived. The numbers are always speculative, but research reveals that, in Kentucky for example, fifty percent more slaves escaped every year after 1830 than had escaped in any year before. Northern Black people helped them. Although these numbers represent a tiny percentage of the growing slave population, the enslavers were disproportionately infuriated by the occasional escape. In one sense they accurately perceived the threat. The fugitives—their stories and the challenge they posed to the racist but slavery-averse majority of northerners—potently fueled abolition.

Black abolitionist David Ruggles accelerated the process of Black people protecting other Black people—runaways and even free Black people—in 1835, when he founded the New York Committee of Vigilance. Soon there were Vigilance Committees all over the North to help Black people get out, and stay out, of slavery. As Ruggles's 1837 report of his efforts reflects, the defenders had their hands full. They watched for the slave catchers and northern kidnapping gangs, rescued free Blacks from being dragged into slavery, and created a network of contacts on ships and trains to identify slaves being transported who might be liberated by touching free soil. In what was a routine experience for him, in 1838 Ruggles opened his door to a young fugitive named Frederick Bailey just escaped from Maryland. The Vigilance Committees and the Underground Railroad network were two arms of the same movement.

Slavery as Courtroom Drama

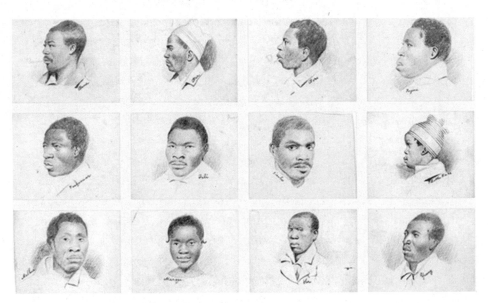

The *Amistad* fugitives. *Sketches by William H. Townsend, ca. 1840. Courtesy of the Beinecke Rare Book and Manuscript Library, Yale University.*

A couple of years after Ruggles's report, the fugitive slave movement hit pay dirt. In 1839 the ship *Amistad,* loaded with a cargo of slaves from Africa, set sail from Havana in the Spanish colony of Cuba for Puerto Príncipe near the other end of the island. The cargo was illegal: Spain had banned the slave trade. The Spanish owners had bought the slaves in a fraudulent system designed to disguise illegal imports as Cuban slaves, since slavery was still legal in Cuba. Led by a Mende African slave, whom whites named Cinqué, the slaves attacked the crew, killed the captain, and took over the ship. They then commanded their Spanish captors to sail them back to Africa. Instead, the white men used the cover of night to steer the ship northwest. A few weeks later, the ship ended up in Long Island Sound, where men from an American naval vessel took the rebellious slaves into custody in a Connecticut jail.

As a dispute on the high seas, the case went to the local federal court, showcasing the great American legal confrontation over the status of human beings as property. The Spanish minister contended that the Black people on the *Amistad* were property to be extradited under a general treaty with the United States to return all "fruits" of piracy. The president of the United States, Martin Van Buren, filed an appearance through his attorney general to represent the nation's international obligations. Midway through the litigation, the Spanish position evolved from a property claim to a claim for extradition of the Blacks as criminals. The American sailors who took the *Amistad* on Long Island claimed the human cargo as salvage. The Spanish "owners" claimed the slaves as property. The abolitionists argued that the African Blacks were free people—born free, free under the prohibition of the slave trade, and free to defend themselves against the criminal Spanish kidnappers. Van Buren of New York, already the target of suspicion from his southern brethren in the Democratic Party, was desperate to prove his proslavery bona fides in the run-up to the election of 1840. His attorney general argued fiercely for the return of the Black captives to Spanish hands, and the administration sent a navy ship to whisk the unfortunates off to Spain, should the African captives lose the legal proceedings.

Local abolitionists called in the troops from New York to argue for the rebels' freedom. *United States v. Schooner Amistad* was an ideal vessel for arguments about the global meaning of slavery. The high seas were a kind of lawless natural world where all humankind came together free of the history and positive law of any one society. Were the enslaved Africans pirates and murderers, to be returned to Cuba to stand trial for their crimes, or were they merely Jeffersonian bearers of rights, asserting their right of self-defense? As with Little Med, when the victims made it to free soil, or free water, were they free by default or, because of the color of their skin, slave? If free was the default, where was the justification for shackling them anew?

The federal trial judge and, on appeal, the federal court of appeals ruled for the rebellious Africans on all counts. They had been captured illegally, the judge said, and were entitled to the natural law of self-defense. They were not pirates or murderers. The American treaty on piracy did not apply. Instead, the American law abolishing the international slave trade governed the case. For thirty years, American law had prohibited the importation of slaves.

But they could not go free. Pending the executive branch action returning them to Africa, both the trial judge and the appeals court refused the abolitionists' repeated requests to let the captives—including the four children, three girls and one boy—out on bail. The judges' opinions on bail were a compendium of racial prejudice. If they were Frenchmen, the judge admitted, of course they would be out on bail. But Africans could not "stand in that point of view." This was a singular case, and "the laws of this country do admit the right of property in men." Enslavement might have been more municipal than national after the decision in the case of Little Med, but still the institution, painfully ill-suited to a nation founded on the Declaration of Independence, persisted. The president's representative in the case filed an appeal with the Supreme Court, and the prisoners would remain imprisoned until the high court ruled.

Amistad was slavery's debut at the Supreme Court. The abolitionists had a superstar to represent them: lawyer, current congressman, and former president of the United States John Quincy Adams. Federalist ex-president son of a Federalist ex-president, Adams was hardly the model of a firebrand. His first foray into abolition, opposing the gag rule in 1836, was not a strike against slavery but rather a defense of people's right to petition their government. But, as with many of abolition's early supporters, his initial recruitment in defense of free people was soon translated into sympathy for the enslaved. From the beginning, he was the *éminence grise* behind the abolitionists' legal strategy in the *Amistad* case.

Adams was as close as you can get to American royalty. Although his involvement was devoutly to be wished, his participation had a fragile quality; he was in his seventies, almost completely deaf, and overwhelmed by his duties as a congressman. To recruit him, Lewis Tappan and Boston abolitionist attorney Ellis Loring had to make a special trip to Quincy, Massachusetts: Help us, President Adams, you're our only hope.

Beginning on February 22, 1841, and finishing on the second of March, Adams stood in the quiet of the Supreme Court and unleashed one of the earliest salvos in the Civil War. Adams and his allies in the New York faction, Lewis Tappan and Theodore Weld, had been amassing their legal armaments since they had met in Washington around 1838. Since Adams was a lawyer with a long career in international law, he saw slavery in the broadest context. What, he began by asking, is the legal status of slavery? The stateless captives of the *Amistad* gave him the perfect opening to try out his theories.

The Declaration of Independence was first, Adams asserted, pointing to the copy hanging in the court's own chamber. Spain, and the U.S. president, he said, were asking a nation founded on the Declaration of Independence to send innocent Black Africans into slavery or criminal prosecution. Adams spent time taking down the Spanish claims under the various treaties and the executive's unseemly eagerness to satisfy the foreigners. As the colonists had laid out in the Declaration, the *Amistad* captives on the high seas were governed only by the law of nature and nature's god: "The moment you come, to the Declaration of Independence, that every man has a right to life and liberty, an inalienable right, this case is decided." Even the United States Constitution, Adams boldly argued, represented slaves as persons, not property. Only local law created enslavement; once foreign slaves touched free northern American soil, they were free.

In 1841 Joseph Story was sitting as an associate justice on the Supreme Court. Story seemed promising for the abolitionist side. Before going on the court, he had been the distinguished author of the treatise *Commentaries on the Conflict of Laws,* where he had embraced the municipal theory of slavery and then featured Justice Shaw's decision in the Little Med case. In the days before regularized collections of court decisions were available, Story's *Commentaries* had been immensely important in publicizing the decision that Little Med was free once her enslaver brought her to free

Massachusetts, thus spreading the idea of free soil throughout the North. One week after Adams finished his argument, Justice Story gave the nation the answer in the *Amistad* case: Adams was right; the treaties with the Spanish did not govern the dispute. As a pure matter of fact, the evidence showed that the Blacks had not been lawfully enslaved, and so they did not come under the treaty.

The implication was clear: had the Africans been lawfully enslaved, say, before the Spanish banned the slave trade, positive law in the form of the treaty would have governed. This was not a good development for the abolitionists, as positive law created and protected slavery throughout much of the United States. So slavery would continue to be legal in the "municipal" regions of the South and any states that came in as slave from the territories. But in 1841, few in the antislavery movement were making more ambitious legal arguments than Story allowed. The Garrisonian moralist wing was making extralegal arguments for everything from moral suasion up to disunion with the slave states. The conservative factions, particularly the upstate followers of Gerrit Smith, were just starting to deploy the argument that slavery was a violation of natural law and thus illegal everywhere.

In the absence of positive law, the court was left with the question the slave empire was most anxious to avoid: How do you justify slavery "upon the eternal principles of justice and international law"? The captives had revolted, killed the captain and the cook, and commandeered the ship. And right they were, Story ruled. In a metaphor familiar to all students of the Declaration of Independence, there are circumstances so dire and unjust that no law provides a remedy: "We may lament the dreadful acts, by which they asserted their liberty, and took possession of the Amistad, and endeavoured to regain their native country; but they cannot be deemed pirates or robbers in the sense of the law." Mutiny, indeed, was the right of the illegally enslaved. And "on those principles, . . . there does not seem to us to be any ground for doubt, that these negroes ought to be deemed free." Without comment, the Supreme Court also treated the newly arrived Black people as persons for purposes of American justice. Their interests could be represented in court just like any other litigants' and, having proved the absence of justification for their enslavement, they were declared free. They could stay in the United States, return to Africa, or go wherever they chose.

By the time the Supreme Court ruled on March 9, 1841, Cinqué and the more than thirty other Mende Africans had lived in various American jails for two years. The abolitionists had formed a rescue committee with preachers, artists, printers, and fundraisers. They located people who could speak the Mende language, and the captives began to tell their stories. They told of their free lives in Africa, evoking the Edenic first chapters of the classic slave narratives. The abolitionists made pamphlets of the tales, complete with pictures of the Africans, especially the handsome leader. All the factions of the shattered national movement played well with others. Garrison covered the trials nonstop in *The Liberator*, including in his coverage praise for his movement rival Tappan for funding the defense. The noisy new force of the penny press took an interest in the irresistible story, and even the proslavery *New York Herald* portrayed the victims in a manifestly human light in a series of articles about the case. One month after the Supreme Court ruled, the rising upstart newspaperman Horace Greeley started the largely sympathetic new newspaper the *New York Tribune*. Abolitionism was no longer confined to journalism's margins.

By the time the successful Black litigants sailed back to Africa, there was a crack in America's founding legal document. Most had always treated the Constitution as protecting slavery where it was legal under local law. Moral suasion, shaming, religious pleading, containment were all strategies for attacking a heavily buttressed legal institution. On its face, the court's recognition of the treaties' authority, where that authority applied, would seem consistent with this repressive regime. If the Constitution protected slavery where it applied, that was the end of the argument.

And yet. Urged on by John Quincy Adams, Justice Story had painted a picture of the act of enslavement as a Hobbesian world where all warred against all and there was no authority to invoke for help. In that circumstance, people were entitled to revolution. Didn't the Declaration of Independence make that clear? The American Revolution was living proof of the explosive force of that starting place. The *Amistad* case began on the high seas. But it was just a matter of time before the ambitious legal thinkers of the New York abolition wing expanded the logic of revolution to penetrate the homeland. Maybe the Constitution would have to be read against a background of the ultimate law of nature so graphically described in the story of the *Amistad*.

Who Lives, Who Dies, Who Tells the Story

In August 1841, a few months after the *Amistad* decision, Frederick Douglass would begin to spread his story of the Hobbesian world of slavery. There were many Black fugitive slave memoirists, and many orators, both Black and even white, slave and free, but Douglass is to the movement as Lincoln was to the Republican Party: the indispensable one. With his whip-scarred back, he was a living manifestation of the "peculiar institution" of chattel slavery. And with his brilliance, his burning sense of injustice, and his wicked humor, he could make the argument as well as be the argument.

Immediately after the Garrisonian Massachusetts Anti-Slavery Society hired Douglass in 1841, it sent him on the road. In some sense, he was on the road for the next half century. At first he traveled with the man who hired him, John Collins, a thirty-something white theology student and

Frederick Douglass on the platform. *Courtesy of Library of Congress.*

general administrator of the Society's affairs. Within weeks, a Philadelphia audience member reported that his address "thrilled through everyone present and compelled them to feel for the wrongs he had endured." "I have come to tell you something about slavery," Douglass announced. When he came north, he said, he was surprised at how much the abolitionists already knew about slavery, its history and horrors. "But they cannot speak as I can from experience, they cannot refer you to a back covered with scars, as I can, for I have felt these wounds."

Douglass compelled his audience to listen. Once he had their attention, he told them what they needed to know, whether they liked it or not. Herein lies the real radicalism of Frederick Douglass: he told them that their Christian religion didn't stop the enslavers one bit. That the abolitionists had to help; the enslaved people knew about abolitionism, and they were counting on it to emancipate them from "slavery and its evils." Douglass relentlessly recited that while slavery was bad, when it came to racism, "prejudice against color is stronger north than south; it hangs around my neck like a heavy weight." He continued, "The northern people think that if slavery were abolished we would all come north," but instead, Douglass predicted, "to escape from northern prejudice, we would go to the south."

Douglass knew about northern views on race: within weeks of his hiring to preach abolition in New England, the conductor on the Eastern Line Railroad threw him off the train for refusing to leave his seat in the "whites only" car. Douglass held on so hard that when he landed on the platform, he was still clutching his train seat.

It is impossible to overstate Douglass's impact. As the historian David Blight describes in his authoritative biography *Frederick Douglass: Prophet of Freedom,* Douglass was uniquely suited for the task. First, because of his authenticity; as he said from the beginning, he could speak from experience. But also because of his energy and commitment. Within nine months of his Nantucket debut, Douglass had spoken in at least twenty towns, often making multiple presentations in a single town, and often staying on for days. By the time Douglass joined the movement, abolitionists had learned the lessons of the Seventy. They stayed in the homes of other abolitionists or anyone who would have them. The abolitionists tried the churches, but establishment Protestants were becoming increasingly alienated from Garrison's movement, and the abolitionists often had to resort to lecturing in secular spaces like town halls or even outdoors.

But Douglass was not just another of the burgeoning corps of abolitionist lecturers—he was a rhetorical phenomenon in the golden age of American rhetoric. "He stood there like an African prince," observer (and famed suffragist) Elizabeth Cady Stanton recalled from 1842, not a year after he started his course, "majestic in his wrath, as with wit, satire, and indignation he graphically described the bitterness of slavery and the humiliation of subjection ... Around him sat the great antislavery orators of the day, earnestly watching the effect of his eloquence on that immense audience, that laughed and wept by turns, completely carried away by the wondrous gifts of his pathos and humor."

Douglass delivered the early speech Stanton heard not on some public green in a remote town but at century-old Faneuil Hall, Boston's first town hall, and the site of critical events of the American Revolution, where he attracted what Stanton describes as an "immense" audience. A speechwriter and speaker of Douglass's gifts would probably have been an attraction anywhere. When he spoke with white Boston abolitionist Edmund Quincy, people in the audience suggested Quincy must have written the speech. How could a lowly fugitive slave "talk so well?"

As with abolition's dependence on the crucial advances in printing technology and on vastly expanding railroads, abolition lectures intersected with another force creating a communal culture: the lyceum lecture movement. The first formal record of the movement appears in 1826, with the founding of the "Millbury [Massachusetts] Branch Number 1 of the American Lyceum." This first lecture society stemmed from the fertile mind of one Josiah Holbrook, a lecturer by trade. Holbrook promoted the concept everywhere he went to lecture. In 1830 he called a convention. Named for the outdoor space where Aristotle taught in ancient Athens, the lyceum was an innovation in moving the social process of learning and transmitting information literally into the public realm. Instead of learned societies with limited memberships or subject matter institutions like Bible groups, the lyceum lecture was open to anyone, and for only a small fee, if any. In a telling parallel to the story of abolition itself, lyceum committees of high-minded (male) citizens sprang up. They raised money and hired speakers. Soon a national corps of renowned lecturers arose in response to the demand, what movement historian Donald Scott calls "newly invented positions based upon some form of conscious intellectual production."

From 1840 to 1860, there were more than three thousand lectures in New York City alone. With their mixture of self-help, entertainment, and moral uplift, the essayist and historian Thomas Wentworth Higginson later rejoiced, the national roster of lyceum speakers wove a "new web of national civilization." Audiences in every town in the system heard the same lectures, and self-consciously participated in making a collective culture.

Higginson was wrong about one thing: lyceums were not national; they were mostly institutions of the Northeast and the old Northwest, what we now call the Middle West. As the historian Eric Foner put it in his foundational analysis of the Republican Party and the Civil War that followed its founding, this cultural divide was critical in the ultimate breakup of the union. In the Oneida Institute and in the entire dignity of labor movement we saw one strand of the unique northern culture, the valorization of work, a concept fundamentally at odds with the valorization of leisure that slavery invokes. The northern concept of labor was not static. A peculiarly American ethos of social mobility framed the years of labor as instrumental. Yes, people worked, sometimes as apprentices or even indentured servants, but the goal of work was the acquisition of an independent farm or business. Self-improvement of the lyceum sort was one of the founding tenets of the northern work ethic, with its end game of class advancement. The South's planter class had scant interest in the self-improvement culture of the northern middle class. Like the railroads, the lectures created not the national civilization of the United States but the culture of what would become the *Union*. Long before 1860, the nation was fracturing along cultural lines.

Even in the North and Northwest, however, the lyceum movement remained more parallel to than overlapping with abolition for many years. The requirement that lyceum lectures be nonpartisan and unemotional excluded most of the meaningful abolition lecture talent and subject matter. Indeed, explicit or implicit rules of racial segregation kept even Douglass off the lyceum platform for more than ten years. Critically, however, the parallel traditions of abolition lecture and lyceum lecture fed each other, as the spoken performance became an essential vehicle for creating a common northern culture. And by 1855, the roster of the Northampton, Massachusetts, lyceum society included, critically, three prominent abolitionists, including Boston stalwart Wendell Phillips. When Douglass finally broke into the lyceum circuit in 1854, he was instantly a national star in a system perfectly set up to amplify his voice. He and the other abolitionist lyceum lecturers disguised their attack on compromise with slavery but thinly as a matter of moral uplift. By that time, the nation was ready.

15

(1841–1842)

The Façade and the Cracks in the Alliance

As THE BRILLIANT YOUNG SPEAKER SET OUT in 1841, the bond between Garrison and Douglass appeared, at first, seamless. By good fortune, when their partnership hit the road, the enterprising editor of the *Hingham Patriot* newspaper attended the seemingly obscure convention of the Plymouth County Anti-Slavery Society in November where Douglass spoke. From his reporting, we can appreciate the full picture of Frederick Douglass's impact on the lecture tour and how his support for Garrison's strategy paid off. The convention had adopted a resolution in favor of moral suasion, a direct contrast to the strategy of the New Yorkers' breakaway branch of abolition, which advocated the ordinary tools of politics. Moral suasion beats politics, Douglass proclaimed, in a dazzling speech, because men's — and women's — hearts could be changed everywhere, but politics had a chance only in the North. The task went deeper than politics, Douglass continued, because slavery was deeply "interwoven" in northern culture as well. Northern churches were as guilty as southern churches, and worse, he emphasized, the North was "pledged by the union" to returning fugitive slaves. Only moral transformation, or, even more radically, disunion, could create real change. According to the minutes of the meeting, "the resolution was then passed."

At every stage of the movement deliberations, Douglass spoke with an authority born of his experience. A few months after the Hingham meeting, Garrison appeared with Douglass in Barnstable for a series of antislavery meetings. When Douglass again spoke in favor of nonresistance, Garrison noted with satisfaction that even a "slave" with "his back all horribly scarred by the lash" still declared the divinity of his pacifist philosophy.

Douglass's unmitigated scorn for the hypocrisy of the churches also fed right into Garrison's dispute with the American and Foreign Anti-Slavery Society over disunion with the churches. At the Hingham meeting, Douglass had shared his experience with his prayerful Methodist enslaver: "a man who could pray at morning, pray at noon, and pray at night" yet "tie up Douglass' poor cousin by ... her two thumbs and inflict stripes and blows upon ... her bare back, till the blood streamed to the ground." This wrenching scene was a centerpiece of one of Douglass's most popular orations.

Douglass Waffles and Douglass Matters

Sometimes Douglass used his authority to differ with the establishment abolitionists. Back in Hingham, Douglass had chosen to oppose the man who had hired him and who was his frequent companion on the lecture circuit, Boston administrator John Collins, to defend the value of massive abolitionist petitions, which had been bedeviling Congress for almost a decade. Petitions were political action, by 1841, at odds with the pure Garrisonian dogma of nonresistance. Slaves knew about the petitions, Douglass informed the white abolition gathering. And they were heartened beyond measure by knowing there was activism. They overheard their masters talking about them as if they were dumb beasts and could know nothing, he angrily reported, and then they disseminated the little bits of good news.

From the beginning Douglass was watching his new brethren for their broader attitudes toward race. Describing his appearance in an early lecture in his first published letter to Garrison, he opens with a description of the integrated seating at the New Bedford town hall: "From the eminence which I occupied, I could see the entire audience; and from its appearance, I should conclude that prejudice against color was not there ... [W]e were all on a level, every one took a seat just where they chose; there were neither men's side, nor women's side; white pew, nor black pew; but all seats were free and all sides free." Boldly, when he was still new to the abolition scene, he opposed the Garrisonian orthodoxy against any dealings with enslavers, including even a fugitive slave buying the freedom of his family.

Garrison had demanded that there be no compensation to slave owners to free their slaves. It was blood money, better spent to fund abolition as a movement. In June 1842, after traveling with Garrison on an extended lecture tour of Cape Cod, Douglass came on board with the radicalism, becoming an even more faithful Garrisonian.

His support was never more meaningful than when he was confronting the issue that had divided the abolitionist movement two years before: Should the movement turn to politics to unseat the slave empire? Although a debate could break out at any time, the abolition factions, most visibly at their respective periodic conventions, argued critical issues like the role of political action. In 1841 the Massachusetts Anti-Slavery Society met in Boston to celebrate its tenth anniversary, and predictably took up the hottest movement dispute: Was moral suasion superior to politics? Douglass rose to defend this, Garrison's, core belief. It was his first appearance before a convention, and by all accounts he stunned the crowd.

Douglass's style of speechmaking, scholars have observed, was the classic setting forth your opponent's argument and then refuting it. But what mattered most at that point was Douglass's unique access to his own biography. The politicos asserted that political action was all that had worked for "the cause." "There are those in Massachusetts," Douglass testified, "who treat me like a man and a brother." "I ask you," Douglass intoned, mocking the contention that politics led to humanity, "what this Legislature has done that has caused you to recognize my humanity?" Surely, he implied—actually somewhat unfairly, since Massachusetts had abolished slavery by law years before—it was the moral stature of the Massachusetts friends that drove their egalitarian behavior, not any legislation their governors had passed. The opposing faction had asserted that those who didn't vote were no better than proslavery men. Would being a Garrisonian, and therefore not voting, Douglass continued, make him, a Black fugitive slave, "proslavery"? The argument answered itself. Douglass, and a few other antislavery orators, were the living manifestation of the error of the political abolitionists' ways. The always astute Maria Weston Chapman recognized at once what Douglass was doing. "It is interesting to see," she recorded in summarizing the convention, "with how few words a man of color like Douglas[s], can beat down the mountain of prejudice, which a white man might work a day in vain to pile up proofs against."

For almost two years Douglass traveled around New England and western New York State, often with Garrison on the New England legs, with never a sliver of light between their positions. In his coverage of Douglass in *The Liberator* during those founding years, Garrison quickly revealed Douglass's value to the struggling Garrison faction of antislavery. Garrison's offhand description of Douglass at Nantucket—"a talented colored young man"—soon gave way. "Douglass," Garrison reported, "spoke ... as the representative of his enslaved brethren and sisters," and was routinely greeted with "a roar of applause." The New York press, slowly paying more attention to abolitionism, sent reporters to the annual meetings of the American Anti-Slavery Society, and the abolitionists wanted to showcase their very best. In 1843 Douglass took the stage at the all-important annual anniversary meeting of Garrison's American Anti-Slavery Society with the greats—the star lecturer and fundraiser Abby Kelley, the foundational Wendell Phillips, and Garrison himself.

But there were warnings, if Garrison had been able to see them. In Hyannis, on the first Cape Cod tour, Douglass started invoking stories other than his own, which he drew from the growing body of abolitionist literature. Later he would explain he had grown tired of telling his own biography again and again. He was, as he had been all those years ago in Maryland, "reading" and thinking. And as his enslaver predicted, the more he read, the more he yearned for freedom, this time not to work for himself but to think for himself.

In their first appearance, at Hingham, Garrison had lauded Douglass for his fidelity to Garrisonism, reciting all the reasons Douglass should be drawn to resistance—bodies lacerated with whips and bound with chains, children sold on the auction block, wives scourged and polluted before their own families' eyes—and marveled at his great soul and Christian magnanimity in forgoing a natural recourse to self-defense. You'd think Garrison's awareness of the bad fit between nonresistance and a proud fugitive from enslavement would have warned him the alliance was fragile. But Garrison was nothing if not confident in his beliefs.

Centrifugal Forces

On March 1, 1842, the Supreme Court gave a big boost to Garrison's absolutism and rejectionism when it decided the first major case of a fugitive slave, *Prigg v. Pennsylvania*. Fugitive slaves were ground zero of legal abolition. The court could decide, as Justice Shaw did for Little Med, that enslavers could not bring their human chattels to free soil and expect the northern legal system to enforce the southern system. The Supreme Court could even decide that the American authorities would not enforce the claims of foreign enslavers to humans tossed up by the sea, as in the *Amistad* case. But *Prigg* squarely presented the core case. Could the northern states turn their backs on their southern counterparts in the union when the humans enslaved under southern laws ran to the North for sanctuary?

Political developments of recent years meant the issue was unavoidable. When the northern states freed their soil by gradually abolishing slavery after the Revolution, they slowly began passing laws making it harder for the slave states to take Black northern residents into, or back into, bondage. Pennsylvania, the oldest refuge of escaping slaves, had a long-standing anti-kidnapping law forbidding the transportation of "Negroes" out of the state for the purpose of keeping them in slavery or enslaving them.

Formerly enslaved Margaret Morgan escaped from Maryland to Pennsylvania in 1832. Many years later, her enslaver sent slave catcher Edward Prigg after her, and he took her (and her children, one born on free soil) back into slavery. The state prosecuted Prigg for kidnapping. In his defense Prigg argued that the Pennsylvania law violated the federal Fugitive Slave Act of 1793 and the Fugitive Slave Clause of the United States Constitution. Would the Supreme Court allow Pennsylvania to protect its Black residents, or would it side with Garrison's pessimistic belief that the Constitution was a slave document?

In a sweeping opinion for the highest court, the esteemed jurist Justice Joseph Story, whose treatise, as we have seen, had popularized the Little Med decision, came close to Garrison's despairing scorched earth position. Slavery was more than a "municipal," local institution. It was the foundation of the nation. Reversing the slave catcher's conviction, he opined that if northern states could throw roadblocks into the slaveholders' efforts to take back their human chattels, the South would never have agreed to the

Constitution in the first place. Pennsylvania's freedom law was unconstitutional. Five justices agreed with the outcome, if not the opinion. Given Story's immense prestige, his opinion was generally taken to represent the court. The Constitution was, the court held, as Garrison had always contended, a union with slaveholders.

Within six months, the Supreme Court's decision to protect the enslavers as a matter of constitutional fealty gave Bostonians a full facial blast of what it was like to be ruled by the South through the bargain the court described. Fugitive slave George Latimer had been living in Boston for years when his enslaver sent catchers after him. Latimer was arrested and thrown in federal jail to wait in confinement until his self-proclaimed master, Virginia's James Gray, could come to Boston and claim his property. Boston abolitionists, perhaps inspired by their success with Little Med, ran to state court to their hero, Justice Lemuel Shaw, for a writ of habeas corpus to release Latimer. No such luck. The Supreme Court's recent decision in *Prigg* v. *Pennsylvania* tied the Massachusetts court's hands, Shaw ruled. While Latimer's enslaver gathered his evidence of ownership, crowds of abolitionists massed in the streets of Boston. Three heads-up youngsters started producing a new paper, the *Latimer Journal and North Star,* to report the daily developments in the case. So many thousands of protesters gathered in Faneuil Hall for a rally that pandemonium ensued. With Douglass at the forefront, the antislavery society launched a series of "Latimer meetings" to use the wrenching facts of the case for its crusade. Latimer's enslaver, faced with the prospect of escorting his enslaved person through mobs of furious Bostonians, took the money the abolitionists offered and let him go.

The abolitionists were not satisfied. Justice Story's otherwise sweeping decision in *Prigg* had left room for states trying to protect the Black people who touched their free soil. The Fugitive Slave Act of 1793, which *Prigg* was intended to enforce, seemed to compel state law enforcement to assist slave owners in recapturing their prey. Here, Justice Story had some doubt. State lawmen could help, he speculated, unless state law forbade them to. This was a big "unless." The federal government did not have a serious law enforcement establishment until much later in American history. If the feds had to catch the fugitives themselves, without local courts and police, they would be hard-pressed. Immediately after they paid off Latimer's pursuer, the Boston abolitionists mobilized to get Massachusetts to pass a law forbidding state law enforcement from participating in capturing fugitive slaves. On March 24, 1843, Massachusetts passed the "Latimer Law" doing just that. The gauntlet had been thrown down. Other free states —New York, Rhode Island—followed suit. The South and the southern representatives in the federal government fumed.

For fifteen years—from the decision in *Prigg v. Pennsylvania* in March of 1842 to the final constitutional slavery decision, *Dred Scott,* in 1857 —Supreme Court decisions played a central role in the conflict. The court was thrust into this role in part because abolitionists kept bringing slave cases back up, probing for weaknesses in the court's constitutional barricade around slavery. As the fugitives escaped and the cases kept dramatizing their plight, the northerners had their noses rubbed in the constitutional bargain the court said they had made. The court's decisions became real on the streets of Boston, as the authorities took George Latimer through those streets in 1842.

The actions taken during the Latimer episode—buying Latimer's freedom, arguing to the courts for a loophole in the constitutional defense of slavery, and making political demands on the state and federal legislatures —all seem deeply antagonistic to Garrison's commitment to shun politics and any bargaining with slaveholders. When *Prigg* was decided, the only escape, from Garrison's point of view, was either to change the hearts of the nation or to withdraw from it. "No Union with Slave Holders," *The Liberator* proclaimed.

But as early as October of 1842, in the heart of Garrison country, the New Bedford Latimer meeting passed a new resolution, with Douglass's full support, in deep conflict with Garrison's antipathy to politics. Invoking the Declaration of Independence, the meeting resolved that no person born in America should be born into slavery. If the principles of the Declaration were to govern, the Constitution would have to be understood quite differently indeed.

Douglass wrote his first published letter, in a lifetime of letter writing, to Garrison—a report on the Latimer case. The symbolism was fraught. The more Douglass learned about the intersection of constitutional law and slave rendition at the heart of the case, the more he questioned Garri-son's passive strategy. Douglass's course, which would ultimately lead him to the momentous break with Garrison, was to be a long, meandering jour-ney between the poles of Garrison's rejection of politics and the siren song of political engagement offered by the breakaway New York factions. The principles of Latimer activism mapped the way.

16

(1837–1843)

Political Abolition Pulls on Garrisonians

GARRISON HAD COINED THE MOTTO "NO UNION with Slaveholders." The cutting-edge legal theorists of the New York faction dared to contest his premise: Did the Constitution have to mean union with slaveholders?

Rise Up

While abolitionists had been invoking the principles of the American Revolution from the start, deploying the founding principles against the Constitution did not come at once. Massachusetts congressman Timothy Fuller had suggested in the Missouri Compromise debates that the Declaration of Independence rendered slavery illegal in any ensuing American government. The dominant argument in abolition for a long time, however, was the relatively moderate contention that the Constitution was, at best, neutral, leaving the federal government to regulate slavery outside the states and the states free to treat slavery as they would—free soil in the North and enslavement in the South.

Even the centrist theory of the neutral Constitution supported a lot of political action. Well before formal abolition revived around 1830, as we have seen, slavery's opponents and their allies lobbied the federal government to limit the spread of slavery, under its residual power to act outside the states. In 1820 Congress passed the Missouri Compromise, barring slavery in states carved from the Louisiana Purchase just north of the thirty-sixth parallel. Early in modern abolition, Garrison and the abolitionists lobbied Congress to abolish slavery in the District of Columbia, a federal preserve.

Pushing the free states' internal power to the fullest, the abolitionists in the North had spent decades pressing their states to pass laws like the Pennsylvania freedom law struck down in *Prigg*. Such freedom laws extended the protection of free soil to fugitive slaves as much as possible: slave catchers had to obtain official warrants, and the alleged slaves were entitled to trial by jury on their status. While this process continued, everyone knew, rescuers, usually Black activists, would be able to spirit the fugitives away to safety.

The movement's petitions to abolish slavery in the District of Columbia predated Garrison's full breach with politics. But when the virtuous Garrisonian petitioning of the legislatures didn't produce much legislative activity to protect the slaves or limit the expansion of slavery into the territories, the abolitionists turned to new, more aggressive tactics. They sent out questionnaires interrogating political candidates about their positions on enslavement. Inevitably, the activists realized that their candidate questionnaires obligated them to vote for the ones who gave the right answers. If abolition was going to be the subject of political action, the Constitution would have to be interpreted as allowing action against slavery.

While the abolitionists were revving their political engines, the southern states waged a campaign in federal courts to limit the neutrality of the Constitution, arguing, mostly successfully, that the Constitution forbade the North to extend legal protections to fugitive slaves even on their own free soil. *Prigg v. Pennsylvania* in 1842 was the first major decision supporting the South's position. Seeking to exploit the tiny hole the *Prigg* court left, northern states responded with Latimer laws, forbidding any state law enforcement officials from engaging in slave capture. Not hindered by Garrisonian scruples against engagement with politics, the slaveholders in turn began lobbying Congress for a more ambitious fugitive slave law to force the northerners to pursue the runaways. As both sides tugged on the Constitution, the neutral theory got thinner and thinner.

As Garrison moved to his position as the absolutist rebel against all forms of authority, he abandoned political activities like petitioning, lobbying, and voting to enact abolition. Garrison—with his right hand, Maria Weston Chapman—was committed to changing people's hearts or withdrawing from union with them.

After the movement finally split, the New York factions, which had broken from the American Anti-Slavery Society in 1840 ostensibly over the woman question, could turn to politics free of Garrisonian pacifism. And indeed, in the years when Douglass was following Garrison, the nonresistant, the runaway New York abolitionists were constructing the very edifice of law and politics where Douglass would ultimately make his home.

Rich Old White Men — and Revolution

For a long time, not even all the New York factions were on board for a political initiative. The breakup of the abolitionist movement in 1840 had left behind not one but two centers of abolitionism competing with Garrison's Bostonians. One was the familiar New York City faction around the wealthy Tappan brothers, which remained deeply church-centered, aristocratic in origins and beliefs, and suspicious of politics. But the second concentration of reformers in upstate New York, led by plutocrat landowner Gerrit Smith, had different ideas.

Smith was one of the richest men in America, son of John Jacob Astor's business partner Peter Smith, a man said to have been raised with slaves in his New York household. Gerrit's father was a mean, bullying, miserly man who kept his son at the edge of actual hunger when in college. By the time Smith graduated from college as the valedictorian, he was a real intellectual and dreamed of becoming a lawyer. But when his mother died, he had to return to run the family business with his father in one of their two hometowns — Peterboro, New York.

Like his wealthy counterparts in New York City, Smith came to abolition first through conversion to the Second Great Awakening, and then from the high-society branch of the Second Great Awakening, the Benevolent Empire. He followed the predictable path into colonization. Influenced by his personal respect for the Black slaves of his youthful household, historians speculate, he was soon alienated by the racist underpinnings of the movement to exile America's Black residents and converted to Garrisonian immediatism.

Gerrit Smith was a doer. When, in 1835, a New York antislavery meeting in nearby Utica was met by the usual mob, Smith was outraged. Typically, he invited the conveners to his mansion in nearby Peterboro for refuge and made sure the guests would be greeted with a good breakfast. The mob had its effect on the powerful, wealthy man: it made him fully commit to abolition, and as we have seen, he joined the Tappans in the American Anti-Slavery Society, quickly becoming one of the largest donors.

Of the three branches of abolition—Garrison's Boston, the Tappan brothers' New York, and Smith's upstate faction—the wealthy and well-connected Smith's New York State Anti-Slavery Society was most centered on old, rich, well-educated men. One Peterboro stalwart was Alvan Stewart, educated as a teacher and a lawyer, and of a social class that enabled him, on a journey through the South in 1816, to meet the author of the Declaration himself, slave owner Thomas Jefferson. Stewart was not impressed with Jefferson's slave empire. "Curses," he wrote a friend from Charlottesville, "on the Dutchman who sold the first cargo of slaves at Jamestown in 1620." (Jefferson himself had also written the Virginia Declaration of Rights, which proclaimed that "all men are by nature equally free.")

In the next twenty years after his tour of the South, Stewart, by all accounts a brilliant legal thinker and speaker, became a leader of radical antislavery constitutionalism. First he suggested that, even if slavery were protected in the states where it was legal, the prohibition of the international slave trade also allowed Congress to outlaw the *interstate* trade in slaves under its power to regulate commerce. This was a wickedly threatening move, because after importing slaves from Africa became illegal in 1808, domestic slaves became a "crop," most raised in the coastal southern states and then sold interstate to the newly developed cotton states like Mississippi and Texas. The ghastly coffles of naked, chained humans personified the interstate commerce in slavery. There was no chance that Congress in the 1830s was going to do any such thing as Stewart suggested, but the suggestion would live to threaten the South for real when antislavery politics finally started to gain traction.

But Stewart did not stop there. He made the much more radical suggestion that the Constitution was not neutral. After all, the Constitution never actually uses the word "slavery." The Constitution was in fact antislavery, Stewart boldly contended in 1837, because the Fifth Amendment, which forbids the taking of liberty without due process of law, outlawed slavery everywhere. Congress and the federal courts were bound to act, Stewart concluded, as directed by the Constitution's abolitionist terms. Before the movement breakup in 1840, its nonpolitical and pacifist factions moved swiftly to quash Stewart's heresy. But his great friend and colleague Gerrit Smith was not sure Stewart was wrong.

The decade following the breach from Garrisonian dogma in 1840 saw the greatest revolution in American legal thinking since the Founding. In 1841, an eccentric Boston chemist, George Mellen, published the first book-length argument that slavery was unconstitutional. In 1844 Stewart had a chance to try out the argument in court. New Jersey had ratified a state constitution that declared in its preamble (as other states had also asserted) that "all men are by nature free and independent." Free and equal New Jersey was still living with the residue of its 1804 gradual emancipation law, which held the offspring of the freed slaves to unpaid labor until age twenty-one. If men are free and equal, Stewart asserted in a pair of cases under the new state constitution, they cannot also be enslaved. He demanded a writ of habeas corpus to free two slaves serving out the last of their enslavement years.

Stewart lost. Like its counterpart in Virginia, another "free and independent" state, the court found that the New Jersey draftsmen had intended no such outcome. The New Jersey court went much further and opined that all the language of freedom and independence was just abstract verbiage with no place in law, and that all references to moral argument and humane feelings had no place in court either. The attack on Stewart's legal theory was not an accident; the judges in his New Jersey cases knew exactly what his motives were and who his allies were, and they wanted to put an end to the development of his argument.

New Jersey was a defeat for radical constitutionalism, but Stewart's brilliant and moving argument went the 1844 version of viral. Almost simultaneously, two Gerrit Smith associates, William Goodell and Lysander Spooner, brought the whole argument together in a flood of articles and two books—Goodell's *Views of American Constitutional Law, in Its Bearing on American Slavery* and Spooner's unvarnished *The Unconstitutionality of Slavery*. Goodell and Spooner largely left behind Stewart's idiosyncratic reading of the Constitution as forbidding slavery for due process and other textual reasons and argued most forcefully for the interpretation or rejection of any law that, like the laws of slavery, went against natural law.

The natural law argument was rooted in Lord Mansfield's foundational free soil decision, *Somerset v. Stewart*, seven decades before. Somerset was, formally, a conflict of laws case. In such a conflict, the English courts had some wiggle room to decide whether to respect the unnatural Virginia law. Stewart, Goodell, and Spooner only added the last turn. It was not a conflicts problem, they said. Even in the land of slavery, they argued, such an unnatural law should be constrained by interpretation if possible; but if there were no escape hatch, the court would have to refuse to enforce it, full stop. Even if it were written into the Constitution. Confronted with natural law, slavery would be unconstitutional. Everywhere.

Politics in the Shadow of the Constitution

The critical contribution was not the constitutional theory; it was the practice. It was a straight shot from the argument that slavery was unconstitutional to the demand that the courts and legislatures act, and not just in the places allowed by a neutral Constitution, like the District of Columbia or the territories. No longer would abolition be restricted to modest proposals or, more passively still, to Garrison's extra-constitutional tactics of pacifist moral suasion. Abolitionists could campaign. They could litigate.

What drives legislatures? What do the courts follow? The election returns. Mogul and small town do-er Gerrit Smith occupied the perfect philosophical ground to stir up a political movement around the natural law of freedom. A child of the Second Great Awakening, Smith, raised by an abusive and distant father, saw little to love in religion. Instead, he looked to nature for guidance, using the natural world as an example of balance among competing forces. He rejected theology, with its dogma, for "religion" and "spirituality." Undivided by sect, he thought his rules of morality applied to all humans. He had a simple touchstone: "All know how they would be done by: and hence all know what to do to others." He was a radical individualist, equally wary of domination by organized religion and by government. He abhorred the domination of one person over others and the role of government in enabling the domination.

Such a libertarian philosophy might seem ill-suited for a political or-ganizer, but, like a true individualist, Smith believed passionately in volun-tarism. When Smith heard that the lawyer Myron Holley had called for antislavery candidates to run for office independent of the existing, flawed political parties, he saw that the obvious move was to start an indepen-dent party. The activists had been laying the groundwork with small local conventions for a couple of years. In the spring of 1840, Smith and his upstate colleagues, including the constitutional natural law theorist Wil-liam Goodell, put out a call for a national convention. Garrison responded with an essay in *The Liberator* titled "Infidelity." "A more ridiculous farce," Garrison continued "we have never had occasion to place on record."

The precepts of the early Liberty Party do seem a little unrealistic. Smith and other deeply rooted local citizens thought they'd build from islands of virtue, like Peterboro, New York, and Smith's other hometown, nearby Smithfield. Seeing the example, they speculated, neighboring towns would turn to antislavery, then all of New York State, and, finally, the entire North. Once they had started the process of converting politics to aboli-tion, they could transform one of the two proslavery national parties and disband their third party.

At no point did the Liberty Party ever exceed five percent of the New York vote. Garrison might be forgiven for having dubbed the new group, in the spring of their founding in 1840, "April fools."

But he was so wrong.

The Politico

Garrison was never explicit about how his campaign for moral suasion would free slaves. In fact, if the constitutional deal, which Garrison called a pact with the devil, put the slave power in firm control of the national government, the new moral awakening caused the enslavers to pull their pillows firmly over their heads.

Moral abolitionism did work, perversely in part because it recruited ac-tivists to Garrison's sworn enemies, the abolitionist political activists. None of these were as powerful a draw as the silver-tongued Theodore Weld.

The examples of Weld's influence on the politicians who transformed

Abolitionist congressman Joshua R.
Giddings. *Courtesy of Library of Congress.*

the arc of abolition are legion. A leader of antislavery in the New York
State legislature, Henry B. Stanton started life in abolition as one of Weld's
upstart "Lane Rebels" at Lane Seminary. Another lawyer and Weld convert, New York's Seth M. Gates was, with Vermont's William Slade, the
rare openly abolitionist congressman. In 1836, Weld spent time in Pittsburgh. When he left, he had converted the Presbyterian synod there to
abolition. Presbyterians were the most numerous denomination in the city.
In 1847 the Whig Party of Pennsylvania adopted a resolution opposing
the expansion of slavery in the territories.

Ohioan Joshua Reed Giddings was just minding his own business,
making money in Ohio real estate speculation, when in 1836 Weld showed
up. Like so many in Weld's audiences over the years, Giddings was a lawyer
and a deeply religious member of his Congregational church, which had
moved radically toward the evangelical, emotive practices and beliefs in
personal responsibility typical of the New Great Awakening. It even had
do-good programs in the fashion of the Benevolent Empire.

Thanks to Weld's past visit, when, in 1838, financial reverses caused
Giddings to abandon business and follow the teachings of his church to
make the world a better place, he knew exactly where to focus. He adopted

Weld's passionate immediatism and started the local Anti-Slavery Society. But he did not stop at that Garrisonian resting place. In 1838 Giddings decided to run for Congress. He joined the Whig Party, which was dominant in northern Ohio, and between two bad choices there, definitely the more antislavery party than the southern-dominated Jacksonian Democrats. And he won, bringing the tally of open abolitionists in Congress to three.

As soon as Giddings arrived in Washington, he immediately formed an alliance with Representatives Slade and Gates. They moved to the same boardinghouse, which quickly became abolition central. The Whig abolitionists were joined by the indefatigable legal scholar Joshua Leavitt, dispatched by the Liberty Party to lobby the largely unresponsive Congress. When the abolitionist congressmen called for more data to fill their pleas and speeches, no less an ally than Theodore Weld moved to D.C. Something resembling a modern movement lobby began to emerge.

How could they start to chip away at the unseemly sight of chained human beings marched to the nation's capital and put up for sale? Slavery's Achilles' heel in the national legislature was always the gag rule, an affront even to politicians indifferent to the fate of their enslaved fellow human beings. Giddings and Slade used the device of a bill for building a bridge across the Potomac River to make their first move. A bridge would only make it easier to transport slaves, Giddings argued. We should move the capital to a place where we don't have to look at people chained together by the neck. And we can't even debate the right or wrong of it in our own governing body because of the gag rule. The House erupted, with abuse from all parties and sections pouring down on Giddings. It took an hour to restore order.

Order would become a scarce commodity. The hotheaded southerners in the Congress had long used the southern culture of violence to maintain their dominance over proceedings and debate, not infrequently brandishing firearms or suggesting a duel. They had become accustomed to dough-faced northerners choosing cowardly retreat from their principles over risking death in a duel with armed defenders of the slave power. Notorious brawler Louisiana's John Dawson pulled a knife on Giddings a few years later, but Giddings did not back down. Brawny six-foot-tall former homesteader Giddings was a new kind of northern representative.

The Scene Is Set

Abolitionist politicians would eventually have to decide if they should switch to the new, purely abolitionist Liberty Party. In 1840, however, after forcing the gag rule fight, Giddings abandoned his dalliance with Liberty and returned to the fold. Although the Whigs nominated slaveholder William Henry Harrison for president and, worse, rabid slavery advocate John Tyler as vice president, Giddings was faithful to the party. But on the local level, the emergence of political abolition showed its fangs. Joshua Giddings took heat from his former allies, editors of abolitionist newspapers, and the newly formed Liberty Party, which had more support in Ohio than in most places. Ohio was Whig territory, and Giddings was handily reelected, but much of his support came from, of all sources, William Lloyd Garrison's purists, striking a blow at their Liberty competitors within the movement by backing the man who had abandoned them. It was an incoherent alliance. Giddings, man of Congress, would not long be a good fit in the Garrisonian organization, which thought abolitionists should not vote. Garrison thought the Liberty Party men were fools. But Giddings would not have gotten into any trouble for being insufficiently faithful to abolition if the New Yorkers had not organized a Liberty Party.

In the years after the Liberty Party's first, inauspicious appearance in the 1840 election, the handful of determined political activists in the "new organization" put on a convincing show of founding an actual political party. They convened, locally and nationally. They fought over a platform and strategic direction. Although many of the decisions were modest—contain slavery to where it exists, rather than Leavitt's and Stewart's more ambitious proposals—the Liberty Party was also admirably frank about the rights of northern Black people. Suffrage, school integration, and hiring were all issues where the Liberty Party was consistent.

One of the Liberty advocates' political strategies was to argue that the slave power was oppressing white people and threatening their economic survival and political freedoms. Starting with the gag rule, the defensive slave politicians gave the abolitionists ample reason to fear their power. Building on the argument that the Constitution did not sanction slavery, political abolitionists claimed that the arbitrary, aristocratic slave politicians had actually overthrown the original national constitutional regime in their enterprise of establishing a slave empire in the southern states after the Constitution was concluded. The next step for the southern aristocrats, they speculated, was to expand the slave power, first to the territories and then to the rest of the states. Liberty founders aspired periodically to attract sympathetic southerners but knew fundamentally that their Liberty Party was a sectional party. No national party would end slavery. It was the North they were after.

Running again in 1844, Liberty may have drawn enough votes away from the Whig candidate, enslaver but political waffler Henry Clay, in New York to hand the presidential election to the Tennessee planter and slave owner, Democrat James K. Polk. Not exactly a victory.

17

(1841–1844)

The Cracks Widen

WHILE SMITH'S LIBERTY MEN WERE DREAMING OF electoral power in 1840, Garrison's faction entered its second decade of writing, speaking, and convening to change people's minds. Douglass had established himself as a critical addition to the New England lecture corps. The Anti-Slavery Society used him well, often pairing him, controversially, with the female lecturer Abby Kelley or his friend, the first Black abolition society lecturer, Charles Lenox Remond, or both.

Garrison and Douglass Together

When the summer of 1842 came, Garrison ventured out of Boston, and in June, as we have seen, the team of Garrison and Douglass toured Cape Cod. It was at their first stop in Barnstable that Garrison realized Douglass's sufferings made him a unique spokesman for nonresistance, a martyr in his devotion to the cause of humanity. "Above all men living," Garrison wrote of Douglass's speech in *The Liberator*, "the slaves of this country would be justified in resisting their relentless tyrants unto blood." As the tour proceeded, Garrison's paper overflowed with encomiums for Douglass. On Nantucket, Garrison announced in *The Liberator*, a skeptical and racist observer reported to the *Nantucket Islander* that he "left that hall with a mountain-load of prejudice tumbling from his back. He had beheld an eloquent Negro ... chaste in language, brilliant in thought and truly eloquent in delivery."

The historical record of this first, momentous long lecture tour featuring the two avatars of abolition is devoid of reported conflict between them. Historians speculate that each might have "rolled his eyes" at the other behind the scenes. Douglass soon became famous for his withering humor, especially, as we have seen, when imitating the pieties of Christian slaveholders, and he later revealed his discomfort with the restrictions of the role Garrison cast him in—telling and retelling his personal story —but in those early years he did not breathe a critical word.

Garrison needed Douglass. He reported repeatedly during the Cape Cod summer of 1842 that the lecturers were struggling to attract large turnouts. In Yarmouth Port, "the audiences were respectable but not large." In Hyannis, "Highly respectable." In Brewster, "not large." The people who came were clearly attracted to Douglass, Garrison readily acknowledged. After the Cape Cod tour, the Society recognized that to build audiences it had to use Douglass as often as possible. Like the professional lecturers of the newly emerging lyceum movement, Douglass was a draw in himself.

Douglass Invades Liberty Party Turf

By the time Douglass's Cape Cod tour ended, the Massachusetts Anti-Slavery Society's managing agent John Collins had a cheeky plan: he would send Douglass and the team, led by the controversial female lecturer Abby Kelley, into the heart of Liberty Party territory, on a tour of upstate New York. Predictably, their political abolitionist competitors were upset with the invasion of their turf by the advocates of dissolving the union "through moral suasion." If they get in our way, the Liberty men threatened, they would resist the Massachusetts abolitionists even to "arms."

Despite the martial rhetoric, in 1842 the movements were still surprisingly permeable across the divide. Once when Garrison team lecturers were in Syracuse at the same time as a Liberty Party convention, at least three of them stopped in to argue with their competitors. (Abby Kelley, whose female presence had exploded the movement three years before, did not join her lecture tour colleagues' detour to the opposition.) Leading theorist of the antislavery Constitution and Liberty Party stalwart William Goodell inveighed against the intruders and urged his followers not to attend their meetings. Garrisonians were often silenced when they tried to argue their side. But no "arms" were drawn.

Encouraged by the good turnout in their first venture beyond New

England after the schism, the planners at Garrison's American Anti-Slavery Society embarked on their most ambitious foray yet. In 1843, from June to December, the Society would hold "One Hundred Conventions" throughout the North. In New York, Pennsylvania, and Ohio, they would penetrate deep into the territory of both the New York City and Gerrit Smith upstate factions.

As they set out on this massive program, two Black lecturers, Douglass and Charles Lenox Remond, and the woman on the lecture trail, Abby Kelley, were clear about their loyalties. But the four white speakers the Society deployed were anything but pure abolition advocates. One was a Quaker who soon disappeared from the annals of abolition, and a second lasted about a year and then declared himself too frail for the circuit and went away to college. George Bradburn of Nantucket, far from rejecting politics, was a Whig politician sitting in the Massachusetts legislature, and so hardly a Garrisonian purist. Most ominously, tour general manager John A. Collins, who had originally hired Douglass in 1841, had a new passion. Collins had a long history of cause shopping. After he radically rejected his original Christian faith for atheism, he turned to a version of French utopianism, forswearing private property. Collins had spent the spring before the new abolitionist tour in Skaneateles, New York, organizing a utopian communalist society in his new anti-property cause, unrelated to abolition.

Opening Skirmish: Summer 1843

Within a few weeks of embarking on their tour, the divisions among the members of the team surfaced. After an anemic showing in Liberty Party territory in upstate New York, George Bradburn went to visit his pal and Garrison adversary Gerrit Smith. Collins stayed behind to attend an anti-property meeting.

Douglass went on alone. He could not have been pleased with his errant colleagues when the group reassembled in late July. In Syracuse, Collins announced he would use the convention venue of the Old Congregational Church the next day for a meeting on the evils of private property. Remond immediately announced that he and Douglass would be speaking on antislavery. After agreeing to limit his anti-property meeting to the

Lecture tour manager John A. Collins. *Courtesy of Massachusetts Historical Society.*

Lecturer Charles Lenox Remond. *Courtesy of Massachusetts Historical Society.*

Frederick Douglass. *Courtesy of the National Portrait Gallery.*

morning, when the time came to turn to abolition the next day, Collins simply would not yield the stage.

Pressed by the audience, Collins finally allowed Douglass to speak. The two men proceeded to go at each other. Douglass allowed that Collins had a right to espouse any cause he chose but could not advocate another project at the expense of abolition. Collins responded by asserting that abolition would be meaningless without his broad program of "universal reform." Collins's invariable invocation—that "no one is free until everyone is free"—didn't resonate with the fugitive slave. If the people in charge of the Anti-Slavery Society didn't shut Collins down from his runaway new passion, Douglass responded, he'd leave the campaign and resign. He had been with the Anti-Slavery Society two years.

Everybody involved in the dustup immediately wrote to Maria Weston Chapman. As founder Samuel May acknowledged years later at the twentieth anniversary of the American Anti-Slavery Society, for decades Weston Chapman (and another woman or two) had "assisted in the preparation of resolutions" and "suggested most pertinent thoughts" in the privacy of the informal Society meetings. And then, having gotten the word from Weston Chapman, "one of the brethren" would utter her ideas. Her adversary in the Liberty Party faction, Lewis Tappan, put it crudely in a letter to his colleague Gamaliel Bailey in 1843: "Chapman manages [the Garrison men] as easily as she could untie a garter."

Given her centrality, Weston Chapman's correspondence provides stunning, unedited insight into the events throughout her years with the Garrisonian antislavery societies. Letters formed a tight web of connection among the activists. In the early years of abolition, steamships, canals, and railroads greatly reduced the time it took for missives to travel between cities, and many big eastern cities also benefited from the rise of competitive private mail carriers. In 1845, in response to pressure from its rivals and from the business community, the United States Postal Service cut the cost of postage for private letters.

As the stresses that would produce later conflict within Garrisonism grew more visible, her political correspondence with the members of the Boston faction and even Garrison himself were heavily focused on the perfidy of Gerrit Smith and the Liberty faction. "Dear old hatter Arnold Buffum, gone to the dark side," Weston Chapman wrote to Garrison in a worried tone about a former colleague. And "doubts about George Bradburn abound. Is he taking money from everyone?" she wondered. "Maybe it's all a matter of little hope, and once they're shown how the Boston way will work, Liberty Party politics will melt away like snow," Weston Chapman's admirer Edmund Quincy wrote to comfort his friend.

In all of this obsessing over the competition with the New York political movement, Weston Chapman failed to take note of the clear warnings that something had gone awry a lot closer to home. The Boston faction had a serious problem with their own manager, John Collins. It should not have been news to them. In February 1842, a full year before the Bostonians sent him to head the massive Hundred Conventions initiative, Collins had written Maria and her sister Caroline a letter of extraordinary length, even by the standards of the wordy Weston correspondence. He told them he was sending them a report on the proceedings of a reform convention that had transformed his life. While they might not agree with everything about the new movement, he was sure they would be deeply interested in its goal: "the complete restoration of the whole family of man from its present fallen, degraded and brutal condition." As to slavery, previously the cause that united Collins with his correspondents, that affront now appeared in a list of wrongs—tyranny, servility, murder, piracy, fraud, poverty, disease, and so on—caused by the "monopolization of the earth by a few individuals." Collins then proposed, after a credulous recitation of his newest theory of everything, that Maria and Caroline join him in a follow-up meeting of the new society to address the question of property and proper community association. He signed, ominously for the already over-taxed abolitionists, "on behalf of the Society," J. A. Collins, "Cor. Secretary."

Nothing in Weston Chapman's correspondence in the months after Collins's bizarre and alarming letter reflects the slightest concern with the man's loyalty to or focus on abolition. Indeed, abolition colleague Edmund Quincy wrote casually to Weston Chapman four months later that Collins had set up a "deal of business" for the Anti-Slavery Society, veritable "steam engine" that he was, a man with "capital" ideas, whose advice on relations with the Liberty adversaries would be well worth taking. So off Collins went, with the crucial first team on the Society's most ambitious abolitionist lecture tour ever after the schism with New York. But first he paused to buy land for his new utopian collective community.

In June 1843, within days of the campaign's launch, Weston Chapman got a harrowing letter from the ever astute Abby Kelley. "Confidential," she underlines, introducing the subject of "J. A. Collins." "He needs someone as a balance wheel," Kelley reports, in his diversionary interest in his utopian property cause. "I have heard most bitter complaints ... against Collins on this score. It may be a little conditioning from the Board would be sufficient. I am more and more concerned of the impolicy and wrong of running a tilt against anything on the anti-slavery platform except 'chatelism [chattel slavery].' I have no objection as you know to the utmost freedom for all discussion but a time for every thing and every thing in its time and a place for everything and everything in its place." When the stresses between Collins and Douglass blew up on the stage in Syracuse a few weeks later, Weston Chapman had certainly been warned.

Kelley was the first to report the scene to Weston Chapman. The "sore" had come to a head, Kelley wrote in a letter dated August 2, when Collins refused to subordinate his anti-property meeting to the antislavery group. On the offending occasion, Collins, Kelley said, called slavery "dabbling with effects" compared to the overarching problem of his pet cause, property ownership. "Remond and the other abolitionists" made the proposition to hold antislavery meetings "coolly and gentlemanly," but "Collins takes fire and blows up abolitionists and especially the agents sky high," and now they had come to a decision not to work with Collins. Kelley thought they would all be better off without him. She was actually surprised that Douglass ever consented to work under Collins, knowing him as Douglass did.

Upon receipt of a return letter (not preserved) from Weston Chapman, Kelley wrote ten days later on August 12 to tell her that Collins had parted company with the antislavery tour and that Douglass, with George Bradburn and one other person, had left for Ohio. She was glad to see Collins go; "he was never very good ... but now he was completely useless, swallowing up all the sympathy for antislavery by scheduling meetings for anti-property right." Kelley certainly wouldn't "force" him to work for antislavery either, his "whole soul wrapped in another idea." Why that would be, she added, innocently, as she pushed Collins out of the abolitionist group, "like slavery."

Apparently aware that Kelley had been communicating with Weston Chapman, Collins's wife, Eunice, wrote to her on August 15 with a summary of her husband's version of events. He was too frail to write himself, but, she began, "you may have been informed of the assault made upon Mr. Collins by Remond and Douglass in this place. It was most ungenerous." Although the assault "failed," according to her, Collins was going to leave anyway, "in justice to the cause and to himself."

From Weston Chapman's correspondence and Douglass's later reply, we know that she wrote directly to Douglass on August 19. The letter is lost, but their conflicting versions of her critical letter tell the central story of this first big crack in the relationship. According to Weston Chapman, reporting about the fracas to another white abolitionist, she had told Douglass at the outset that she was speaking informally, as the board had not heard Douglass's and Remond's accounts. While she deprecated the abolitionist movement making itself responsible for Collins's "enterprises," his other pursuits were none of their concern. She hoped her agents would have achieved by now "the victory over their temper." But the outburst had been a "trifling error in conduct" on their part, and the board had "entire comprehension of the feelings which would prompt high-spirited young men to take the action" they did. "I think the Board would have approved of every word" of her letter, she concluded to her correspondent, giving herself high marks for her handling of the explosive situation.

On September 10, Douglass wrote to Weston Chapman in response to her self-described understanding and gentle admonition. In Douglass's version, Weston Chapman's letter sounds substantially less agreeable. There was no friendly, informal report, according to Douglass—instead, she purported to inform him of a discussion by the "Board of managers of the Massachusetts antislavery society" about his confrontation with Collins. The board's discussion led her to feel "called upon" to speak to Douglass of the "Gratitude and respect" he "owed the Board." Weston Chapman also threatened Douglass's pay—a scary prospect to someone who lived from week to week and was at that very moment pleading with her for money for his wife. Hearing of Weston Chapman's threat to dock Remond's and Douglass's pay, Kelley quickly wrote to her that "R[emond] and D[ouglass] should not have their pay stopped." They had been greatly "provo[ked]," and "Collins was not fit for the work to which he had been appointed."

Weston Chapman's August 19 letter to Douglass is central to understanding how his loyalty, so robust in these early years, came apart relatively quickly thereafter. When Weston Chapman wrote to school Douglass in his duty of loyalty to the Society and threaten his pay, she likely had only Abby Kelley's scathing report on Collins's behavior before her. According to Kelley, Collins was entirely at fault, and Remond and Douglass were in the right. Yet Weston Chapman treated both sides as if they were equally culpable.

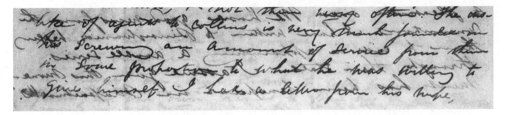

Maria Weston Chapman states her opinion of Douglass. *Courtesy of the American Antiquarian Society.*

"Poor dear Collins!" Weston Chapman wrote on August 24 to David Lee Child, Harvard graduate, diplomat, and lawyer, whom she valued with the "fine assurance which high rank gives (as well in the anti-slavery ranks as any other)." And "poor dear Douglass and Remond," who, as she saw it, had been "provoked by the enemy [unnamed] into assaulting [Collins] in one of his property meetings." What a shame that her agents were "beset by egotism," she lamented, adding, "I think they will be very sorry for it."

Weston Chapman explained her thinking further in a letter to Kelley on September 3. Actually, she wasn't happy with her Black lecturers' work habits. The two men didn't like Collins, she suggested, because he was driving them to work too hard: "The dispute of agents w/Collins," who had just abandoned the abolition tour in July to attend an anti-property meeting, "is very much founded on his screwing an amount of service from them in some proportion to what he was willing to give himself." She had received "a letter from [Collins's] wife," she continued, "saying that the course of Douglass and Remond has soured his convention, that he should not, in justice to the cause or himself, continue in this agency." Maybe he shouldn't, Weston Chapman admitted, but "I want to hear again from him. He had my entire confidence and esteem though I wish that he not have right in his vow to call property meetings." Of course, Weston Chapman wrote forgivingly, "as it had in his head, he had no choice but to call them."

Weston Chapman also informed Kelley that she had, "at the intimation given me to do so in our board, written to them all advising adherence to the original plans, and saying, unofficially what the board thought. As I wrote in the spirit of forebearance and friendship, regret and exhortation which the case demand, and, I think it did good. I thought you would have exactly approved the letter [saying] that we know how to differentiate the difficulty of their situation and that they might ever rely on our friend-ship . . . if they could but finally gain the control of it and hear and forbear as all who love the cause."

It is not hard to imagine how Weston Chapman's idea of a good let-ter sounded to the man who, five years earlier, had been enslaved. When Douglass finally replied on September 10, he opened by saying he had thought he didn't need to tell her the story, as a "third party" (Abby Kelley) was supposed to have reported it. But as Weston Chapman's letter seemed based on a misunderstanding, Douglass continued, he would now set forth the facts. When he saw Collins wasn't going to yield the stage from his property lecture, he asked if there wasn't going to be an antislavery meet-ing. In response, Collins unleashed a speech "respecting the bigotry and narrowmindedness" of abolitionists. Remond responded, charging Collins with using antislavery as a "steping stone to his own favorite theory of the right of property." Collins defended himself on the grounds that the "Board" thought him more valuable. (Douglass doesn't say who Collins was comparing himself to, but the obvious target was the two Black lec-turers who were challenging him.) Collins concluded with the incendiary suggestion that "antislavery . . . is a mere dabbling with effects." Douglass told the assembly that if the board thought Collins was right, he would resign.

Douglass closed his letter to Weston Chapman with a paragraph that would reverberate through the rest of his time in Garrisonian abolition. Although he had spent two years in the movement, apparently Weston Chapman, everybody's "dear friend," did not, he wrote, "know me as many others do." Had she known him, he averred, "I do not think you would have felt yourself called upon . . . to have said anything to me, of the Board entitling them to my Gratitude and respect."

And then he warned Weston Chapman and his other managers: "I trust I have as far as one can have, a just sense of their claims to my grat-itude and respect." No one but Frederick Douglass would be the judge of who had the right to make a claim upon his person, whether for gratitude or anything else.

Weston Chapman's "sharp reprimand" after the Syracuse confrontation came as "a strange and distressing revelation" to him, he wrote many years later in his third and final memoir, and one of which he would not be "soon relieved." (Clearly not, as his retelling of the 1843 story appears almost four decades later.) He thought he had only done his duty and, as he reiterates in his memoir, "I think so still."

As Douglass was realizing, no matter how dutifully he proceeded, the circle of "dear" friendship that enclosed the managerial Maria Weston Chapman and the rest of the Boston clique seemed closed to him. To her, Douglass, like the mayor of Boston and the recalcitrant ministers, was not a friend but someone she expected to labor on her behalf. And in that role, as she quickly noted, he wasn't working hard enough to suit her. This last accusation, leveled only at Douglass and the other Black lecturer, Charles Lenox Remond, simply cannot be separated from the issue of race. Before the dustup, the two white lecturers, as we have seen, had abandoned the tour, Bradburn to visit rich pal Gerrit Smith and Collins for another cause that interested him more than abolition. For weeks before the contretemps, only the Black lecturers Douglass and Remond stayed on the job. And for that they were described as not working as hard as Collins, the boss who had abandoned them.

Of the Boston group, Garrison, poorly educated and born dirt poor, appears to have been the least cliquish. From the beginning, he demonstrated a sincere gratitude to the Black people who jump-started his movement and enabled his paper to survive. Yet in the crucial autumn of 1843, Garrison seemed nowhere to be seen. When the conflict erupted in late July, he and his family were at their annual summer retreat at the Northampton Association, a utopian farm community run by his brother-in-law. Weston Chapman was pinch-hitting, writing and editing for *The Liberator* again and, as the correspondence reflects, basically running the Boston antislavery operation. She may not have found the men to be as easily managed as her garter, but it cannot be a coincidence that after the incident, everybody wrote immediately to Weston Chapman, not to Garrison, the titular head of the movement. On August 16, in the middle of the conflict, Garrison led his wife, Helen, and her mother into a wagon accident, breaking Helen's arm and his mother-in-law's leg. When he finally ended his silence on September 9, he told Weston Chapman that he had been consumed by caring for the invalids and his children.

Garrison apparently had heard by then about the scene in Syracuse. He expressed in anodyne terms his "gratitude" to Collins and his regret at his colleague's ill health. As to Collins's divided loyalty, Garrison disagreed, but it was a free country. His letter reflects that Garrison was taking his position on the basis of Weston Chapman's "statement" that Douglass and Remond had confronted Collins at a utopian "no property" meeting. Prior to learning that version from her, Garrison had assumed the truth: that the disagreement was over whose cause took precedence at a meeting of the antislavery tour. He was "astonished" to learn of Weston Chapman's account (which he had likely read in her August 24 letter to David Lee Child) but was committed to withholding judgment until he heard Douglass's and Remond's "side of the story."

Aftershocks

Fortunately for the future of abolition, the solons in Boston did not have to choose between the familiar white man from their circle of friends and their star orator: Collins pleaded sickness and resigned. Douglass, Remond, Bradburn, and the rest of the group began to make their way to the remainder of the One Hundred Conventions. When he and Douglass arrived in Buffalo next, Bradburn decided the audiences were unworthy of him and again went off, this time to Cleveland to visit his family. Remond, however, came to join Douglass, and the two turned the visit into a triumph, outgrowing the abandoned post office where they started and then again overflowing the Baptist church that had welcomed them. The huge crowds would form in the great outdoors, listening to the two lecturers in the park.

Abandoning their dates farther west, Remond and Douglass stayed in Buffalo to attend the first National Convention of Colored Citizens held in eight years. Douglass and Remond were the only Garrisonians at the Black convention, a meeting organized by the breakaway Liberty Party faction. The newborn Liberty Party had attracted potent Black support by this time. New York had imposed a $250 property condition on its Black citizens for suffrage. The revived Black convention movement was driven, in no small part, by the fight for equal rights in New York, culminating in an unsuccessful referendum in 1846, three years after the convention. People deprived of the right to vote on racial grounds were predictably unhappy with the Garrisonian disdain for suffrage.

The convention was Douglass's first confrontation with the radical Liberty theory that the Constitution prohibited slavery, rather than protecting it everywhere or even only in the slave states. In addition to this challenge, Douglass witnessed one of the most momentous statements on behalf of abolition: Liberty faction leader and fugitive slave Henry Highland Garnet's great speech for violent resistance. Garnet, who had escaped slavery in Maryland, was educated and became one of the few high-ranking Black leaders in the mostly white New York movement. Going beyond the legal arguments of the Liberty activists, Garnet called on the enslaved people to take on their oppressors. "You had far Better all die — die immediately," he counseled, "than live ... slaves." Douglass, the Garrisonian nonresistant, fought Garnet furiously, and ultimately defeated a motion to issue the barnburner speech officially from the convention. A seed, nonetheless, was planted.

It was only a matter of weeks before Douglass himself resisted, verbally, against his own allies. In October, he and Remond were on a platform in Indiana with George Bradburn. Someone asked Bradburn about northern racism, a subject of increasing interest to Douglass. In response, or non-response, Bradburn announced instead his intention to address a list he had made of twenty objections to antislavery. After consuming the rest of the afternoon disposing of five, he proposed to resume with the remaining fifteen the next morning. Douglass moved to refuse him the floor. When the chair denied Douglass's motion, Remond erupted. Within days the usual flurry of letters to Weston Chapman arrived in Boston. Abolitionist and general utopian activist Abraham Brooke wrote from Ohio, reporting what he had heard secondhand from Indiana: "Remond took the floor, called the chairman a jackass [and] appealed to the meeting," and when the meeting sustained the chair, Remond remarked, "They must be a set of monkeys out here in the West." Five days later, Brooke wrote again, having talked to Douglass directly. The revised story was that Remond had not called the chair a jackass but in fact Bradburn had called the two "colored men" and their conduct "monkeyism." Whatever happened, Brooke advised Weston Chapman, in essence, send these guys (Douglass and Remond on the one hand and Bradburn on the other) to different gatherings.

On December 7, 1843, the tour ended at the tenth anniversary celebration of the founding of the American Anti-Slavery Society in Philadelphia. By then, Douglass had other plans.

18
(1844–1845)
Douglass Writes and Garrison Publishes

DOUGLASS HAD BEEN TELLING HIS STORY OF enslavement and escape since he first stood in the Nantucket Atheneum over two years before. In 1844 he decided to leave the lecture trail and write his memoir. Although Douglass would define the genre, his turn to the book-length narrative was not, as we have seen, unprecedented or even unusual. Many other Black Americans, like Venture Smith and William Grimes, had already shared their stories. Indeed, the fugitive slave narrative was just starting to gain popularity. At least nine such stories had appeared in the 1830s, and more than twice as many were forthcoming.

Douglass was mostly silent about his ambitious plan. Nowhere in his voluminous letters do we find any mention of his project. As David Blight relates in his rich portrait of Douglass, he simply disappeared from the lecture circuit for weeks at a time between October 1844 and the spring of 1845 to write and be at home with Anna Douglass and the children, including their fourth baby. Some trusted friends, like Wendell Phillips, knew the memoir was coming. Speaking at the Concord Lyceum in March 1845, just before Douglass finished, Phillips recounted that Douglass had mentioned his book project to an audience in his former hometown of New Bedford, and they had protested against his writing and revealing his name—and his master's name—lest it expose him to the slave catchers.

And yet Douglass had no choice but to risk the truth. Five years earlier, in 1838, the New York Anti-Slavery Society had published the memoir of another fugitive slave using the pseudonym "James Williams" with the identifying details of his escape from Alabama, including the names of his enslavers, altered. In but a matter of months after an Alabama booster challenged the facts in the narrative, the Society renounced the story and pulled it from distribution.

The shadow of James Williams's rise and fall weighed heavily on Douglass's venture into the exploding world of the slave narrative. Williams had surfaced in abolition circles in Carlisle, Pennsylvania, in 1838, telling a story of fleeing Alabama on foot. The locals sent Williams to Lewis Tappan in New York. Thinking his story might make the Society some badly needed money, the New York group put him up at a boardinghouse, where the then obscure poet John Greenleaf Whittier was also boarding. Soon, Williams was telling his life story to the New England poet and abolitionist. According to Williams, he had been enslaved by a Virginia plantation owner, "George Larrimore," whose family then moved with all their slaves to Greene County, Alabama. Much of the book consisted of Williams's tales of terrible abuse at the hands of his Alabama owner, an overseer, and neighbors, each of whom he identified by name.

In early February 1838, the American Anti-Slavery Society published the first copies of *Narrative of James Williams, an American Slave, Who Was for Several Years a Driver on a Cotton Plantation in Alabama.* The book proudly proclaimed it was produced in "NEW YORK: Published by the American Anti-Slavery Society, No. 143 Nassau Street. BOSTON: Isaac Knapp, 25 Cornhill. With an introduction by John Greenleaf Whittier." You don't get more mainstream abolition than that in 1838. In exchange for James Williams's story, New York activists bought him a one-way ticket to free soil in Liverpool, England, where he disappeared from view. The Anti-Slavery Society sent copies of Williams's book to every member of Congress and launched an unprecedented advertising campaign for it in the abolition press.

In the Alabama county where Williams's story takes place, a newcomer from Washington, D.C., John Beverly Rittenhouse, editor of the *Alabama Beacon,* took offense. Beating, torture, injury—all inflicted according to the narrator by the good citizens of Greene County, including plantation owner George Larimore. Rittenhouse set out to find George Larimore. No such citizen of Greene County existed, much less owned vast plantation acreage there. Rittenhouse checked the tax records: none of the other landowners Williams named could be found in the county either. So began a back-and-forth, familiar to modern readers, but not so common in 1838, between the publisher of a supposed nonfiction memoir and the investigative journalist who had his doubts.

The abolitionists desperately tried to find the enslavers where Williams placed them. Rittenhouse, perhaps with more experience of research than the abolitionists, found a George "Larimer" in a Virginia county a hundred miles from where Williams's story began. Larimer told Rittenhouse a version, using what turned out to be Williams's real name, of a slave who had tried to poison his owner when he discovered he was being sold to Alabama and the name of the Alabama plantation owner who had bought the Virginia slave. Getting that close to finding a real story behind the slave's memoir, Alabama newshound Rittenhouse stopped asking questions. Meanwhile the abolitionists wasted their efforts trying to impeach Rittenhouse's source.

And then the abolitionists gave up. On October 25, 1838, they published a letter in *The Emancipator:* "They could not, with propriety ask for the confidence of the community in any of the statements contained in the narrative. Resolved, that the publishing agent be directed to discontinue the sale of the work." A year later, the anti-abolitionists were still dancing on the Society's grave — the story they had hawked so loudly turned out to be a lie, crowed Whig politician Calvin Colton in his 1839 anti-abolition pamphlet *Abolition, a Sedition.*

Whatever the truth status of "James Williams's" story, six years later Frederick Douglass felt he had no choice but to accurately name his enslaver, Hugh Auld. His text is also surrounded by testaments to his trustworthiness and authorship by abolitionist icons, a preface by William Lloyd Garrison, and a laudatory letter by Wendell Phillips.

Publication Day

On May 9, 1845, *The Liberator* carried a notice, "Narrative of the Life of Frederick Douglass," followed by the text of Garrison's full preface to Douglass's book. Historians, especially biographers of Garrison and Douglass searching for fault in the ultimate breakup of their relationship, have placed different weight on the decision to announce Douglass's stunning and movement-altering publication with an excerpt not from the book itself but from Garrison's introduction.

The actual wording of the notice is revealing. "It will give our friends as much pleasure to hear," the announcement begins, "as it does us to announce, that 'Narrative of the Life of Frederick Douglass,' written by himself, is in press, and will be published in a few days. The subject and the author of the Narrative is too well known, too highly admired, and too deeply beloved by abolitionists to render any commendation of his highly reflective mirror of slavery, necessary at our hands." *The Liberator* continued, "The value of the work is greatly enhanced by a Preface from the pen of Mr. GARRISON, and a brief though animated and thrilling Letter to the author ... from Wendell Phillips." This self-serving elevation of the white abolition leaders' brief contributions is not, however, as much of an overreach by Garrison as it appears. Garrison was in New York, the May 9 announcement reveals, for the annual meeting of the American Anti-Slavery Society. "Mr. Garrison being in New York ... for lack of other matter from him," one "Y," the author of the announcement, "transferred [the preface] to the editorial columns of the Liberator." The identity of "Y" is not a mystery: *The Liberator* was printed at that time by "J. Brown Yer-rinton," as the paper announces on the very first page. We now know that Garrison often left *The Liberator* in the hands of others while he traveled or rested. Absent any evidence in the historical record that Garrison ordered the decision to print his preface in full, the text of the announcement provides an innocent explanation.

Frederick Douglass's *Narrative* was, as James Williams's had been, "published at the anti-slavery office, No. 25 Cornhill, 1845." Although it is unlikely that Garrison himself set the type—he had long since employed typesetters like Yerrinton at 25 Cornhill—Garrison biographer Henry Mayer credits him with seeing "it through the press." Clearly conscious of the James Williams debacle, everyone involved with the *Narrative*'s publication vouched for its authorship and reliability. "Mr. Douglass has very properly," Garrison writes in his preface, "chosen to write his own Narrative in his own style, and according to the best of his ability, rather than to employ some one else. It is, therefore, entirely his own production."

As *The Liberator* notice reflects, the Garrisonian abolition forces put their muscle behind their star orator's written debut. Within days of the opening sale, a rave review appeared in Horace Greeley's *New York Tribune,* which was becoming the largest circulating daily in New York: "Considered merely as a narrative, we have never read one more simple, true, coherent, and warm with genuine feeling . . . We wish that every one may read [Douglass's] book and see what a mind might have been stifled in bondage,—what a man may be subjected to the insults of spendthrift dandies, or the blows of mercenary brutes, in whom there is no whiteness except of the skin, no humanity except in the outward form, and of whom the Avenger will not fail yet to demand—'Where is thy brother?'"

Douglass's *Narrative* Versus the Slave Power

Frederick Douglass's story delivered an explosive message. He demolished slavery's defenses, modeled a powerful argument for freedom, and highlighted the aspect of slave power most threatening to the enslavers' white allies in the North: that the enslaved were fully human.

They recognized the threat. The antebellum South was not a hermetically sealed and foundationally different political society from the northern territory of abolition. The South's hysterical response to the abolition pamphlet campaign of 1836—death threats, book burning, post office quarantine—showed that the southern authorities were keenly aware of the danger in abolition's arguments.

In the years that followed the revival of abolition, the South and its northern allies generated a body of argument in favor of slavery. They had their work cut out for them; slavery is a problem in an age of emancipation. There's a reason why William Lloyd Garrison opened his welcoming speech to the young Douglass that first night at Nantucket with an invocation of the American Revolution. If "all men are created equal," as the Declaration of Independence proposes, it's a heavy lift to justify white people buying Black people and working them to death.

But the defenders of slavery soldiered on. Their arguments eventually reduced to the contention that Black people were inferior to white and so not equal. Either they were inferior human beings or, most extreme, not human at all. And if they were subhuman or not human, their treatment was unassailable, no different from the way farmers treated their horses or cattle.

Since the teachings of Aristotle, one argument for being human is the capacity for speech and reason. Christianity added the alternative that humanity was a gift from God—men were, as the Declaration had it, "endowed by their creator with . . . inalienable rights." Introducing Douglass's book, Garrison homed in on the defining markers of humanity. From the first time he met the author, he tells his readers, he could see that Douglass was "in intellect richly endowed—in natural eloquence a prodigy." For the religiously inclined, Douglass was "godlike," "in soul manifestly created but a little lower than the angels," and yet, Garrison concluded, "a slave."

Douglass's eloquent, disciplined memoir is a material manifestation of his unparalleled mastery of those two very human characteristics, speech and reason. His wrenching description of how enslavement compelled even his mistress, kind at first, to deny him his humanity is, perversely, the unimpeachable evidence of that very status as a full human being: "In the simplicity of her soul she commenced, when I first went to live with her, to treat me as she supposed one human being ought to treat another. In entering upon the duties of a slaveholder, she did not seem to perceive that I sustained to her the relation of a mere chattel, and that for her to treat me as a human being was not only wrong, but dangerously so."

(Or, as Justice Roger Taney would say in his opinion in *Dred Scott v. Sandford,* just over a decade later, "the Negro has no rights which the white man is bound to respect.")

Even if they were human, slavery's defenders argued, they were not civilized humans, so enslavement was good for them. The enslavers were benign masters, they argued, enabling the uncivilized people to learn the virtues of European civilization and even in some cases learn Christianity.

In refuting the "good master" narrative, Douglass took his place in a long line of fugitive slave writers who used the most potent weapon— the description of horrific physical torture. Douglass brilliantly links the institution of slavery with its brutal torment: the first scene he presents, immediately after he leaves his grandmother's house to take his place in enslavement, is the horrific beating of his enslaved aunt, Hester, by their master. "Soon the warm, red blood (amid heart-rending shrieks from her, and horrid oaths from him) came dripping to the floor." Douglass reports, "I had never seen anything like it before." He calls his experience of Master Anthony's beating his aunt "the blood-stained gate, the entrance to the hell of slavery."

Compared to this terrible and graphic report of cruelty, the explicit contrast between slavery and Christianity might seem less potent. Yet, as in his lectures and speeches, Douglass's *Narrative* is filled with rage at the hypocrisy of the "Christian" slave regime. His signature performance of the hypocritical "Slaveholder's Sermon" we saw very early in his lecturing career. In preaching to the slaves, Douglass informed his audience, the clergy always took as their text the injunction to "servants" to "obey their masters." After all, he continued, mimicking the slavers' preachers, look at your muscular frames, your hard, horny hands, and see "how mercifully he has adapted you to the duties you are to fulfill."

Douglass hated the sugar-coating of enslavement with the religion of the Golden Rule, because the divinity and righteousness of the gospel, "more than chains, or whips, or thumb-screws, gives perpetuity to this horrible system." The sermonizing slaveholder in the *Narrative* was Thomas Auld, Douglass's third and irredeemable master. Preachers came to dine, as his house was the preachers' "home." But this only enabled him to find "sanction for his cruelty," Douglass writes. "I have seen him tie up a lame young woman, and whip her with a heavy cowskin . . . and in justification of the bloody deed, he would quote this passage of Scripture — 'He that knoweth his master's will, and doeth it not, shall be beaten with many stripes.'" Ministers at the dining table "used to take great pleasure in coming there to put up; for while he starved us, he stuffed them." Douglass clearly understood the power of the abolitionist argument that slavery violated the core meaning of Christianity, and he spent precious pages of his memoir hammering the point home.

In addition to rebutting the argument the slaveholders made, the *Narrative* also fed a counternarrative of freedom that turned out to resonate powerfully with currents running in the free lands. In the antebellum North, the rising men of the working class valued their capacity for self-ownership. They owned their labor and could sell it freely to employers, always knowing, as the historian Eric Foner puts it, that a free worker was able to leave his job. "No one who enters the factory," Foner describes a prewar Waltham, Massachusetts, laborer reporting, "thinks of remaining there his whole life-time."

Slavery was the polar opposite to this optimistic picture. The slaves labored for their masters, coerced into lifelong service by brute force. Douglass describes the experience of losing freedom in the moment when a master's death led to the gathering of all his slaves for distribution among his heirs: "After the valuation, then came the division. I have no language to express the high excitement and deep anxiety which were felt among us poor slaves during this time. Our fate for life was now to be decided. We had no more voice in that decision than the brutes among whom we were ranked." The slaves' loss of self-ownership was the exact antithesis of the free men's vision of what they valued most.

Having complete, arbitrary control over the lives of other humans was the very definition of the aristocracy that provoked the original American Revolution. Douglass's description of his master whipping his aunt with a passionate fury at her being caught with a young man who had been "paying her attention" can only be read as mad sexual passion enabled by arbitrary aristocratic power. The many accounts of plantation owners acting like the European aristocrats of the ancien régime allowed abolitionists to frame the South not as a partner in the American constitutional experiment but as an alien political power — the "slaveocracy." Ohio Democratic senator Thomas Morris coined the phrase "slave power" in 1839 to call out the growing threat of the South's politics to the rest of America. (He lost his seat over it.)

Douglass's story of an alien slaveocracy sold almost five thousand copies in four months. Slave narratives were, as the historian Manisha Sinha has called them, the "movement literature of abolition." Until Harriet Beecher Stowe's fictional *Uncle Tom's Cabin* seven years later, nothing came close to the impact of Douglass's *Narrative*.

19
(1845–1847)
Frederick Douglass, International Superstar and Publisher

DOUGLASS USED HIS PLATFORM AT THE ELEVENTH anniversary meeting of the American Anti-Slavery Society in New York on May 6, 1845, to raise the anticipation for his book release two days later. For the first time, Douglass told the packed auditorium, he would name his master and identify where he had been enslaved: "I lived on the plantation of Col. Lloyd, on the eastern shore of Maryland, and belonged to that gentleman's clerk." He knew his boldness would endanger him—Wendell Phillips had warned him the previous month. But he would do it anyway, he revealed, "hastening the day of deliverance" for all the enslaved.

Sailing to Freedom

Douglass did not mention the shadow of James Williams's "hoax," which hung heavily over any slave narrative claiming the movement's support. But the cowardice of the New York abolitionists abandoning Williams did force Douglass to take the risk of naming Auld and provoking him to come north to recapture him. Douglass so feared, as he said later in 1855, that he would be "spirited away, at a moment when my friends could render me no assistance," that he began to plan a trip abroad.

As it turned out, this second flight from southern enslavement also introduced him to a society freer of the racism that permeated the so-called "free" North. Just as he'd sailed the waters to get to New York, he would cross the sea to find another birth of freedom.

On August 6, 1845, he set off for England and Ireland aboard the steamship *Cambria*. Cunard, the British steamship company, consigned

Douglass to steerage, lest the American passengers take offense at his presence. Douglass was accompanied on his speaking tour of the U.K. by stalwart Garrisonian James N. Buffum, the humble Quaker, later mayor of Lynn, Massachusetts. Buffum, by all accounts a decent person, assigned himself to steerage as well, calling it an economical measure.

Douglass, the natural thespian, set the scene of his voyage in his letters home: "We had nearly all sorts of parties in morals, religion, and politics as well as trades, callings and professions. The doctor and the lawyer, the soldier and the sailor . . . the scheming Connecticut wooden clock-maker, the large surly New-York lion-tamer." More importantly, "the Whig and the Democrat, the white and the black were there." They had "anti-slavery singing and pro-slavery grumbling; and at the same time [slave owner and South Carolina] Governor Hammond's letters were being read"; so too "my Narrative was being circulated."

As the ship neared the free soil of England, some Europeans onboard asked their famous passenger from steerage to deliver a lecture on slavery. He prudently waited for the captain to second the motion. Douglass was right to be cautious. Once the captain got behind the idea, and Douglass walked up to the saloon deck from steerage to begin his speech, proslavery passengers reared up at once to shut him down. As Douglass spoke, describing the treatment of Black Americans, his critics screamed that he was lying, and when he responded with verbatim readings from the slave codes, they threatened to throw him overboard. In a harbinger of his better world to come, an Irish passenger informed one obstreperous white American that if he threatened Douglass again, two could play at the violence game. Finally, the captain quieted everyone down by bringing up actual irons and promising to throw the unruly crowd into them. "An AMERICAN MOB ABOARD A BRITISH STEAM PACKET," Douglass later described the scene to Garrison.

Like the American slave James Somerset seventy years before, Douglass found that his status changed definitively when he set foot upon the free soil of England. After he and Buffum checked into their hotel in the port town, they went to see a local great house, Eaton Hall. Lining up for entry into the tourist site, they ran into some of the proslavery Americans off the *Cambria*. "We all had to wait," Douglass reported to Garrison, as only one party could go in at a time. "They looked as sour as vinegar and as bitter as gall, when they found I was to be admitted on equal terms with themselves. When the door was opened, I walked in, on an equal footing with my white American fellow-citizens."

Keeping an Eye on Frederick Douglass

Douglass left almost immediately for Dublin, to rendezvous with Richard D. Webb, the co-founder of the Hibernian Anti-Slavery Society. The Bostonians had designated Webb to manage his British tour.

Webb was a Quaker and a noncombatant in the perennial conflict between the Protestant English governors and the mostly Catholic Irish subjects. As a Quaker, he had a well-established affinity for abolition, and, as with many British reformers at the time, his agenda included a wide range of programs for human improvement. (Temperance, or teetotalism, was a pressing issue in Ireland.)

The role of carping outsider suited Webb well. Quakers were one of the last remaining religious groups banned from public office in modern England, but they were renowned for their success in the precincts of the marketplace. In Webb's case, his family had risen into the middle class through the linen trade. Like Garrison, Webb apprenticed in the printing business and opened his own printshop. His Quaker circle helped him, the disproportionate number of Quakers in business providing him with a steady stream of business printing to support what was often a volatile trade. The Webb printshop turned out profitable runs of train tickets and labels for myriad Quaker enterprises, as well as reform literature for its own interests. Temperance pamphlets and religious tracts flowed from its presses.

In 1840, three years after helping found the Hibernian abolitionists' society, Webb had met Garrison at the World Anti-Slavery Convention. The London meeting quickly became infamous for the Brits' refusal to seat female Garrisonian delegate Lucretia Mott. The British and Foreign Anti-Slavery Association, the primary English abolitionist group, was firmly on the side of the New York anti-woman faction of the American movement. Webb, by contrast, was a natural ally for Garrison. A skeptic about religion (Webb would later become a Unitarian) and an early publisher of suffrage literature, the radical, dissenting Webb embraced Garrison, Garrison's female delegate, and the purist Garrisonian wing of abolition. As usual, for the Garrisonians, Webb fell into the habit of corresponding not with Garrison but with Maria Weston Chapman. In their extensive and extended exchanges, Webb arranged to send her goods for the antislavery fair, and he bought subscriptions to *The Liberator* for his British friends. He gossiped and he carped: the clergy were bigots, the Brits immune to the claims of abolition, and Garrison's fame carried no weight at the big antislavery convention. The legendary Daniel O'Connell, who was working to get the British to lift restrictions on Catholic participation in politics, he confided to Weston Chapman, was "immoral and inauthentic."

In 1842 Garrison himself finally penned a letter to Webb with a long and flowery apology for not having written sooner. Unlike Weston Chapman, when Garrison wrote, he usually wanted something specific. This time it was to introduce Webb to Thomas Davis, an early antislavery activist who was coming to England and Ireland for his health. Unbeknownst to Garrison, after hearing from the titular "boss," Webb immediately wrote to his friend Weston Chapman. Thomas Davis is seeking our hospitality, he informed her. "Do tell me about him." Being the correspondence czar gave Weston Chapman many advantages.

Douglass had no reason to know it, but his prospective host Webb had lined up on Collins's side of Douglass's conflict with his errant colleague in 1843. Collins had been a great favorite of the British activists since the Garrison ally's fundraising visit to Britain in 1840–41. The Webb circle had made an alliance with Collins against the New York faction's British counterparts, the British and Foreign Anti-Slavery Association. Collins was a "really able man," British ally Mary Walsh wrote to Weston Chapman after the brouhaha in 1843. She was sorry he was not well.

Webb was not so fond of the other emissaries from American abolition. When the radical Boston abolitionist Henry Wright arrived in Ireland in 1844, Webb complained nonstop. Wright dumped a huge packet of papers in his usual terrible handwriting on Webb. (Webb had been publishing some of Wright's work, with little success.) Wright spent most of his days writing in his room, thinking he was shaking the world, "an exaggerated idea of the influence of his effort" and, Webb thought, "vastly disproportionate to the greatness of his design." Wright was so extreme that even the Garrisonians pulled out of his lecture agency in 1837, but Webb's com-

plaint was not about the virtue of Wright's politics but that he was neither an amusing visitor nor a marketable author. Even Garrison was not
immune from Webb's sharp pen. "He is too lazy," Webb writes, accusing
Garrison of neglecting the paper and losing the competition with political
abolition. Of course, Webb did not like Gerrit Smith any better, calling
his constitutional theory "Jesuitical, Machiavellian, and unworthy of him."

By the time Webb turned his dyspeptic gaze on his next guest, Frederick Douglass, he was prepared for anything. "Frederick is a fine fellow,"
he began his first dispatch to Weston Chapman, "and I hope his visit to
these countries may be a happy experience." Though he added a caveat: "I
hope he has no money making effort in view other than to ... defray the
expenses of his journey."

Managing Frederick Douglass

Weston Chapman also worried that Douglass would try to enrich himself
on the trip, "aiming at [some]thing for himself in the prosecution of a
philanthropic enterprise." And she was afraid he would be tempted by the
popularity of the New York faction in England and go over to their side.
"This is his first trial," she writes, revealing how paramount loyalty was in
her lexicon. "I hope he will be strong enough to endure it."

Though she was worried, Weston Chapman didn't want Douglass to
know she was trying to control him from across the sea. She wrote to
Webb in advance of Douglass's arrival to ask him to manage Douglass for
her, without her "incurring the odium of telling him myself." She wished
Webb "might feel a call to do one thing, i.e., to warn Douglas [sic] of the
effect it has on a man's respectability to be aiming at anything for himself,"
adding, "I hope Douglas will be wise enough to be helped, for he has the
wisdom of a serpent." In case Webb didn't know how to carry out her man-
date, she gave him a script: "Pray strengthen him with the case example of
Garrison, [Wendell] Phillips, and [Edmund] Quincy." Would Douglass
be that wise? she wondered. "He has uncommon ability of a practical and
useful sort." But would it be enough? Could he understand, as Weston
Chapman did, that the Boston society was the perfect uncompromising
fount of truth?

Speaking of serpents, Weston Chapman wrote quite a different letter

Douglass triumphs in Ireland. *From* The Uncle Tom's cabin almanack, or, Abolitionist memento. *For 1853 (J. Cassell, 1852).*

when she thought Douglass would see it. The open letter she handed to Douglass introducing him to Webb as he left the United States said, "The bearers of this letter, James M. Buffum and Frederick Douglas have been for many years the devoted advocates of the Anti-Slavery cause, as well as highly esteemed personal friends of my own." No management problems there.

Two weeks into their visit, Webb "like[d] them both exceedingly," finding Douglass "an excellent fine fellow." Of Buffum, he enthused, "I have not had the sense as a man I could trust more fully than JNB ... He is true blue." Douglass was the draw, attracting crowds in the thousands, and generating enough demand for a run of two thousand copies for Webb's first printing of Douglass's *Narrative*. By late September, however, Webb's tone had changed. After Douglass made a joint appearance with the Irish nationalist Daniel O'Connell on September 29, Webb reported to Weston Chapman, "Frederick is vastly delighted with Dan — and I don't wonder that any dark man should be." But Webb had tired of the "dark man" in his guest room: "Frederick is touchy, huffish, haughty, & I think selfish." Of course, Webb mentioned, Douglass was useful—"as an advocate & orator . . . he is a wonder indeed. But he is uneven and unreliable." Maybe that's what "geniuses" are like, Webb mused.

By October 12, he writes, Frederick was traveling to Cork. He was scheduled to stay there with the Jennings family. Webb was happy he was leaving—Douglass's difficult nature had almost driven away the endearing Buffum. Full of "suspicion and jealousy . . . his habit of talking in half jest, half comment, leaves it very difficult for even those who relish a joke very much to know whether he is in jest or correct." Like many marginalized and oppressed people, Douglass used humor as a weapon, and Webb couldn't figure it out. But Webb's strongest complaint about Douglass was that he would not take Webb's advice. Ignoring his managers, Webb felt, Douglass harmed the antislavery cause, especially by criticizing the local churches for the policies of their American branches. Jealousy, pride, contempt—Webb's judgment of the famed author and orator reads like a recitation of a catalogue of sin. It's not personal, Webb says; he was just worried about the damage Douglass would do to the movement.

Don't tell him about my criticism, he hastened to add. "In speaking so freely as I do . . . I only speak for your guidance. I don't think there would be any good done by reflecting back to inform Frederick ever so gently anything I have said. He is unnecessarily injudicious and jealous." Like Weston Chapman, Richard Webb worried about Douglass being "spoiled by all the petting and flattery" his British audiences and admirers offered. Webb portrays Douglass like some child whose character is imperfectly formed. He had been puzzled when "Maria C" had given him "hints" for Douglass rather than telling Douglass directly what she thought he should do, but now Webb understood why she did not confront Douglass directly.

For someone supposedly so spoiled and obnoxious, Douglass did famously well in his next visit, with the Jenningses in Cork. Beverage manufacturer Thomas Jennings, a Unitarian in religion and the head of the Hibernian Anti-Slavery Society, presided over a large, liberal, music-loving family in his capacious household. In November, after Douglass's visit, Jennings's daughter Jane wrote a rapturous letter to Weston Chapman. Each day, she enthused, "only increased our affection and respect for him."

And they were not generally considered easily pleased, she confessed. But "Frederick!" He "won the affection of every one of us," and the family parted from him with regret, hoping he would return. Isabel, the oldest of the Jennings girls, wrote to share more details about Douglass's turn in Cork: "There never was a person who made a greater sensation in Cork . . . and in private he is greatly to be liked. He has gained friends everywhere he has been—he is indeed a wonderful man." After a month the Jenningses concluded that Douglass was indeed "worthy of all the praise of Garrison and Wendell Phillips." Isabel understood that it was "only natural that he should excite more sympathy than any of the others," being the first "intelligent slave who has ever visited."

Douglass, too, loved his experience in Cork, later writing to Isabel Jennings of his cherished memories of his visit, and of the life, warmth, and humanity that flowed from her and her family and friends. Douglass was particularly struck by the sponsorship of the reformist mayor of Cork, Richard Dowden. He wrote Dowden a touching thank you, recalling having been "tramped, reviled and maltreated . . . by white people during the most of my life." He had since met many benefactors, but never "one, in your station, having so many public cares and weighty responsibilities to bear and yet so ready . . . to devote time talent and official influence to the advancement of benevolent objects."

As Douglass made his way from town to town, he collided, unavoidably, with all the preexisting fractures in Irish movement politics. Irish activist Daniel O'Connell's Catholic emancipation movement was but one strain in the widespread landscape of reform so typical of the early nineteenth century. The Catholics were at odds with their British Protestant rulers, and later reform religions like Quakers and Methodists with the mainstream brethren. Layered over these political disputes was a robust temperance movement led by a crusading clergyman. To some extent, the strains were familiar to Douglass, coming, as he just had, from his clash with Collins over the primacy of property reform within the antislavery society. And then there was the potato famine. Many people in Ireland were less concerned with worrying about oppressed slaves across the ocean than with their own ragged and starving people.

Leaving Ireland for Scotland, Douglass wrote Garrison a wrenching description of the poverty he had witnessed. "I spent nearly six weeks in

Dublin," he recalled, "and the scenes I there witnessed were such as to make me 'blush and hang my head to think myself a man.'" The beggars Douglass reported — and this was before the crop failure descended into actual famine — "would move a heart of iron." But Douglass adamantly refused to take the bait of comparing victimizations. However horrible the conditions of the poor were, he asserted in a speech in Limerick, "Negro-slavery consisted . . . not in taking away a man's property, but in making property of him, and in destroying his identity." Douglass provided an example of the difference: "The slave must not even choose his wife . . . for the slave holder had no compunction in separating man and wife, and thus putting asunder what GOD had joined together." Jane Jennings exulted in Douglass's success at this next stop, and even Webb reported he was getting on swimmingly. Webb could not help but add that Douglass was "very proud" and that he would no longer give the star orator advice.

In November, Webb had bad news for Douglass: the rigid and controversial Henry Wright was coming back from America to Britain, and Douglass's Boston bosses thought he should take Wright on the English leg of his tour. Douglass refused. Wright was well known for his assertion that British churches should cast off their American branches for their support of slavery and send back the money from the tainted source. This did not make him popular in the U.K. "Friend Wright," Douglass wrote frankly, "has created against himself prejudices which I as an abolitionist do not feel myself called upon to withstand." Furthermore, "he is truly," Douglass added, perhaps a touch sarcastically, "a reformer in general. I only claim to be a man of one idea." Never again was Douglass going to arm wrestle with a John Collins for the platform at a lecture hall filled with audiences intended for himself. His gratitude to the movement for getting him an audience at all was running out.

I'm Sorry He Feels That Way

From late November to December of 1845, Douglass made a brief return to stay with Webb, whose request to take on Wright he had bluntly refused to accommodate. Then he took off again to lecture around Ireland — Belfast, Ulster — and for an extended tour in England.

Two months after Douglass's visit, in February 1846, James Buffum wrote to Weston Chapman to tell her that Douglass was very unhappy with her. In addition to the original, confidential letter Weston Chapman had sent in June 1845 to ask Webb to keep an eye on Douglass, she also wrote a second letter to Webb in January: "If Douglass can but keep from the temptation to 'get into his own head,' (as we call being drunk with vanity)," she wrote, "he will not only do the cause great good, but receive and deserve a high place in the list of public benefactors. If his good sense prevails all will go well." It is unclear which of the two letters was the trigger.

"Buffum tells me that Douglass is displeased at an intimation in a letter of mine to you," Weston Chapman wrote to Webb on February 24, 1846, "that he would be tempted by offers from the London Committee [which was roughly allied with the New York faction of American abolition] to desert the Am. Society." Incredibly, she tells Webb that she cannot figure out why her letter about Douglass's susceptibility to making a deal with people she called "Satan" in earlier correspondence would have made him unhappy. She didn't *think* he would yield, she says, and accusing someone of weakness to temptation wasn't insulting because after all, even Jesus was "tempted." All she wanted to do was "help," in case "his circumstances and inexperience, together with his characteristic peculiarities might put him in the way of temptation." She then sent Douglass a gift of a much-sought-after item from the annual bazaar—an annual antislavery collection of writings she compiled, published as *The Liberty Bell.*

In March, a month after Buffum had warned her, Douglass wrote to Weston Chapman himself. Ostensibly a thank you for the copy of *The Liberty Bell,* the letter is a rhetorical masterpiece. He starts by informing her that he has done her the favor of putting notices about her bazaar in copies of the very popular *Narrative* he was selling. "I have done so from no sordid motive," he continues. Indeed, "I have never received any pecuniary aid directly from [the antislavery cause]. I lived in a small house, indulged in no luxuries, willingly, in the thin but brave ranks of our noble pioneer William Lloyd Garrison." Since coming to Europe, he has lived on the proceeds of his own book.

Why does he talk about his finances, he asks? "Because I have felt somewhat greaved to see by a letter from you … that you betray a want of confidence in me as a man and an abolitionist." She told Webb to keep an eye on him, Douglass continues, but not to keep an eye on Buffum, he

Douglass tells Weston Chapman not to manage him. *Courtesy of Boston Public Library.*

surmises, because Buffum was rich and therefore not susceptible to being bought by the London committee. Maria's suspicious and sneaky missives did him a "great injustice" and "are very embarrassing." She "whispered in the ear of a stranger," he chides, "to whom I look up as a friend." Until he heard Webb read the insulting letter from Chapman, Douglass thought he, like all the other Boston activists, had her confidence. Now "I am disappointed," he writes. Money would never alienate him from the Garrisonians, he says, but her lack of confidence in him would do exactly what she feared. "If you wish to drive me from the Anti-slavery Society, put me under overseership and the work is done." Then he takes a swipe at Webb: "Set someone to watch over me for evil and let them be so simple minded as to inform me of their office and the last blow is struck."

The letter offers a glimpse into Douglass's heart—rarely seen in all the reams of paper he produced. Why didn't you tell me "face to face"? he asks. Why didn't you "write me a kind letter, as did my friend Mr. [Wendell] Phillips, warning me against the London Committee." If she had done that, Douglass tells Weston Chapman, "my feelings toward you as to him would be those of ardent gratitude." When he left Boston, he felt himself "armed with the confidence reposed in me by yourself and the Board." But now, "not sustained as I supposed myself to be," he concludes, he nonetheless has "neither compromised myself nor the character of my friends."

Carping behind one another's backs is a hallmark of the Boston clique's correspondence. Webb produced so much vitriol in his letters, he could have fueled a generation of Borgias. He thought Remond was ineffective, Wright a useless scribbling egomaniac, and Garrison a lazy loser. Edmund Quincy compared Garrison to Falstaff in one clever little missive. Even Abby Kelley complained about John Collins's increasing engagement in

extrinsic social causes before the blowup at Syracuse. Much of the complaining and tattling was communicated explicitly to Weston Chapman,
manager, moral arbiter, and enforcer of strict Garrisonian orthodoxy. Douglass's extensive and varied correspondence is straightforward by comparison. He writes in clear anticipation that his words will be published, as
they often were. He focuses mostly on the politics of the task at hand and
almost never shares his opinions about his fellow activists. His refusal to
tour with Wright, for instance, is entirely centered on Wright's threat to
Douglass's pure abolition message. Unlike Webb, with his endless nitpick-
ing about his houseguests, Douglass is silent about Wright's qualities as a
companion or anything else.

As Douglass observed with his usual astuteness, it seemed "simple
minded" of Webb to share Weston Chapman's secret instructions with
the object of her management. Weston Chapman responded to Douglass's furious letter by writing to Webb again. There is no copy of Weston
Chapman's letter, but from Webb's letter back to her, it seems she had "express[ed] her dissatisfaction" with his breach of "confidence." Webb admits
he did read Douglass Weston Chapman's letter wishing that Douglass
might not yield to temptation. It is his custom, he informs her, when he re-
ceives letters from any of his American friends, to read them at the weekly
meeting of his small antislavery society. Guests are welcome, but of course
they then hear the declamation of the recent letters. So it was with Douglass. Right after he and Buffum arrived in Dublin (which would have been
around June 1845 or possibly on one of their later visits), Webb wrote, they
were present at the weekly meeting. The "mischief was done" not by Webb
wanting to lord it over his "haughty, self-possessed" houseguest, but "by my
supposing Douglass was a sensible man and that this advice or suggestion
from one of his best friends would be taken in good part."

Webb garlands his exculpatory version of events with a cascade of
attacks on Douglass as being "ridiculous, magnify[ing] the cause of discomfort or wounded self esteem . . . reacting extravagantly when he thinks
himself hurt." Of course, "I may not have been quite judicious in reading
[Weston Chapman's letter] to him," Webb concedes, but the indiscretion
was at worst "a venial sin." It was Douglass's fault, Webb concludes, for
taking offense. Had he been less self-involved, it would not have been a
problem for him to take direction from "one of his best friends."

Drifting Away

Whatever the motives, the damage was done. Douglass, always patrolling his borders, reassured Weston Chapman in a later letter that nothing could ever harm their friendship. Meanwhile, in May, he did exactly what she was afraid of—he lent his enormous presence to the annual meeting of the dreaded British and Foreign Anti-Slavery Society. Indeed, he lectured for them not once but twice.

Weston Chapman and her circle saw the British society as the counterpart to the breakaway New Yorkers' organization at home. They had good reason. The Brits had refused to seat Lucretia Mott in 1840, presaging the ultimate schism with the Tappans' New York faction over the woman question in America. Joseph Sturge, a Quaker who founded the British society to address slavery internationally after the abolition of slavery in the British West Indies, was a close friend to Lewis Tappan. Not coincidentally, when Tappan broke with Garrison over his attacks on the churches and advocacy of women, the Tappan faction named its new organization the American and Foreign Anti-Slavery Society, in homage to its British counterpart. As of 1846, the British group had followed a pro-church line, refusing to participate in pressuring British churches to send back dues they received from their slaveholding American branches. American abolitionists had been particularly focused on the Free Church of Scotland, which got ample funding from the Presbyterian churches of the slaveholding South. The last thing the Garrisonians wanted was for their star orator to fall into the Brits' orbit.

Douglass, the British Lion

But Douglass was becoming a lion. Without Garrison's assistance, he attracted the attention of the movers and shakers in British reform. He met British and Foreign Anti-Slavery Society founder Joseph Sturge in Birmingham in December, probably through Webb and the Quaker connection, and spoke with other wealthy, powerful Quakers as well. It should not have been a surprise, then, that someone from the British society invited him to attend the annual meeting in May. Regardless of how his Boston patrons were going to take it, Douglass immediately decided he would go to London to accept the invitation. Douglass may have acted preemptively to share the unwelcome news with Garrison because he knew it was going to appear in the press. He softened the blow by telling Garrison that the competition had attracted a very small turnout. More to the point, he reported, he had helped persuade the hitherto pro-church society to sign on to the campaign against the Free Church of Scotland to "SEND BACK THE MONEY."

So taken with Douglass was the former anti-Garrisonian British society that Sturge invited him back that very week to a meeting with a much bigger audience. Indeed, Douglass now reported to Garrison, he filled "one of the biggest chapels in London," and the meeting was presided over by "Sir Edward North Buxton, Bart."

While he was there, the British society passed a "broader and nobler platform." It is true that the British society had sided with the New Yorkers and the Liberty Party in the past, Douglass says to Garrison, but whose fault is that? "The fact is they have known very little of our efforts since 1840." The British secretary tells me, Douglass reports, that while he dutifully sent Boston his annual report, he never got one back, and was left, therefore, to gather information of our movements as best he could. Why would we leave them in the dark like that, Douglass wonders innocently to Garrison. Some accident must have befallen the reports from Boston. Oh, well, he concludes, "a new and better way is marked out" now. The British abolitionists are now resolved to cooperate with American colleagues. "Let this resolution be universally adopted . . . and there will be a happy termination to the bitter jarrings which have during the last six years marred and defaced the beauty and excellence of our noble work."

And so the migration of Frederick Douglass out of the Boston clique and toward political abolition begins, not with a direct confrontation, but in a foreign venue a little removed from the American schism, and fueled by his seemingly innocent desire that they should all get along. Maria Weston Chapman was right about one thing. The prosperous British solons of the Anti-Slavery Society did open their wallets as soon as Douglass made himself available to them. In the same letter to Garrison about their good intentions toward Boston, Douglass revealed that they were so eager to keep him in Britain, they raised five hundred dollars to bring his wife and children overseas, to ease his homesickness.

Predictably, Douglass's appearance at the British society earned him another scolding from Weston Chapman. "I have no confession to make or pardon to ask for my conduct in the matter," Douglass responded. He went at the urging of "good friends, friends who are as anxious for the emancipation of the slaves as any." No longer was Douglass confined to the Boston faction for friends who would emancipate the slaves. He outright denied her accusation of "money temptations," assuring her, "No such was offered and . . . no such temptation would have been availing." This last is indeed peculiar, since it was Douglass himself who revealed that the Brits had offered to pay for his family to come join him. But it was never about money. Crucially, Douglass warned the Bostonians that he had a purpose greater than their obsessive factionalism: "I will speak in any meeting where freedom of speech is allowed and I may do anything toward exposing the bloody system of slavery."

While Douglass's Boston administrators were focusing on the schism within their movement, Douglass, homesick and lonely, was crisscrossing the U.K., from Belfast to Edinburgh, lecturing for the emancipation of the slaves. In a wrenching cry for help, he wrote to a faithful friend of the movement, William White, who had fought off a proslavery mob with him early in his career. "I shall never forget," Douglass reminisced, "how like two very brothers we were ready to dare—do and even die for each other." He had written to White because he wanted some help. "Do you think it would be safe for me to come home this fall?" It would not be safe. Although he had long been known as a fugitive slave, now that he had identified himself, he had reason to fear his old enslaver would send slave catchers to hunt him down. (Later recollections include his receiving rumors that his former master was intent on recapturing him.) It would not be very hard to find him; his every appearance was preceded by a flood of publicity. Traveling alone to the much-publicized events meant he was constantly away from his support system and vulnerable to being seized. He imagined the payoff in "avarice and vengeance" for capturing Frederick Douglass. He was a sitting duck.

Living in London was not an option for Douglass. His wife, Anna —the woman who had helped him to escape from enslavement, and the mother of his four small children—was manifestly unable to move the family from Lynn, Massachusetts, to London, England. She was born free, by barely a year after her mother's manumission. She was, until the day she died, largely illiterate. Visitors to the household recall an almost completely silent woman, who served food to her husband and his visitors but never participated in his public activities. When Douglass left for two years abroad, she was living a private life, focused on her children and her garden, and doing piecework for essential household income. Although her daughter Rosetta, the eldest, wrote a positive memoir of her in 1900, even Rosetta's scant recollection of her mother's supposed antislavery work is unsupported by any public record. She does not appear as an active participant in the African church in Lynn. When the time came to educate Rosetta, the Douglasses sent her to white Quaker abolitionists in Rochester, New York.

In her daughter's words, Anna was hard to know. She left almost no historical record at all, other than as framed by her husband. In 1844, six years after he escaped, Douglass reconnected with another runaway slave from his Maryland neighborhood, Ruth Cox Adams. For several years Adams lived with the family, providing the crucial link of literacy, reading Douglass's letters to his wife and writing to him of his family's doings. The reader catches a reflection of his idea of Anna Murray Douglass in Frederick Douglass's letters to Ruth, in which he enclosed letters to Anna: "Read the enclosed letter which I send to my Dear Anna over and over again till she can fully understand its contents." Douglass complains more openly about his discontent with his spouse a decade later, in an aggrieved letter to one of his many female admirers, Lydia Dennett, in Rochester. Anna is sick in every "member except one," Douglass writes. She "still seems able to use with great ease and fluency her powers of speech—and by the time I am home a week or two longer, I shall have pretty fully learned in how many points there is need of improvement in my temper and disposition as a husband, and father!" However imperfect his family life, though, Douglass felt keenly his exile from home.

The Price of Freedom

When he arrived in Newcastle in August 1846, Douglass's spirits were low. He had been away from his family and on the road for a year. In Newcastle, Douglass stayed with another Quaker family, the Richardsons

—siblings Henry and Ellen, and Henry's wife, Anna. The Richardsons, a successful family in the grocery business, focused their abolition efforts on getting customers not to buy slave goods like cotton. Ellen, an unmarried schoolteacher of modest means, observed Douglass's sadness and homesickness when on a family outing one afternoon and decided to try to buy his freedom. But she didn't tell him what she was up to, because she knew he was of the "Garrisonian party," which brooked no "barter in human flesh." Instead, she wrote to a group of famous reformers around England, including the great British radical John Bright, and raised funds to pay for Douglass's liberation. Barred by Garrisonism from consulting with her beneficiary about her scheme, she turned to her sister-in-law, who brought in the Richardsons' Philadelphia lawyer to find Douglass's enslaver, Hugh Auld, and start the process of buying his freedom.

A veritable chain of lawyers got involved: Little Med's Boston lawyer Ellis Loring, New York attorney Walter Lowrie, and ultimately a representative in Baltimore. Finally, Douglass's prospective liberators told him what was going on. Homesick and worried about wife Anna waiting for him long after he had said he'd be home, Douglass was beyond anxious for his British patrons to make the deal with his enslaver. Still he remained in Britain, now waiting for the agonizing last negotiations over the $711.66 payment for his freedom to conclude.

While he waited, Garrison came to London. He had plans to launch yet another antislavery organization, to compete with the hated British and Foreign Anti-Slavery group with which Douglass had been flirting. Garrison and Douglass lectured together all over Britain the summer and fall of Douglass's manumission, finally ending in October. Garrison dispatched his lecturers, including Douglass, according to his notions of what the movement needed. As of that fall, he needed the radical Henry Wright in the United States immediately, he believed, but although "sighing to see his wife and children," according to Garrison, Douglass should not come home until spring. "People [in Britain were] everywhere desiring his presence," and the movement could not accept the loss of what he was securing for them. Garrison was sure that Douglass's flirtation with the "chaff" of the British and Foreign Anti-Slavery Society had passed. Unconcerned as he was about Douglass's personal feelings, Garrison revealed himself at the same time to be concerned with Douglass's "personal safety." He was unlikely to pose a roadblock to the plans for his emancipation, as Douglass's rescuers feared.

Not that there was any shortage of Garrisonians to condemn the purchase of Douglass's freedom. Learning of the initiative, Henry Wright, the most ultra of the ultra-Garrisonians, took up his pen to share his objections to the manumission plan with Douglass. "I wish you would disown it," Wright advised him, "never recognize that hateful Bill [of sale]—nor to refer to it, as of any authority to establish the fact that you are a *Freeman* and not a slave." Wright made the standard Garrisonian argument against paid manumission: Douglass's argument was not with Hugh Auld but with the entire American republic. It was the wicked laws and Constitution that kept him, on northern soil, still enslaved. Worse, by focusing the wrongdoing on one enslaver, Wright elaborated, Douglass sacrificed his enormous asset as the "slave of the Republic." His symbolic role was the source of his influence, his strength, and his "truly manly . . . position." He urged Douglass to renounce the claim that America put on him and three million of his fellows, rather than try to humble the Americans with a poisonous bill of sale for one. You got away, Wright said. "He has no more power over you." If Douglass came back, he'd be sheltered by the sympathies of millions.

Douglass's answer to Wright is a tour de force of argument and a revelation of his unique role in this most critical American social movement. Wright is entitled to his opinion, Douglass begins, and, in a sidelong dig at Weston Chapman, it is to his credit that he states it directly. Nevertheless —and here Douglas reveals the unbridgeable gap between him and his fellow abolitionists—as to his enslavement, he is the "party of all others most deeply concerned." The American republic would hold him in bondage. What to do when an irrepressible force threatens your very survival? People who eat pay the British duty on wheat, although they fiercely oppose the tariff. A creditor who falsely claims a debt must be paid anyway if the alternative is prison. Douglass uses an example from Wright's own life: Wright opposed the use of national passports as a violation of the right to travel. But he got and used a passport while traveling abroad. Similarly, Douglass's free status is a "bit of paper, signed and sealed."

Douglass brilliantly rebuts Wright's argument that Auld is of no consequence because the United States is the real adversary. Auld *is* the United

States, Douglass piercingly asserts. Aided by the American government, "[he] can seize, bind and fetter, and drag me from my family, feed his cruel revenge upon me, and doom me to unending slavery. The slaveowner is the representative of that government and the commander in chief of its army and navy, so thoroughly has the slave interest captured and conscripted the entire power of the Republic." This could hardly be disputed in 1846, when the national army and navy had, that very year in fact, provoked war with Mexico by taking an expansive Texas as a territory, with the expectation that it would make one or many more slave states.

He does not waste time on the "million friends" who would defend him, should the slave catchers come. Only his few British friends took the necessary steps to release him from that "terrible liability" and, he writes, "place me on an equal footing of safety with all other antislavery lecturers in the United States." To be raised up to his northern managers, he had to go to Britain. American antislavery saw him as an asset; Wright had argued forcefully that his value to the cause would be reduced by relieving him of his terrible liability. After all, he had been instructed, "Tell your story, Frederick." We'll take care of the rest. As to my loss of value to you, Douglass concluded, I never made it about myself. I was always arguing for "the three millions now in chains."

Henry Wright was not alone. The Philadelphia Female Anti-Slavery Society passed a resolution condemning the ransom as "impolitic and inexpedient, taking from Douglass one of the strongest claims to the sympathy of the community." Perhaps incited by the divisions in the movement, Elizur Wright, former Garrisonian, now a deserter to the New York faction, wrote a scathing letter in his self-published newspaper *The Daily Chronotype*. "We abominate such a transaction," Wright inveighed. It was bad enough when the abolitionists bought out George Latimer, the escapee who fueled such excitement when slave catchers chased him in Boston in 1842. But Douglass wasn't in danger in England, he protested. Wright imagined Douglass must have exaggerated his fearfulness and played the credulous Brits. "Cheapened" and "discrace[d]," he thundered, in sum.

Garrison reprinted Elizur Wright's column in *The Liberator* to answer it on Douglass's behalf. Garrison dissented from both the "logic" and the "spirit" of the diatribe and expressed the collective gladness that Douglass was now free and could return to the bosom of his family. The next week's *Liberator* carried another similar column, but also a long rebuttal by Garrison himself, "The Ransom of Douglass." Garrison's argument graphically reveals his love for Douglass. From his earliest years in the movement, it was Garrison's intransigent consistency that gave him his outsized strength. Whenever offered the easier road of compromise with the powerful forces of slavery, he spurned the temptation. Although they would never free Black people and live among them, racists and enslavers might agree to send their slaves back to Africa, argued the "colonization" movement. Not a chance, said Garrison in his earliest appearance in abolition, a decade and a half before. Black people are Americans, many here longer than their would-be colonizers, and the movement reflects nothing but hatred for the race. Most recently, he had spurned the imperfectly abolitionist churches, even the liberal churches of the North. "Come out," he implored his followers; separate from the sin of slavery. It broke up the abolitionist movement. But he compromised to support Douglass's freedom.

Garrison, so insistent on logic, was particularly exercised that opponents of ransoming Douglass accused him of violating the principles he himself had laid down when founding the American Anti-Slavery Society in 1833. The founding document clearly says: "We maintain that no compensation should be given to the planters emancipating their slaves: Because it would be a surrender of the great fundamental principle, that man cannot hold property in man." No surrender, Garrison argued when Douglass was involved; all the ransom did was concede the power of power. Like pirates, the enslavers held their friend and champion. So they had to be paid. Though paying Douglass's enslaver, his rescuers still maintained the wrongness of slavery. Of course, that argument could have been made in any of Garrison's prior controversies — colonization, come-outerism, voting in elections corrupted by compromise. Not only did uncompromising Garrison compromise his principles for Douglass, but also he even "contributed his mite" to the ransom fund. The document reads:

> Know all men by these presents: That I, Thomas Auld, of Talbot county and State of Maryland, for and in consideration of the sum of

one hundred dollars, current money, to me paid by Hugh Auld of the city of Baltimore, in the said State, at and before the sealing and delivery of these presents, the receipt whereof I, the said Thomas Auld, do hereby acknowledge, have granted, bargained, and sold, and by these presents do grant, bargain, and sell unto the said Hugh Auld, his executors, administrators, and assigns, ONE NEGRO MAN, by the name of FREDERICK BAILEY, or DOUGLASS, as he calls himself—he is now about twenty-eight years of age—to have and to hold the said negro man for life. And I, the said Thomas Auld, for myself, my heirs, executors, and administrators, all and singular, the said FREDERICK BAILEY, alias DOUGLASS, unto the said Hugh Auld, his executors and administrators, and against all and every other person or persons whatsoever, shall and will warrant and forever defend by these presents. In witness whereof, I set my hand and seal this thirteenth day of November, eighteen hundred and forty-six (1846).

THOMAS AULD.

Signed, sealed, and delivered in presence of
Wrightson Jones, John C. Lear.

The authenticity of this bill of sale is attested by N. Harrington, a justice of the peace of the State of Maryland and for the county of Talbot, dated same day as above.

To all whom it may concern: Be it known that I, Hugh Auld of the city of Baltimore, in Baltimore county in the State of Maryland, for divers good causes and considerations me thereunto moving, have released from slavery, liberated, manumitted, and set free, and by these presents do hereby release from slavery, liberate, manumit, and set free, MY NEGRO MAN named FREDERICK BAILEY, otherwise called DOUGLASS, being of the age of twenty-eight years or thereabouts, and able to work and gain a sufficient livelihood and maintenance; and him, the said negro man named FREDERICK DOUGLASS, I do declare to be henceforth free, manumitted, and discharged from all manner of servitude to me, my executors and administrators forever.

In witness thereof, I, the said Hugh Auld, have hereunto set my hand and seal the fifth of December, in the year one thousand eight hundred and forty-six.

HUGH AULD.

Sealed and delivered in the presence of
T. Hanson Bell, James N.S.T. Wright.

On April 4, 1847, Douglass sailed home, a free man.

Coming Home

Even without constant fear of recapture, it must have been hard for Douglass to come back to America after living so far from the race hate of the nation structured around slavery. It must have been hard as well to resume his role as the favored lecturer of the Garrison wing after Weston Chapman's ham-handed efforts to "manage" him from across the sea and the frank words of abolitionists defending his enslavement as an asset to the movement.

Unbeknownst to the Boston abolitionists, Douglass and his British admirers had been discussing quite a different plan for him: he should have his own newspaper. While he was in Britain, some of the same activists who had raised money to buy his freedom had hatched the idea of buying his economic as well as his bodily independence. But Douglass did not want an annuity; he wanted to work. Heavily aided by Douglass's female British supporters, a group of donors began a campaign to purchase a steam printing press. Right after Douglass got back to Lynn, one of them, the wealthy British Quaker Mary Howitt, wrote to ask him if he'd like to have a "printing press." "Yes, yes!" he answered, not for himself but "as an aid to a great cause."

At the same time, the circle of female Douglass admirers deluged the Boston office with fan mail. "It was very delightful . . . to receive intelligence of the safe arrival across the Atlantic of our dear friend F. Douglass," one English abolition stalwart wrote to Weston Chapman upon Douglass's return. "Many here have become deeply attached to him & feel an intense interest in his welfare." Douglass biographer William McFeely writes that one of these emotive correspondents accidentally revealed the plan to set Douglass up with his own paper in a letter asking Weston Chapman if she had talked to Douglass about his new venture.

Her reaction was predictable. Even once the secret had been revealed, the relentlessly epistolary Boston bunch managed to keep most of their discussions about Douglass's new venture out of their letters. But the attitude of the major players — Edmund Quincy, the Weston sisters — peeks through in their correspondence and reveals how their behavior in the face of Douglass's ambitions derailed the promise — always fragile — of interracial alliance at the top of the Boston movement.

Douglass himself left a record of how he perceived the reactions of his former colleagues in the introduction to the second, 1855, version of his memoir, *My Bondage and My Freedom.* He replaced the testimonials from white sponsors Garrison and Phillips that had accompanied the earlier, 1845, version with a paean to his unstoppable rise from the Black abolitionist doctor James McCune Smith. Smith, clearly speaking for Douglass, tells the reader that Douglass had at first benefited from "the society of Wendell Phillips, Edmund Quincy, William Lloyd Garrison, and other men of earnest faith and refined culture." Soon, however, Smith continues, "these gentlemen, although proud of Frederick Douglass, failed to fathom, and bring out to the light of day, the highest qualities of his mind; the force of their own education stood in their own way: they did not delve into the mind of a colored man for capacities which the pride of race led them to believe to be restricted to their own Saxon blood." His stay in Britain among supporters not crippled by such pride of race "awakened him to the consciousness of new powers that lay in him." From the "pupilage of Garrisonism," Smith tells us, "he rose to the dignity of a teacher and a thinker."

Given her centrality to the breakup, Weston Chapman's absence from the list of inadequate white colleagues in the new introduction is puzzling and may account for her neglect by historians. Douglass was certainly clear on the role that women played in the movement in general and his fate in particular. Indeed, right after listing the failed white male colleagues, Smith credits an unidentified female supporter with the idea of a Black-published paper. As a result, Smith explains, Douglass turned to the project of publishing a newspaper. "This proceeding was sorely against the wishes and the advice of the leaders of the American Anti-Slavery Society." But Douglass went ahead anyway, the triumphal narrative continues.

Overseership

The real story is less straightforward. For a few months in the summer of 1847, Douglass waffled on the newspaper project. The Boston clique overtly tried to stave off his journalistic ambitions by offering him a column in the newspaper of the American Anti-Slavery Society, the *National Anti-Slavery Standard.* He announced that he had given up the idea of having his own paper.

Pro-Douglass letters flooded in to *The Liberator* suggesting he had been strong-armed by the "Boston Board." Garrison wrote a column explaining why the Society didn't want Douglass publishing. A Douglass paper would not fill a void of papers with colored editors, Garrison argued, because while Douglass was abroad, no fewer than four other such publications launched. The prospects for Douglass were not enhanced by the experience of these publications, which were struggling. Nor would Douglass's name automatically confer success where others had failed. Finally, Garrison contended, Douglass's skills as a lecturer were proven and his value to the Boston movement unparalleled. In typical fashion, Douglass also wrote an answer assuring the public in angry tones that no one, especially not the board, had made his decision for him.

Still, Douglass was clearly unhappy. He asked for a big fee from the *Standard.* His demand did historians everywhere a service, because it fi-

Edmund Quincy to Caroline Weston on his opinion of Douglass. *Courtesy of Boston Public Library.*

nally provoked Edmund Quincy into saying what he really thought of the Bostonians' Black ally: "Talking of unconscionable niggers," Quincy wrote Maria's sister Caroline Weston in July, Frederick Douglass had the effrontery to demand two dollars and fifty cents per column for the *Anti-Slavery Standard*. Quincy was trying to bargain Douglass down to a hundred dollars for a year's worth of columns, but when he consulted with Boston solon Wendell Phillips, Phillips warned Quincy against trying to "beat him down." After more back and forth with Douglass, Quincy reported, he agreed to take some version of his proposal to the board. "Those niggers like kings," Quincy expostulated, "are kittle cattle to shoe behind and I suppose it is better worth while to pay him."

"Kittle" means difficult to deal with, unsafe to meddle with. But Quincy's use of the n-word could not be justified in any way, including by the mores of his times. The word was toxic in 1847. Douglass himself calls out the slur as a term of opprobrium in making the contrast between how he was treated in Europe versus in the United States in his first report from his sojourn away from American race relations. Reminiscing about an early encounter with American racism after his escape from slavery, "I remember," Douglass wrote to Garrison, "there was in Boston . . . a menagerie. I had longed to see such a collection . . . never having had an opportunity while a slave . . . I went, and as I approached the entrance to gain admission, I was met and told by the door keeper, in a harsh and contemptuous tone 'We don't allow niggers in here'!" After reciting a half-dozen such American encounters to Garrison, Douglass reports that, in Ireland, he had gone to dinner with the Lord Mayor of Dublin. "What a pity," Douglass continued, "there was not some American democratic, Christian at the door of his splendid mansion, to bark out at my approach, 'They don't allow niggers in there.'"

The refined and self-consciously literary gent Edmund Quincy didn't shrink from putting the hateful term to paper, not once but twice, in his letter to Caroline Weston, supposedly another abolitionist stalwart. Writing to one of the tight band of Weston sisters, Quincy seems to have been unafraid of their reaction to his words, all because Douglass was asking to be paid a couple of dollars for his writing. We can't pay him more than the "others," Quincy wrote in a quick follow-up letter to Caroline. In case she thought he meant other white contributors, he quickly made clear who the "others" were. Paying him more would "set the flax in a flame, or at least all the *wool*."

Garrison Floats Above the Fray

Garrison's absence from the hateful correspondence was typical. Writing to rabid Douglass critic James Webb at this same time, Garrison noted that both Douglass and the Quaker Buffum were by his side, in fine spirits, and "begging me to proffer to you, and all the Dublin friends, their loving regards."

Regardless of how his close associates talked in private about their star orator and author, Garrison enthusiastically set out with Douglass for an Anti-Slavery Society tour of the West. After all, the need to keep Douglass deployed on the lecture stage was the Bostonians' rationale for trying so hard to thwart his editorial ambitions. The two departed from Philadelphia on August 3, 1847, to tour Pennsylvania, western New York State, and Ohio, areas that had lately shown promise for abolition. They immediately received a taste of the angry resistance that would be a feature of their western jaunt. Since the trains in Pennsylvania didn't enforce segregation, Douglass was sitting quietly at the window when an angry white man demanded he get out of his seat. Douglass did not resist but lectured the attacker about his bullying. Garrison reports the incident to Helen in what is clearly a tone of sorrow and indignation. Once in Harrisburg, Garrison reports, he lectured without incident, but when Douglass rose to speak, a mob gathered, hurling bricks, eggs, and firecrackers. "It was the first time," Garrison wrote, "that a 'nigger' had attempted to address the people of Harrisburg in public." Garrison's indignant use of the word reflects again how everyone in the movement knew exactly how obnoxious it was. Garrison expanded on the word in another letter to Helen, saying it was not him talking, of course; it was the "slang term" of the "rowdies." And abolitionist Edmund Quincy.

For a month the two men, once mentor and mentee, now privileged white companion and international star orator, traveled as one. Garrison's letters reflect an unreserved indignation at the treatment Douglass received — separated from Garrison and barred from the dining table for two long hungry days on the stagecoach to Pittsburgh. "Only think of it,"

Garrison wrote, "and then of the splendid reception given to him in all parts of Great Britain!" Garrison was astute. Douglass was exhausted and his voice was increasingly unreliable.

In Pittsburgh, Garrison reports, the tour met "several . . . colored Pittsburgh friends," including "Dr. Delaney [*sic*] (editor of the *Mystery*, black as jet, and a fine fellow of great energy and spirit)." Regardless of Garrison's opinion of his skin tone, Martin Delany was about to play a critical role in thwarting Garrison's plans. Delany was one of the leading Black supporters of the Liberty Party, and an active campaigner for Liberty candidates in increasingly abolitionist Pittsburgh. Douglass, meeting Delany for the first time upon the abolitionists' visit to Pittsburgh, enlisted the editor of the new antislavery paper to join forces with him in putting out a paper of Douglass's own.

Evidently, Douglass had not given up on becoming the editor of a newspaper. From Pittsburgh he wrote to lawyer Sydney H. Gay in New York, asking Gay to represent him in examining the books of a Black-owned newspaper, *The Ram's Horn*, published in New York by two Black editors, Willis A. Hodges and Thomas Van Rensselaer. If the books were good, Douglass wanted to become a third party in the concern. If the paper turned out not to be a sound investment, Douglass offered to write for *The Ram's Horn* for free or, indeed, to donate to it if it was in financial distress. Gay's role in this is mysterious, as he was at the same time the editor of the Garrisonian *National Anti-Slavery Standard*, where he printed Douglass's "public" letters.

Nothing in Douglass's official letters to Gay, reporting from the road in Ohio, reflects any disloyalty to Garrison or the cause. Right after asking Gay to investigate investment in *The Ram's Horn*, Douglass wrote a long, effusive missive for publication. In his telling, "Mr. Garrison is the honoured centre of every circle into whose midst we are brought. His conversational powers are inexhaustible . . . Our friends eagerly flock around to hear his words of strength and cheer."

The signs were good. Huge crowds gathered everywhere they went, thousands filling a giant portable tent in Ohio. According to Douglass, Garrison was the star; according to Garrison, Douglass was. "We are having a real anti-slavery revival," wrote Douglass. Ohio, he speculated, could be more important than Massachusetts within a year. By 1847, the booming states of the upper Midwest were fertile ground for the movement.

Even the competition in the movement, the Liberty Party men, Garrison reported, were less adverse in the more courteous Midwest than in the ideological heartland, the East. Called to debate the core Garrisonian position that abolition must make no union with slaveholders, Garrison was struck by the respect extended by his debating opponent, Ohio congressman Joshua Reed Giddings, one of the founding fathers of political abolition.

Respectful or not, Giddings was the opposite of Garrison's idealistic and extremist model of refusing to belong to churches or engage in politics. Indeed, when he met Garrison on tour, Giddings was coming off a stunning performance in the fiercest political battle over slavery to date, concerning the extension of slavery into the territories gained in the American war with Mexico.

But, oblivious that the momentum of the movement was shifting from his lecture halls to the halls of Congress, Garrison was having a wonderful time telling abolitionists the answer was to secede from the government and come out of their churches. In Ohio he realized a life's wish and attended the theology department's graduation at Oberlin College. Two of the theology graduates took the occasion to speak against Garrison's program of disunion from politics and come-outerism with the churches. Although a faculty member denounced the graduates' lack of zeal, Garrison himself wondered privately in a letter to his wife where zealous followers of his own ideology would find congregations and salaries to live on. If Ohio congressmen like Giddings wanted to pursue political programs, and Oberlin theology students wanted to stay in the churches they hoped would employ them, it was potent evidence that Garrison's disunion and come-outerism might not be the best plan.

Then, around September 13 in Cleveland, Garrison began to feel unwell. His collapse came as he and Douglass were about to embark on a speaking tour to Buffalo. Garrison had to forgo the tour and stay at the Cleveland home of a local supporter. As was the custom, he urged Douglass to go ahead to Buffalo to keep their obligations to the locals, expecting to follow shortly. When Douglass left, Garrison was in the hands of a Black doctor, Dr. Peck.

Garrison was so sick that his hosts called a second doctor, who thought it might be typhoid. On September 17, Douglass wrote to Sydney Gay to report on the tour for the *National Anti-Slavery Standard:* "Mr. Garrison and myself are still pursuing our Western course, and steadily persevering (although much worn with our labours)." There then ensued four pages of description of the means of transportation, the geography of the Buckeye State, the quality of their hosts, and a poem by contemporary poet Robert Nicolls, but not a word about Garrison's condition. Before Douglass's next dispatch, the *Standard* picked up from a Cleveland publication that Garrison had been too sick to go to Buffalo.

On September 26 Douglass wrote to Gay again, noting that the news about Garrison had reached the *Standard* and "deeply regretting that [he had] omitted all mention of his illness" in his previous letter. He had thought Garrison would recover quickly, he explained, and above all, he did not want to worry the family. When he got to Rochester on the six-teenth, Douglass continued, he had gone to the post office, looking for a letter about Garrison; Dr. Peck had promised to keep him informed. Two fruitless visits later, on the eighteenth Douglass heard from Dr. Peck that Garrison was quite ill and would quit the tour and go home. Garrison had asked Peck to tell Douglass not to alarm the family. On the twenty-third, Douglass informed Gay, he had sent a telegram to Cleveland inquiring about Garrison but had to leave for Syracuse before he got an answer. He would return to Cleveland, he wrote from West Winfield, if he heard that Garrison was no better. "I have reproached myself for leaving him at all," he wrote.

And then, silence on the subject of his ailing colleague.

The Boston abolitionists sent Garrison's old friend Henry Wright to Cleveland to get him and accompany him home. His colleagues raised enough money to pay his doctors' bills.

Frederick Douglass Does Not Write a Single Line

On October 20, in his last letter from his sickroom in Cleveland, Garrison opened his heart to his wife. "Is it not strange," he asked, "that Douglass has not written a single line to me, or to any one, in this place, inquiring after my health, since he left me on a bed of illness?"

Garrison is technically accurate; there were no letters directly from Douglass to Garrison or to his hosts in Cleveland in the archives, but Douglass did stop on his way through New York at the home of Garrison's dear friend the preacher Samuel May, who had recently taken a parish in western New York State. After Douglass passed through, May wrote a note to Garrison on October 4 and shared both Douglass's efforts to get news in the early days after their parting and his shock and dismay when he did not find Garrison recovered and waiting for him at May's house, as the two had arranged.

Broken relationships often turn on a lost letter. By then, however, the real issue between the two — Douglass's return to the newspaper idea — was everywhere. As he left Garrison in Cleveland on September 14, he had already concluded his business plans for a paper, *The North Star.* The prospectus for Douglass's newspaper appeared in the Ohio abolitionist publication the *Anti-Slavery Bugle* on September 17, just as Douglass was reportedly searching the post offices for news of Garrison's health. That the *Bugle* got the scoop about Douglass's new plans is not surprising; one of the primary participants in that Ohio paper, Samuel Brooke, was listed on the prospectus as one of Douglass's sponsors. Brooke had led Douglass astray, Garrison speculated to Helen in his October letter complaining about Douglass's neglect; he wanted to tie his struggling Ohio paper to the stronger brand. Apparently Douglass acting without a white mentor was inconceivable to the abolitionists. The *Anti-Slavery Standard* picked up the item about Douglass's venture a week later, with a passive-aggressive endorsement: "We still believe that he would be more useful as a lecturer, than as an editor, but as he is determined to enter the *corps,* we give him a most hearty welcome. We know he will make a good paper for his readers — we hope he will make a profitable one for himself."

Garrison told Helen in a plaintive postscript what he really thought: "It will also greatly surprise our friends in Boston to hear that, in regard to his project for establishing a paper . . . he never opened to me his lips on the subject, nor asked my advice in any particular whatever. Such conduct grieves me to the heart." And Garrison thought it was a bad idea, "impulsive, inconsiderate, and highly inconsistent with his decision in Boston" not to pursue such a plan.

Letters to London

Douglass was writing—just not to Garrison, who thought his project was a bad idea. He wrote in October to his British sponsor, Julia Griffiths, who had emerged as one of the most dedicated of Douglass's mostly female British supporters, to thank her for a collection of books his British friends had sent him.

Griffiths's relationship with the star would soon become the subject of fevered speculation. As befits her mysterious role, her origins are cloaked in some shadow. Her father, usually described as a London stationer, publisher, and bookseller, went bankrupt more than once, and Julia was raised mostly by her aunt and uncle. Unlike much of Douglass's British circle, the Griffithses were not Quakers, and they certainly were not wealthy. The extent of their involvement with the movement is unclear. Was Julia's mother a friend of the great British abolitionist William Wilberforce, as one historian speculates? No one knows. Even how the two met is unclear. Douglass says Julia and her sister Elizabeth, usually called Eliza, met him during his stay in London and showed him around. Julia had a more romantic memory of their meeting at his goodbye party his last night in London. Don't you remember, she wrote Douglass, "that Eliza pinned that white camellia in your coat?"

Regardless, Julia Griffiths soon emerged as the leader in efforts to raise money for Douglass's journalistic ambitions. The abolitionist activists Jane and Jonathan Carr, another example of brilliantly successful Quaker merchants (baking), acted as treasurers for the fund to buy Douglass's steam press, which had caused such agita in Boston already. Alongside the usual Quaker Douglass admirers, Julia raised money for the press and the books Douglass had received so gratefully. On October 1, 1847, Carr sent him a draft for more than four hundred pounds. Douglass informed Carr that he had already bought "an excellent and elegant press" with the money. The other "coloured"-run papers, he assured Carr, were already on their last legs or ready to fold into Douglass's enterprise. Therefore, the original project of a unique Black-run press was intact.

Douglass finished his tour in New York, while Garrison languished in Cleveland. Stopping in Rochester, Douglass reconnected with his old and dear friends Isaac and Amy Post, mainstays of antislavery in western

New York. Five years before, Amy Post had overseen the creation of a network of abolition societies, consisting mostly of her Quaker friends. Plain in aspect and unadorned in garb, Post stood as an irresistible contrast to Weston Chapman, the Contessa. Like her eastern counterpart, she was the center of a circle of abolitionist family and friends and a faithful correspondent. The tone of the letters to and from Amy Post, unlike Weston Chapman's, reflects a warm and inclusive attitude toward the always fractious movement. In a lovely letter revealing an unusual degree of trust, Douglass had written to Post from England about how much she meant to him: "You loved and treated me as a brother before the world knew me as it now does."

The schism between Garrison and the two New York factions had cost Post's operation dearly, as many affiliates disassociated from her society in favor of Gerrit Smith and his political abolitionists. Post, like Weston Chapman, tried to fund the operations with bazaars, and she, like Weston Chapman, asked Douglass to get his British supporters to send her articles to sell. Better still, she thought to ask Weston Chapman to lend her Douglass as a speaker, when he returned from Britain, but Post got nowhere. One can only imagine what the conversations between the two old friends consisted of when Douglass showed up in Rochester funded for a newspaper, ignoring the preferences of Weston Chapman, and leaving Garrison behind.

On October 28, Douglass wrote to Amy Post from Boston to announce his decision. He would move to Rochester and publish his newspaper there.

The North Star Rises

The debut issue of *The North Star* appeared in Rochester on December 3, 1847.

Like the first *Liberator*, the first issue of *The North Star* opened with its editor's declaration of purpose: "It has long been our anxious wish to see, in this slave-holding, slave-trading, and Negro-hating land, a printing-press and paper, permanently established, under the complete control and direction of the immediate victims of slavery and oppression."

"Brethren," Douglass pleaded, "the first number of the paper is before you. It is dedicated to your cause. Through the kindness of our friends in

THE NOR

FREDERICK DOUGLASS, } EDITORS.
M. R. DELANY,

RIGHT IS OF NO SEX—TRUTH IS OF NO COLO

VOL. I. NO. 23.

ROCHESTER,

The NORTH STAR is published every Friday, at No. 25, Buffalo Street,

(Opposite the Arcade.)

TERMS.

Two dollars per annum, *always in advance*. No subscription will be received for a less term than six months.

Advertisements not exceeding ten lines inserted three times for one dollar; every subsequent insertion, twenty-five cents.

THE object of the NORTH STAR will be to attack SLAVERY in all its forms and aspects; advocate UNIVERSAL EMANCIPATION; exalt the standard of PUBLIC MORALITY; promote the moral and intellectual improvement of the COLORED PEOPLE; and hasten the day of FREEDOM to the THREE MILLIONS of our ENSLAVED FELLOW COUNTRYMEN.

PUBLISHER'S NOTICES.

☞ All communications relating to the *business matters* of the paper, names of subscribers, remittances, &c., should be addressed to WILLIAM C. NELL, Publisher.

☞ Agents, and all others sending names, are requested to be accurate, and give the *Post Office*, the *County*, and the *State*. Each Subscriber is immediately credited for money received.

☞ Any person sending in the payment for four subscribers, to be forwarded to one address, may have a fifth copy for one year.

☞ All letters and communications must be post paid.

LIST OF AGENTS.

MASSACHUSETTS.—R. F. Walcutt, 21, Cornhill, Boston; Nathan Johnson, New Bedford; Horatio W. Foster, Lowell; James N. Buffum, Lynn; George Evans, Worcester; Roscoe Spooner, Plymouth; Charles H. Seth, Springfield; David Ruggles, Northampton; H. Carpenter, Upton.

MAINE.—Oliver Dennett, Portland.

VERMONT.—Rowland T. Robinson, North Ferrisburg.

CONNECTICUT.—Jonathan Leonard, Meriden.

NEW HAMPSHIRE.—Weare Tappan, Bradford.

NEW YORK.—Sydney H. Gay, 142, Nassau Street; James McCune Smith, 93, West Broadway; Joseph Post, Westbury, Queen County; Mary Harper, Albany; Elias Doty, Marcellon; Willetts Keese, Peru, Clinton County; William S. Baltimore, Troy; J. F. Platt, Penn Yan; J. Jeffrey, Geneva; E. L. Platt, Bath.

RHODE ISLAND.—Amaraney Paine, Providence.

PENNSYLVANIA.—J. M. M'Kim, 31, North Fifth Street, Philadelphia; G. W. Goines, 8, Exchange Place, Ditto; H. Vashon, B. Bown, Pittsburg; William Whipper, Columbia; Isaac Roberts, Jacob L. Paxon, Norristown, Montgomery County, Milo A. Townsend, New Brighton.

OHIO.—Christian Donaldson, Cincinnati; G. W. Carter, Ditto; Valentine Nicholson, Harveysburgh, Warren County; Samuel Brooke, Salem.

MICHIGAN.—Robert Banks, Detroit.

INDIANA.—Joel P. Davis, Economy, Wayne Co.

Communication.

REV. JOHN LELAND.

DEAR DOUGLASS:—In looking over your paper of the 7th inst., I saw, under the head of "Reminiscences of a Slave," a thing that grieved me much. In a fictitious work (written by an ex-judge of Otsego county), entitled the

ernment, destructive of every human and benevolent passion of the soul, and subversive of that liberty absolutely necessary to ennoble the human mind. Let me ask whether heaven has nothing better in store for these poor negroes than those galling chains? If so, ye ministers of Jesus, and saints of the Most High, ye wrestling Jacobs, who have power with God, and can prevail over the angels, let your prayers, your ardent prayers, ascend to the throne of God incessantly, that he may pour the blessing of freedom upon the poor blacks. How would every heart rejoice to see the halcyon day appear, the great jubilee usher in when the poor slaves, with a Moses at their head, should hoist up their standard, and march out of bondage! Or what would be still more elating, to see the power of the gospel so effectual, that the lion and the lamb should be together; all former insults and revenges forgotten; the name of master and slave be buried; every yoke broken, and the oppressed go free but not empty away!"

In a pamphlet entitled the Virginia Chronicle, published in 1790, Elder Leland has given to the world a more extended view of slavery, from which I beg leave to extract a few sentences to show his extreme unlikeness to that portion of the American clergy which the author of the above fiction intended he should represent:

"The whole scene of slavery is pregnant with enormous evils. On the master's side, pride, haughtiness, domination, cruelty, deceit, and indolence; and on the side of the slave, ignorance, servility, fraud, perfidy and despair. If these and many other evils attend it, why not liberate them at once?—Would to Heaven this were done! The sweets of rural and social life will never be enjoyed until it is the case. The voice of reason (or perhaps the voice of covetousness) says it is not the work of a day; time is necessary to accomplish the important work. A political evil requires political measures to reform."

Again, after speaking of some imaginary obstacles to their emancipation, he says:

"But one thing is pretty certain, that fancy can hardly point out how they could serve the whites worse than the whites now serve them. Something must be done! May Heaven point out that something, and may the people be obedient. If they are not brought out of bondage in mercy, with the consent of their master, I think they will be, by judgment, against their consent."

I regard them as a mongrel species, half man and half ape."

As the book above alluded to is put forth under the auspices of a respected citizen, and as many of its readers will regard it as generally accurate in its illustrations of the distinguished characters alluded to, I have deemed the above extracts from the Works of Elder Leland worthy of publication, as a just defence against the foulest of all aspersions that could be cast upon the name of that highly distinguished Christian and patriot.

CUYLER TANNER.

RICHFIELD, N. Y., April 22.

Selections.

LETTER FROM ROBERT DOUGLASS.

Our friends in Eastern Pennsylvania will be glad to see the letter from Mr. Douglass, late of Philadelphia. It will interest our readers generally to know that Robert Douglass is an artist of skill and promise, who, in this country, was unable to gain a livelihood by his profession, though he added to it that of a Daguerreotypist; and has therefore emigrated to a country where he hopes the colors he uses, and the way he uses them, will be the test of his merit, rather than that upon his own body, which he neither put on nor can rub off.—*National Anti-Slavery Standard.*

KINGSTON, Jamaica, }
Feb. 29, 1848. }

FRIEND GAY:—We arrived here safely after a very tolerable voyage. I was much impressed with the beauty, as seen at a distance, of the high mountains of this island, their greatest elevation being, I am told, eight thousand feet above the level of the sea. One, in particular, resembled a giant reposing, his profile distinctly visible against the soft light of the evening sky, the mist surrounding his capacious brow, giving the idea of a proper-fitting nightcap. On landing, we found the city of Kingston exceedingly hot and dusty, and the walking scarcely endurable.—The great numbers of the lower order running to and fro, almost all black, formed a striking feature. Most of them were chanting some air or ditty, which, upon listening to, I discovered to be a hymn. I was impressed with their devotion, and inclined to believe that a population so fond of sacred music must certainly be a very honest one.— We must have had dealings with the

attendants, h
continuing his
The white c
was said, bec
to most ex
voters.

I have had
my residence
large party e
evening, in t
longing to
"Dove," an
tain. We te
"Ponds," w
islands, with
—such a m
in the tropic
and interesti
tifully trans
every objec
swimming to
other or in
row passage
a few mome
the "Dove"
with their a
figured, ra
trices, apps
irons, plant
along until
slept that n
Mansion H
The nex
started for a
mountain.
the entrance
stationed fo
sharks, or
we took a
We break
cave. This
a great nat
up by an is
of the mou
ed to a gr
selves by r
pieces of r
considerab
Green Bay
Louis Cal
the great
Port Roy
shock by
caped by
years afte
Thence w
immense w
were amaz
tifications,
the most i
quantity
implement
intelligenc
and expla
and the r
correct w

H STAR.

THE FATHER OF US ALL, AND ALL WE ARE BRETHREN.

WILLIAM C. NELL, Publisher.
JOHN DICK, Printer.

RIDAY, JUNE 2, 1848.   WHOLE NO.—23.

ne of march,
e proceeded.
re-elected, it
s had gone
bribing of

cursion since
Royal. A
ston in the
of them be-
ry schooner
by her Cap-
ge called the
with little
to guide us
to be found
ry was novel
ter so beau-
could see
and the fish
suit of each
In a nar-
aground for
wers, part of
ic Africans,
ed, or dis-
zontal cica-
ed with hot
ned the boat
freely. We
oyal, in the

y early, we
the opposite
our boats at
and having
p away the
r approach,
n the sea,—
within the
considered
t is lighted
e at the top
we clamber-
mused our-
stones and
ined here a
en went to
the tomb of
owed up by
h destroyed
by another
sea; he es-
lived many
he story.—
Augusta, an
gston. We
of the for-
cannon, of
uction, the
, and other
ar." The
ho showed
s language,
ch he gave
s appertain-

I called it a glorious meeting. It
could not be otherwise. The very
name of Faneuil Hall could not be pronounced at such a time without a glorious offect. For that word is synony-
mous with resistance to wrong. It
wakes the remembrance of a day when
MEN trod these streets—when generous
hearts found nerve to second their noble impulses—when an iron will was not
wanting to a pure conscience, to make
deeds of its high behests. To think of
that day, to admire those men, to ap-
prove their deeds, is to catch their
spirit, if we be not dead.

But is the object of our meeting accomplished? Why, for what did we go
up to that Hall? Was it to applaud
thrilling speeches? Was it to burn
once more with idle indignation at the
wrongs of slavery? The day for that
is past. Or did we need to be told that
our fathers were so wicked as to wish
to legalize slavery, or so stupid as to
attempt it? We hear enough of that in
Congress. Or did we go up merely to
resolve? We have been amusing our
masters with resolves these dozen
years, until the very word fills our tyrants with hope, and ourselves with
mutual distrust. The conviction has
spread through Massachusetts that the
time has come for action, if we be not
slaves.

We need no formula of words to ensure harmony of feeling. The humanity within impels us in one direction,
carries us all to one point. All the
suggestions of the present time, and
all the memories of the past, centre in
one thought—It is no sin to be free—it
can be no crime to aid men to freedom.
Our desire for justice, and our respect
for law; our love of man, and our fear
of God; all concur in this one purpose
—to aid men to be free in this free
land, shall not be punished as a crime.
We have a Constitution— engrossed
upon parchment; laws — hid in the
books. We will know if they can
command justice to those three noble
sailors. In Congress, it would seem,
all is lost by our former supineness;
but the crisis Providence has now forced
upon us, we will meet—

"Rest, rest, perturbed spirit of our fathers"—
we will meet it like men.

"In such a case," said Otis, "I despise a fee."

The Otises are dead, though the
cause remains. Therefore the fee
must be raised. My thought was to
raise a fund of one or two hundred
thousand dollars, the interest to be ap-
propriated to the defence of the present
case, and such others as may arise,
until the Constitution shall "establish
justice." The principal could then be

sponse. Enthusiasm would kindle from
Cape Cod to Mount Washington, and
a response would come back to aston-
ish our friends and appal our enemies.
I seem to see a reason why a fund of
this sort should be raised, in prefer-
ence to raising donations outright, sufficient to defend the present case. It
can be more easily, more cheerfully,
more promptly done. The interest
would be more available, a more safe
dependence for carrying the trial thro'
triumphantly. Besides, and more than
all, the moral effect would be incalcula-
ble. You may hear again from
JUNIUS.

PROGRESS OF POETRY.

In the natural progress of society, the
songs which are the effusion of the feelings of a rude tribe, are gradually pol-
ished into a form of poetry still retain-
ing the marks of the national opinions,
sentiments, and manners, from which it
originally sprung. The plants are im-
proved by cultivation; but they are still
the native produce of the soil. The
only perfect example which we know,
of this sort, is Greece. Knowledge and
useful art, and perhaps in a great measure religion, the Greeks received from
the East; but as they studied no foreign
language, it was impossible that any
foreign literature should influence the
progress of theirs. Not even the name
of a Persian, Assyrian, Phenician, or
Egyptian poet is alluded to by any
Greek writer: the Greek poetry was,
therefore, wholly national. The Pe-
lasgic ballads were insensibly formed
into Epic, and Tragic, and Lyric poems:
but the heroes, the opinions, and the
customs, continued as exclusively Gre-
cian, as they had been when the Hel-
lenic minstrels knew little beyond the
Adriatic and the Ægean. The literature of Rome was a copy from that of
Greece. When the classical studies
revived amid the chivalrous manners
and feudal institutions of Gothic Europe,
the imitation of ancient poets struggled
against the power of modern sentiments
with various event, in different times
and countries—but everywhere in such
a manner, as to give somewhat of an
artificial and exotic character to poetry.
Jupiter and the Muses appeared in the
poems of Christian nations. The feelings and principles of democracies were
copied by the gentlemen of Teutonic
monarchies or aristocracies. The sentiments of the poet in his verse, were
not those which actuated him in his
conduct. The forms and rules of com-
position were borrowed from antiquity,
instead of spontaneously arising from

billet of wood at your back if you aint
off at once. You, without a cent in
your pocket, to think to impose upon
me!"

The old man walked off without ut-
tering a word. The captain turning to
a person who came near at the moment,
told him the story, pointing to the old
man, who turned and looked at them,
and then continued his way.

"Do you know that old man?" asked
the person to whom the captain now
spoke. "No, sir!" "Well, dis-
charge your cargo; I rather guess he
can pay for it." The captain soon felt
his error, and in due time the lumber
was landed at the wharf. The next
morning the old man was there again.
"So, young man," he said mildly, "you
concluded to accept my offer?" The
captain, humbly approaching the old
man, said, "Sir, I did not know you.
Please excuse—sir—I—sir"—The old
man was too busy examining the lumber to notice the stuttering apology,
and merely heard enough to know for
what it was intended. "Give me the
surveyor's certificate," said he. It was
given him. "Your bill, sir." It was
also given. "This is correct, and
there's a check for the amount."—
"Sir," interposed the captain, feeling
very anxious to atone for his error—
"Young man," interrupted the pur-
chaser, and he emphasized young with
a peculiar tone of voice, "all is settled
if you will allow me one word of advice
—never again judge a man by his coat.
Farewell!"

The check was duly paid, and had
the captain but observed the circumstance, he might have seen the name
of the giver of the check, and that of
the President upon the bills received
for it, belonged to the same person.

The above anecdote is strictly true,
and carries a good moral with it.—
Transcript.

THE TELESCOPE AND MICRO-SCOPE.

While the telescope enables us to see
a system in every star, the microscope
unfolds to us a world in every atom.
The one instructs us that this mighty
globe, with the whole burthen of its
people and its countries, is but a grain
of sand in the vast field of immensity
—the other, that every atom may
harbor the tribes and families of a
busy population.

The one shows us the insignificance
of the world we inhabit—the other
redeems it from all its insignificance,
for it tells us that in the leaves of every

England, we are in possession of an excellent printing press, types, and all other materials necessary for printing a paper. Shall this gift be blest to our good, or shall it result in our injury? It is for you to say. With your aid, co-operation and assistance, our enterprise will be entirely successful."

There was poetry ("The Fugitive Slave's Apostrophe to the North Star") and prose (the short story "The Dying Slave") as well as wedding announcements and music reviews. The heart of the issue was a long piece by Douglass. In the run-up to the 1848 presidential election, Whig politician Henry Clay had given a speech about not expanding slavery to the territory gained in the American war with Mexico. Clay had said that his opinions on slavery were well known, consistent, and long-lived. Well known, Senator Clay, Douglass responded, but none of the rest. You confess that slavery is "a great evil and a wrong to its victims." But, he continued, "you are yourself a slaveholder at this moment." And, "speaking of 'the unfortunate victims' of this 'great evil,' you hold this most singular and cowardly excuse for perpetuating the wrongs of my 'unfortunate' race." My race.

Clay had barely lost the presidential contest of 1844, and he remained a potent force and a leading presidential contender in the Whig Party, in part because of the stubborn support of the growing cohort of antislavery, or "Conscience," Whig politicians. The conflict between his unrepentant enslavement of his personal victims and his seductive flirtation with the antislavery wing of his party was his weak spot. And Douglass went right for it. And so *The North Star* ascended to confront the leading politician of the era on a claim of inauthenticity that no white editor could make: my race.

Five days after *The North Star* appeared, so did upstate New York abolition leader Gerrit Smith. Welcome to New York, he wrote to Douglass on December 8. He enclosed five dollars for a two-year subscription to the paper. He had added Douglass to his beneficiaries of forty acres of land each, part of Smith's project to make Black New Yorkers property owners and therefore eligible to vote. James McCune Smith, who would later write the introduction to Douglass's second memoir, had also just joined Gerrit Smith's beneficiaries. Although McCune Smith did not need Gerrit Smith's generosity, it made the ambivalent Garrisonian a member of the upstate community, later named "Timbuctoo," drawing Douglass into the

Upstate abolitionist Gerrit Smith. *Courtesy of Library of Congress.*

upstate New York faction and putting Smith on Douglass's radar. "Your friend and brother," he signed off, "Gerrit Smith."

It was not all presents and scoops for the paper. Douglass, Delany, and William Cooper Nell, a great friend of Garrison's who was listed in Rochester as "publisher" of *The North Star,* were struggling. The press Douglass had bought with his British funding turned out to be a mistake, and he had to pay a commercial printer to produce the newspaper. At two dollars a year, the subscriptions barely covered the cost of contract printing. Douglass sent Delany out into the field to speak and drum up new supporters. Douglass's correspondence with Delaney from the early months of the paper is filled with frustration, Douglass pleading with his partner for reports of his success and submissions to publish in their paper. Would *The North Star* survive, Douglass fretted, or would the predictions from his colleagues in the "old organization" be sadly realized?

The Garrisonians would not use their established platform to support Douglass's competing paper. As soon as he got started, the Weston sisters cut him off from the fount of funding, the antislavery fairs. Douglass's friend Amy Post asked if Anne Weston would send for her western New York fair some of the fetching European goods that made the Boston fairs so successful, as well as copies of *The Liberty Bell*. Weston said no, refusing to help Post because of her support for Douglass's project.

Within months of the first *North Star*, Weston Chapman was engaged in a robust correspondence with her British friends about Douglass's failings as a person and newspaper owner. Having learned nothing from Webb's disingenuously "sharing" her confidential critical letters just two years before, this time she wrote to the British poet and litterateur Mary Howitt about how "selfish" Frederick Douglass was and that he should not have received presents from the English, as they were "taken from the cause." Weston Chapman's ire was probably aroused by a gift of ten British pounds that she had recently received from the British philanthropist Anne Milbanke (briefly Lady Byron) with instructions to forward it to Douglass. In Weston Chapman's letter forwarding the money to Douglass in September of 1848, just nine months after the first issue of *The North Star*, she expressed herself as regretting that he needed the money and attributed his financial troubles to the "perplexing business operation," but she deferred to his own "best judgment in the management of [his] affairs."

As luck would have it, when Weston Chapman's letter to Mary Howitt criticizing Douglass arrived, Howitt was entertaining Douglass's passionate British supporter Julia Griffiths. Griffiths immediately wrote to Douglass to tell him what his Boston colleague was saying about him behind his back, and "wondering" that "this woman would dare to write about you in such a manner." Maria's sister Anne was in the Boston office when Douglass, who was still circulating in the Boston movement, picked up Griffiths's letter, and she witnessed how sad and offended he was. Maria shouldn't have written to Mary Howitt, Anne told their sister Caroline in a letter detailing the whole sorry affair. Douglass was "weak" and "touchy." Why provoke him? You should be careful, Anne reminded Caroline, and so should Maria, about what you say and write.

But Weston Chapman didn't seem to care. She had shared her opinion of *The North Star* with another of her many British correspondents, the reformer Joseph Lupton. Her letter is lost, but in his reply, Lupton says he was "sorry to hear her report," as he had hoped for Douglass's success, because "a paper edited and managed by a colored man would be of great service to the cause." But then Lupton concluded that the aforementioned man of color probably did not have "sufficient business habits" for "such an important enterprise."

As usual, Garrison was more passive-aggressive. In 1848, planning the Anti-Slavery Society meeting for May, he wrote that, of many possible speakers, "of course we must have either Douglass, or WW Brown or [Charles L.] Remond." Of the three Black men listed, only one would be chosen, and Douglass was now one among many. Douglass, not yet separated from the Boston clique, agreed to speak at this most prestigious Society meeting, and Garrison then dropped the other Black leader, Remond: "At our other meetings he will find frequent opportunities to speak."

Douglass made one last appearance as a member of the clique. One year after the 1848 Society meeting, in May of 1849, he came to speak again. But he was scheduled so late in the proceedings that he had to cut off his presentation.

PART IV

---◆---

DOUGLASS TO THE POLITICAL SIDE

20

(1844–1849)

Slave Power Rises and Abolition Power Rises

DOUGLASS COULD NOT HAVE CHOSEN A BETTER time to separate from Garrison's version of abolition. Just as he broke free of the Boston group in 1847, political abolition was gaining some major traction, and Garrison's vision was losing steam.

The ascendancy of political abolition had unlikely roots in the presidential election of 1844. As the contest between the Whig slaveholder Henry Clay and the Texas annexationist Democrat James K. Polk loomed, the Liberty Party nominated activist James G. Birney and seemed poised to be irrelevant. We'll just wait until the presidential campaign is terminated, Garrison wrote to his purist colleague Henry Wright about the threat from the competing movement. And then we'll make our "onslaught on public sentiment," preaching our solution to national slavery: "disunion."

The Election Turns Out to Be about Slavery

The Liberty Party barely did better in 1844 than it had in the local elections in the years since 1840. Despite its poor showing, however, and contrary to Garrison's prediction, the issue of slavery turned out to be central to the election.

The catalyst was the long-standing issue of whether the United States should annex the Republic of Texas. An independent Texas had emerged from the 1835 rebellion of Americans whom Mexico had foolishly invited to tame its remote and empty land. Most of the Texas settlers had come from nearby slave states like Louisiana and Arkansas, and despite Mexico's abolition of slavery in 1829, they brought their slaves with them. It was

an unstable arrangement, and in 1835 the American "Anglo-Texans" revolted. There was powerful support in the United States for annexing their
territory; the sentiment stemmed from many sources, ranging from the
national ethos of spreading America's superior republican values to greed
for the desirable farmland.

For the first time, however, there was meaningful, organized resistance
to American expansion. People feared war with Mexico if the United
States annexed Texas and doubted that the government could easily ad-
minister vast new regions. But a lot of the resistance also came from the
new abolitionist movement. The most potent evidence of the linkage between Texas annexation and the slavery issue is that it was John Quincy
Adams, the aging but powerful New Englander who had fought the gag
rule for the abolitionists, also leading the opposition in Congress to annexing Texas. As the abolition movement was slowly staggering to its feet in
the years after the Republic of Texas emerged in 1836, the editorial pages
and the petitions of the new movement all doggedly fought to keep slave
Texas out of the United States. Texas, hanging out there, "independent,"
for eight years after 1836, was an irrefutable argument for the rising power
of abolition.

Despite the growing opposition, however, the prospects for annexation
reached a high-water mark before the 1844 election. Democratic president Tyler's secretary of state was the slave power firebrand, former South
Carolina senator John C. Calhoun, and he was all for annexing Texas. The
Tyler administration sent a treaty to do so to the Senate, but annexation
fell short of the two-thirds vote needed for confirmation.

As the election of 1844 neared, former president and New Yorker Martin Van Buren confidently publicized his opposition to annexing Texas,
joining the growing ranks of candidates who would underestimate the slave
power. Southern-dominated Democrats rejected the obvious front-runner,
Van Buren, and chose as their candidate Tennessee slaveholder James K.
Polk, an open supporter of annexation. Polk's opponent, the Whig Henry
Clay, was evasive on the subject. As the historian Corey Brooks describes
the improbable results, the election was so close that the seemingly unim-
pressive fifteen thousand New York votes for the Liberty Party cost Clay
the state and threw the Electoral College to Polk.

Taking Polk's election as a sign of support for annexation, lame duck

President Tyler, in a raw exercise of power, submitted the rejected treaty to Congress as a joint resolution. Resolutions pass by majority vote, not the two-thirds vote that had thwarted the treaty before the election. Despite the seriously suspect constitutionality of ratifying a treaty as a resolution, the resolution passed, and the United States annexed Texas. In this exercise of raw and questionably legal political might, the North got a full facial blast of the power of the "slave power."

Watching the contest, New York abolitionist Lewis Tappan had predicted that a win for the annexationist Polk in 1844 would actually help the abolitionist cause. As Tappan foresaw, when the southerners wielded their legislative might to force the addition of slave Texas after Polk's election, cracks began to appear in the two-party system. Despite its sponsorship by the Democratic president, about a third of northern Democratic representatives voted against annexing Texas. New Hampshire congressman John P. Hale rose to oppose the resolution and opened a crevasse in New Hampshire politics, splitting the Democrats there wide open over the expansion of slavery. The alliance of antislavery Democrats, Whigs, and Liberty men in the New Hampshire legislature worked so unexpectedly well that the antislavery forces took over the state legislature and appointed Hale to be their senator. (Senators were still appointed by the state legislatures in those days.) Annexing Texas predictably led to war with Mexico, and after the United States' victory, which added even more potential slave territory in the Southwest to the mix, President Polk asked Congress for money to make peace.

A Proposal to Contain Slavery

As the raw exercise of slave power began to erode the two-party consensus on placating the South, David Wilmot, a hitherto marginal Pennsylvania Democrat, proposed that slavery should be banned in any land acquired in the Mexican War. In 1846 Wilmot attached his proposal as a proviso to Polk's spending bill for the Mexican peace process. The proviso tore the wraps off the sectional divides in both of the major parties. Northern Democrats, already unhappy with their party for rejecting their native son Martin Van Buren in 1844, found an outlet for their ire in sponsoring Wilmot's Proviso.

In the scorching debate in Congress, Whig abolitionist representative Joshua Reed Giddings took the opportunity to weave the extension of slavery into Texas and the Southwest as part of the political abolitionists' larger story of slave power dominance over the whole nation. This time a handful of Whig congressmen and senators from abolitionist Maine and Massachusetts joined Ohio's abolitionist Giddings to speak out for limits on the spread of slavery. The two drivers of political disunion — the western spread of slavery and the political might of the slave power over the whole United States government to ensure it — came together in one issue.

Southerners responded to the Wilmot Proviso with predictable fury. Senator John C. Calhoun, in his last term before his death, took the most extreme position. Slaves were property, he contended, and the Constitution protected property. Therefore, any law to impede southerners from taking their slaves anywhere was unconstitutional. A decade later, a variant of Calhoun's argument would be adopted by Chief Justice Roger Taney in *Dred Scott v. Sandford*. For now, the confrontation between Wilmot's non-extension proviso and Calhoun's everywhere extension theory threw Congress into an uproar. President Polk, wielding all the power of his office, including, reportedly, unlimited amounts of pork, managed to defeat the proviso in the Senate and make favorable peace with helpless Mexico.

But for the first time in national politics, slavery was not merely on the table. It was, in fact, the centerpiece. In almost no time, the two-party structure began to collapse.

The Birth of Mainstream Antislavery Politics

The cause of antislavery politics was blessed by the presence of a politician in equal parts radical and ambitious. Lawyer Salmon P. Chase came to abolition by seeing his client's printing press trashed in a riot in Cincinnati in 1835. As early as 1840, the increasingly radical Whig member of the local city council was expressing his inclination toward an abolitionist third party. By 1842 he was openly allied. He adopted Liberty Party legal theorist Alvan Stewart's theories about why slavery was unconstitutional, and he used the arguments, although with little success, in a robust law practice defending fugitive slaves. But he was also legendarily ambitious, and throughout his Liberty Party years he was a consistent voice for alliance,

Free Soil Party organizer Salmon P. Chase.
Courtesy of Library of Congress.

electoral effectiveness, and pragmatism. He would not require Liberty men to call themselves "abolitionists," and he proposed after the disastrous Liberty Party campaign in 1840 to replace the obscure James G. Birney as the Liberty standard-bearer.

As the slavery issue rose in importance in the 1840s, the arguments against slavery fell along a continuum. More conservative antislavery advocates focused on resistance to the expansion of slavery into the territories and to the threat of the slave power, especially the constitutional structures that empowered the slave interest. More ambitious abolitionists advocated for immediate abolition of slavery everywhere and, most ambitiously, for full citizenship for all Black Americans. For the party platform, Chase consistently chose the popular theme of resisting the slave power and its expansionism over the moral claims of enslaved Black people for immediate emancipation and equality.

In the aftermath of the Wilmot Proviso fight, the largest antislavery faction in mainstream politics, the antislavery Whigs like Giddings negotiated with Chase and like-minded Liberty men for an alliance. After a long negotiation, the plans collapsed. Chase, however, was clearly the entry point for some kind of collaboration, as the antislavery politicians in each party started to come loose. The antislavery sentiment in the Democratic Party coalesced around New York's Martin Van Buren. Not an obvious abolitionist hero, Van Buren when president had tried to reassure his slaveholding Democratic colleagues that he was reliable by pressing to return the *Amistad* escapees to their fate in Spain. But when he lost the nomination in 1844 over his stance on Texas, he moved further toward the antislavery cause. Van Buren brought with him his substantial Democratic Party following, called "Barnburners" (as in people who would burn their own barn to get rid of the infestation of slavery), who were unhappy about many things beside the annexation of Texas, especially their being cut off from patronage when their man lost the nomination.

While the political parties dithered, social change moved forward, as it often does, on the back of new media, in this case the explosion of ideological newspapers. In the years since the first Liberty Party convention in 1840, the nation had seen an eruption of cheap niche publications. There were Barnburner papers, Whig antislavery papers, and of course the several Liberty papers that were stirring the pot like mad. Maybe even more than Congress, it was those papers that were the target of Liberty Party maneuvering in Washington. Whenever the handful of lobbyists in Giddings's boardinghouse would raise the rhetorical temperature in Congress, the papers would pick it up and report it around the North, and the movement would expand.

Chase, ever the schemer, wanted to hold off the Liberty Party convention in 1848 until after the two major parties had made their choices, hoping that two enslaver nominees would drive the dissidents to his third party. But the left is never that orderly. The convention would not put off its decision. Sniffing out a taste for compromise among his formerly radical political abolitionists, the real radical Gerrit Smith left the Liberty Party and organized a fringe group, the Liberty League, committed to abolition first and last. Despite displeasing one of their founders, the Liberty Party did choose a more mainstream candidate than its prior nominees, the newly selected New Hampshire senator John P. Hale, who accepted Liberty's nomination on the condition he could reconsider if a better antislavery coalition came forward.

And that's exactly what happened.

First the Whigs cracked. The northern, or "Conscience," Whigs took the position that the Whig Party had to nominate a Wilmot Proviso supporter in 1848 as a condition of their continued party loyalty. The dominant southerners in the Whig Party ignored the demands of their northern brethren and nominated slaveholding Louisiana planter and Mexican War general Zachary Taylor. Northern Whigs were in play. On the other side, anti–Van Buren Democrats seized control of the home state New

York convention, and the Barnburners were conclusively driven out of the Democratic coalition, putting them in play as well. The Democrats nominated Lewis Cass, a Michigan senator perceived as proslavery for his support of letting the territories decide the issue for themselves. Chase was ecstatic. He began to circulate a call to a convention, a "People's Convention," of all "who prefer Freedom to Slavery." On June 21, 1848, his convention issued another call—for a meeting of all "Friends of Freedom" in August. Now the emboldened and alienated dissidents from both major parties were ready. They gathered in Buffalo, united in opposition to the extension of slavery, and tried to see if they could work together.

The Birth of the Free Soil Party

The Friends of Freedom convention was made to test every abolitionist activist's ideology. William Lloyd Garrison thought voting in elections held by the slave nation was immoral, so he would have little interest in a political party convention. The voluntarist Gerrit Smith was very attracted to political action, but he thought that any program short of complete and immediate abolition and racial equality was inadequate. Frederick Douglass would go to any meeting where abolition was advanced. And recent antislavery convert Martin Van Buren thought the Democrats should have nominated him in 1844, despite his opposition to the annexation of Texas.

At least Van Buren got something.

When the dissidents met in Buffalo, they established a weird but practical procedure whereby all three factions of the newly created Free Soil Party—Whigs, Democrats, Liberty—had equal say. Since Liberty had never polled more than a minuscule number of votes, the prominence of the Liberty men at the August convention was quite an acknowledgment of how much they had started to matter.

The ubiquitous Salmon P. Chase wrote the platform. The refugees from the Whig and Democratic Parties lobbied for a platform that stuck strictly to the most conservative position—the non-extension of slavery into any new territories. The platform explicitly included that commitment. But the Liberty delegates to the platform committee succeeded in including language stating that "it is the duty of the Federal Government to relieve itself from all responsibility for the existence or continuance of slavery wherever the government possesses constitutional authority to legislate on that subject, and it is thus responsible for its existence."

No one knows how far this language would have gone. Certainly it was a directive to the federal government to end slavery and the slave trade in the District of Columbia. More boldly, the national government might simply refuse to legislate pursuant to the Fugitive Slave Clause, limiting the prospects for the refugees' recapture once they had made it to the North. Many northern states had enacted Latimer laws, forbidding their officials to pursue the fugitives. Leaving the enslavers to their private remedies alone would have rendered the North much more protective of the fleeing enslaved. And that wasn't the end of the possibilities. As we have seen, Liberty Party legal theorist Alvan Stewart had already proposed that the federal government could outlaw the interstate slave trade, even if it could not outlaw slavery within the southern states, an even more deadly attack on the economic foundations of the slave states. The platform of a newborn third party was hardly about to become the law of the land. But it does reveal how far the political landscape had changed in the decade since a couple of radical legal theorists had suggested that the Constitution might allow for some political action against slavery.

The Liberty faction happily traded their nominee Hale for the Free Soil platform, and Van Buren became the nominee for president of the new Free Soil Party. Former Whig Charles Francis Adams Sr., John Quincy Adams's son, was the candidate for vice president.

As usual, Garrison was not there. He was in Northampton at an infirmary taking the umpteenth cure for his health. His ailment is obscure. His biographer Henry Mayer reported that he lacked "zest." The day he arrived at the cure establishment, he met abolitionist David Lee Child, who was touring the county drumming up support for the Free Soil convention. Although Garrison reports that he and his fellow activists spent the entire visit to the spa "discuss[ing] the affairs of the nation," he spent the rest of the long letter to his wife discussing the details of his water cure. He took all different kinds of baths—half baths, sitz baths, rubdowns with wet sheets; he ate prunes and drank cold water, eschewing milk. Writing to his political ally Weston Chapman, he devoted pages to explaining the various cures and his responses to each and every one, the spraying, the compresses, the spartan diet. After many days' bathing, he noted in passing to his wife, Helen, that he was going to a local "Free Soil" meeting. What he really wanted, he told Helen, was "the day when the great issue with the Slave Power, of the immediate dissolution of the Union will be made by all the free States." He thought that Free Soil would lead to that day, and so he hailed it as the beginning of the end.

As the convention got under way, Garrison's enthusiasm waned. His main attention was on his physical regeneration, as he gave himself up to being "packed, showered, drenched, etc." But learning by telegraph of the business in Buffalo, he advised the Garrisonians to "take great care." The Free Soilers were right that under the Constitution, nothing could be done in the states. But limiting your ambition to keeping slavery out of free soil was a far cry from disunion, which had long been the Boston position. Worse, this moderate platform might tempt people to vote. Garrison took the opportunity to swipe at the competition: Gerrit Smith was so impulsive and unstable, Garrison said, he might even abandon the Liberty Party for the new bunch, which of course Smith did not. They were not radical enough for him.

The Liberator reported on the new party proceedings in a workmanlike way: who was nominated, what the resolutions were. In its first report, the paper was struck by the fact that "several colored men were present as delegates." The editor learned from *The North Star,* the paper reported, that Douglass (not a delegate) had given a major speech. A week later, *The Liberator* published a letter from Samuel May, again suggesting a lukewarm response to the appearance of Free Soil. So nice that so many of our "countrymen" have come so far, the letter read. And it would be churlish to hold back because they haven't gone further. We veterans of course see that there is much further to go, to make the real moral argument. But, May suggested shrewdly, I'll bet the Free Soil Party looks pretty scary to the oppressors on the other side.

It sure did. Even though the Free Soil ticket picked up only ten percent of the vote in the end, the South's response was incendiary. John C. Calhoun wrote, and forty-eight other southern politicians signed, the Southern Address, printed in the *Charleston Courier.* In it, Calhoun exhorted the South to act as one in order to protect its "peculiar institution." If the North proceeds, he argued, as he foresaw, after the Free Soil campaign, they will destroy the South and the union. There will be no place for the

South in such a union. The Southern Address is known mainly for its role in advancing the doomsday scenario that, ten years later, led the South to secede.

Calhoun's Southern Address is a paean to the antislavery activists he had been fighting for a decade and a half, "the Abolitionists," who, since 1835, had been working to "bring about a state of things that will force emancipation on the South. To unite the North in fixed hostility to slavery in the South, and to excite discontent among the slaves with their condition," Calhoun warned.

How did they do it? Calhoun asked. "Societies and newspapers are everywhere established, debating clubs opened, lecturers employed, pamphlets and other publications, pictures and petitions to Congress, resorted to, and directed to that single point, regardless of truth or decency; while the circulation of incendiary publications in the South, the agitation of the subject of abolition in Congress, and the employment of emissaries are relied on to excite discontent among the slaves. This agitation, and the use of these means, have been continued with more or less activity for a series of years, not without doing much towards effecting the object intended." Indeed, he concluded: "The great body of the North is united against our peculiar institution. Many believe it to be sinful, and the residue, with inconsiderable exceptions, believe it to be wrong."

Letter by letter, lecture by lecture, squabbling every step of the way, the dozen white men who gathered in a Black refuge on that stormy night in Boston to found the first modern antislavery society in 1832 along with their altruistic and indefatigable Black brethren and female colleagues— however undervalued and disrespected the Black men and women and the white women were—these people were all doing what Calhoun decried. And they did it in less than twenty years. Calhoun was doubtless overstating the threat. The Free Soil Party had garnered only ten percent of the vote. In several northern states, however, the margin was much greater than the difference between the Whigs and the Democrats.

As Calhoun astutely noticed, "the measures of aggression proposed in the House" might not be adopted in the current session. But "there will be in all probability a considerable increase in the next Congress of the vote in favor of them, and that *it will be largely increased in the next succeeding Congress under the census to be taken next year* [emphasis added]." As the 1850 census revealed, the population of the free states had increased by fifty percent from 1840, while the total (slave and free) population of the slave states grew by less than a third. Since slaves counted for only three-fifths in calculating the states' representation in the House and in the Electoral College, unsurprisingly, the free states' dominance of both went up and the South's went down. The northern demographic numbers were there. It was just a question of political will.

Frederick Douglass Approaches and Retreats

Frederick Douglass was not taking any water cures. He was too busy trying to keep his newspaper from taking on water. Still, he did make time to attend the Free Soil convention in Buffalo in August 1848. Even there, he was clearly holding back. He was called upon to speak—to the customary resounding applause. The Free Soil coalition was hardly a friendly gathering; the formerly Democratic Barnburners included plenty of overt racists. But for Douglass the gathering erupted in cheers. Douglass said he could not give a speech—his throat would not allow it.

On August 21, *The North Star* broke its silence. "This grand movement," Douglass raved, "so long desired and so long maturing has at last assumed a definite and tangible form . . . The members of the Convention . . . were evidently thoroughly imbued with the spirit of freedom. . . . Slavery has rallied its friends . . . under the leadership of [Lewis] Cass and [Zachary] Taylor. The one is a cringing sycophant . . . the other a swearing, swaggering manstealer." In typical Douglass style, he poses the argument against himself. The abolitionists could condemn Free Soil for not doing more, but their platform, of course, Douglass answers, is what the American Anti-Slavery Society adopted at its founding. The Free Soil Party demands that slavery be abolished wherever the United States has the constitutional right to do so. What course ought we, the colored people, Douglass asks, and our friends to pursue? He goes on, "While we are as deeply convinced as ever of the slaveholding character of the American Constitution, and are satisfied that it is the duty of the *free* States to separate from the slaveholding States, and are disposed in no way to abate or modify our testimony on that point, we feel no hesitancy in proclaiming our deep and sincere God-speed to this *free soil* movement."

And yet, and yet.

On September 1, Douglass personally returned to his Garrisonian roots. It is true, he admitted, that the platform of the new party was deeply inadequate. And that the candidate, Martin Van Buren, had at best a checkered past on a range of antislavery issues. But, he concluded, "the course of the colored voters should not be determined by the past transgressions of the members of the *Free Soil* party, but by what they now are, and what they are now aiming to accomplish." As for himself, he confessed, pivoting, he would not vote for any of the candidates. In a pure Garrisonian moment, he castigated the ballot box as a "fiery furnace" in a pro-slavery American Constitution. Then, pivoting a second time, closed by advising any readers who would vote anyway to be sure to avoid the two major parties.

Surely Douglass did not expect the new party to win the presidency. When it lost, taking only ten percent of the votes cast, however, he was disappointed. And in the aftermath of all the effort he asked the right question: "What good has the Free Soil Movement done?" Very little, he concluded. After the party lost, it did not leave a legacy. It did not send lecturers around the country. It founded no societies. Its politicians merely tried to make deals with the two major parties. Worse, the party did harm. It sucked resources from the authentic Liberty Party and left the public confused with its half measures. But significantly, Douglass was not ready to fall back to Garrisonism either. Don't mistake this criticism, he said, for a denunciation of politics. Some political party is inevitably going to arise in the wake of antislavery.

The New Territory Provokes the Fight

Douglass was prescient. Free Soil could do some damage to the slave-driven two-party system. Even after the paltry showing, the antislavery faction in Congress was big enough that the House of Representatives could not pick a leader. Just thirteen years after Congress passed the gag rule forbidding antislavery petitions even to cross its threshold, nine Free Soil representatives stopped the election of a Speaker of the House. The indefatigable Joshua Reed Giddings saw the problem clearly: "confusion," he wrote to his wife, in the major parties' ranks. The Speakership mattered in part because the Speaker had unreviewable power to make committee assignments, and the fate of the massive lands gained in the Mexican War was still very much on the table. Would some version of the Wilmot Proviso pass in the new Congress? Or would each northern congressman be forced to vote for or against and then be answerable to his district? Much depended upon who chaired the committees.

The House of Representatives went through sixty-three votes over three weeks. Every time the Free Soil caucus seemed to support a candidate from either side, the southerners in that party immediately abandoned him. In the 1849 Congress, it was impossible to satisfy a major party. Finally the two parties got together and voted, by a coalition of some members from each side, that choosing a Speaker no longer needed a majority vote of the House. Whoever got the most votes got the job. And thus Democrat and slaveholder Howell Cobb became a minority Speaker of the House of Representatives.

Gold was discovered at Sutter's Mill, and California adopted a free state constitution. The legislature that couldn't pick a leader was about to confront the hottest issue in American politics again. A free state from the territory gained from Mexico in the war wanted in. Would enslavement be extended into the territory won from Mexico, or would the South be left to its declining demographic fate?

21

(1848–1850)

The Private Lives of Public Activists

As DOUGLASS FORESAW, JUST AS THE BATTLE over the extension of slavery heated up, Free Soil unraveled. Once the scent of political power wafted across the movement, compromise was the order of the day. The faithful Free Soil Ohio congressman Joshua Reed Giddings took the first hit. In 1849, because of a bizarre set of unrelated disputes, the canny Free Soil forces held the balance of power between the evenly divided Whigs and Democrats in the Ohio state legislature. The prize for siding with one side or the other was that the state legislature had the power to appoint Ohio's United States senator. While Giddings stayed nobly in Washington, hoping the Free Soil representatives back home would elevate him, former Democrat and wheeler-dealer Salmon P. Chase was working the halls in Ohio. He wooed away a couple of Free Soil reps back to the Democrats, and in exchange they put him in the U.S. Senate. He was the second abolitionist senator, and number one, New Hampshire's John P. Hale, was exultant.

But Chase's gambit split the Ohio Free Soil Party right down the middle and drove the furious Whig Free Soilers back to the mother ship. Giddings tried his best to hold the idealistic alliance together, but to no avail. Free Soilers everywhere started seeking out their former major party partners to make deals for public office. Poor Giddings. When the second Ohio Senate seat came open, the Free Soilers made a "Chase deal" with the Whigs this time and sent another mainstream politician to Washington.

With the forces of antislavery looking for a way back to their ancestral parties, the wily old master Henry Clay saw an opportunity. If he could put together a package of legislation to deal with the Mexican-American

War lands, he might get it passed piecemeal by coalitions of neutrals with the northern interest for some proposals and coalitions of neutrals with the slave faction for others. A compromise. The Compromise of 1850, as it is known.

The Contessa Leaves for the Old World

Antislavery was facing its biggest challenge and opportunity since 1820. And yet it seemed as if the three movement leaders were all turned inward.

Maria Weston Chapman was no longer in the country. In the summer of 1848, just as she sent her last letter berating Frederick Douglass for his effrontery, she gathered her three children and sister Caroline and moved to Paris.

By 1848 she was a wealthy widow. Although no one dealing with her in the movement would have known it from her public presence, her husband, shipping magnate Henry Grafton Chapman, had died of tuberculosis six years before, in 1842. On his deathbed, the story has it, he left her "to the Cause." She did not miss a beat. Self-righteous, energetic, reliable, and utterly confident, she continued editing the *National Anti-Slavery Standard* newspaper, stepping in for Garrison at *The Liberator* during his many absences, financing the movement with her fairs, and managing the Boston group with a combination of tea and correspondence.

In 1846 and 1847, however, her late husband's parents died, and she inherited a family fortune. At the same time her son, Henry Jr., had become a terrible nuisance. Bad boys seem to have run in the Weston family, and Maria's sisters, still managing her children for her, had to pull him out of school in Weymouth. Without much explanation, Weston Chapman decided to take a European tour — with the family. She would see if a stint at the famous Heidelberg University would set her troublesome fifteen-year-old son on a better path.

The Weston Chapman family also enjoyed getting away from the social stigma attached to abolition in America to the more welcoming precincts of European society. Rather than going to London, where she had spent formative years in her uncle's care, the wealthy and sociable Weston Chapman household — Maria, children, various sisters — settled in Paris.

Garrison professed himself bereft. What, he asked his dear friend Elizabeth Pease, would the movement do without the "indefatigable" Maria Weston Chapman? "How the cause will get along without her immediate presence here I cannot tell," he mourned. When bidding her farewell, he confessed he was unable to figure out how to reconcile himself to her departure, well considered though he acknowledged it was. I know there is no amount of water in the Atlantic, he wrote hopefully, to separate your philanthropy from the cause you have labored in for so long. In classic Garrison fashion, he could not manage to pay her a farewell call, however. He was just so busy getting ready to go to Northampton for his water cure.

Weston Chapman stayed away for seven years. She solicited her affluent French friends to send items for the antislavery bazaars, and the Weston Chapman residence in Paris was still a center for foreign antislavery activism. But she was gone. By the time she returned in 1855, chasing the exasperating Henry, whom she had sent home to break up an unsuitable relationship, the American landscape had changed irreversibly. The road to the Civil War was clear, and a newborn Republican Party was on the rise. She later moved to New York to be where her errant son was working in the family business. She raised more money for Garrison's branch when she returned, but she was never at the heart of the action again.

Frederick Douglass Finds Help but at a Cost

Douglass had no such option. Although it is impossible to know if he would have stayed in London in 1847 had Anna Douglass been able to thrive abroad, it is difficult to imagine him living, in the critical years, thousands of miles away from the struggle.

Since Douglass could not flee to the loving community of supporters he had left behind in London, his most ardent admirers—Julia Griffiths and her sister Eliza—came to him instead. On May 2, 1849, he walked into Isaac Post's pharmacy in Rochester fresh off the train from New York. I have brought my "English friend," he told his loyal supporter Post. Come and meet her at my house today. Post surely knew who the friend was; Douglass had written to him weeks before while impatiently awaiting Griffiths's arrival in New York. Nonetheless, Post's discomfort at the social situation is palpable. When he got to the Douglass house, he found

Julia Griffiths, bonnet still on, organizing the distribution of presents from Europe for the Douglass children. When she looked up at last, he says, strangely, he realized she was white. Douglass came in and the two began chattering away about their writings with such fervor that Post, seeing no tea table being set, cut the visit short and went home.

Griffiths didn't materialize out of thin air. Douglass had written her at least one sad and worried letter about the state of *The North Star*. As anyone reading the paper would have seen, it had little advertising and not remotely enough subscribers to pay the cost of producing it. Douglass was especially angered and saddened by the failure of Black supporters. Worse, the white subscribers were mostly in places like the U.K., where sending the paper was expensive. Douglass mortgaged his own home to try to keep the paper afloat. The Posts, whose western New York Anti-Slavery Society was donating to help the paper, threatened to pull their support unless Douglass would submit to a financial manager. They had stood by and let him mortgage his only property, and now they wanted to manage the paper. Douglass was furious.

Douglass also suspected that he was caught between the two abolition factions — too political for the nonresistant Garrisonians and not political enough for the Liberty wing. Although the archives are full of letters from the Boston circle criticizing Douglass in the harshest terms, in these early years, Garrison and *The Liberator* were exquisitely discreet. *The Liberator* reprinted some of Douglass's most aggressive articles, most notably his long, anguished "letter" to his former enslaver Hugh Auld. Garrison re-iterated Douglass's pleas for subscriptions, as a sign that "colored people" could successfully run such an enterprise, and noted the first anniversary of the paper's maiden edition in January of 1849.

The Weston sisters, however, were not so disciplined. Douglass came to Boston to give one of his very good speeches, Anne wrote to Maria in June 1849. But he was "very cool to us," although "we behaved very civilly and easily," Anne self-reported her own perfect behavior, "not going out of our way or saying anything about him. Miss Griffiths, the woman who made mischief of your letter to Mary Howitt," she noted, "is travelling in this country." Griffiths was in fact with Douglass on his speaking trip to the Boston area, in a group with Amy Post and Julia's sister Eliza (who was, Anne observed gratuitously, a very plain woman).

Things did not remain civil. In a letter to Anne Weston a few months later, in April 1850, sister Debora related that she had learned the editor of *The North Star* was sending copies of the paper to Weston Chapman (actually to the Boston Anti-Slavery office). "Stop them at once!" Anne ordered the hapless office administrator who had delivered the unwelcome news. Of course, she added, "do it as politely as you can." Learning later that the issues were still coming, Debora tried to double down on stopping them without revealing it was the Westons who were behind the decision.

The unsolicited copies of *The North Star* that so offended the Weston sisters were part of Griffiths's program for the paper to offer gift subscriptions to drum up interest. Whether the Garrisonians liked it or not, Griffiths was there to stay. After the Griffiths sisters finished sightseeing around the United States, they moved into the Douglass house and began to manage Douglass's affairs. Julia Griffiths, who had come from the British abolition world of people like the Richardsons and the British and Foreign Anti-Slavery Society, had no history with the Boston clique and no inclination to depend on it for help. First, she and her sister assumed Douglass's mortgage. Then she started campaigning for more subscriptions for *The North Star*. According to Douglass, she doubled the paper's readership, a serious step toward financial solvency.

Soon Douglass was seen everywhere with a Griffiths sister on either arm. White society responded predictably. The week the Griffiths arrived in New York from London, their hotel refused to seat them in the dining room with Douglass. The passengers on the riverboat taking them to Rochester came close to a riot when the three tried to have lunch together. The management soon appeared and physically threw Douglass out. When the sisters accompanied Douglass to the annual Anti-Slavery Society meeting in New York City in 1850, the trio made the mistake of walking around the fashionable Battery together while waiting for a boat trip, and a mob of thugs attacked them, managing to punch Douglass in the face before the three could get to the shelter of the vessel.

This was old news to Douglass. He had lived as a Black man in racist America since birth, since his flight to free soil, and even since he had bought his freedom. As usual, Douglass turned his life into art. He wrote movingly about his experience being seen with white women in fancy neighborhoods as challenging his inequality rather than his skin color. After all, he noted, Black men are intimately paired with white women when they drive their carriages down the streets of New York. What could be causing the commotion? It must be his "impudence," he wrote, asserting that he was their equal.

The worst part was that the anger and disapproval were not confined to the in-the-open oppressors. Almost immediately after the Griffiths sisters appeared in 1849, Boston abolitionist and writer Caroline Healey Dall—an avid Douglass fan and supporter—writing in her journal, asked herself about "this woman," Julia. "Her manner to Douglass is peculiar," Douglass's supporter mused. "His to her still more so." Things got worse when, within a year after their arrival in the Douglass household, Eliza Griffiths fell in love with and married John Dick, Douglass's Scottish printer. The newlyweds moved to Philadelphia, leaving Julia boarding alone in Douglass's house and office.

The mail routes buzzed with speculation. Within a month of the wedding, Douglass's first publisher, the formerly disaffected Garrisonian William Cooper Nell, an erratic soul who had since left Douglass and returned to the Boston fold, wrote to Amy Post: Would Julia now follow in her sister's footsteps and take a husband of her own, Nell wondered. An activist in faraway Ohio wrote to Amy Post in 1850 asking where Julia was now that Eliza was married. Finally, by late 1851, Douglass got an earful from his close associate, publisher Samuel D. Porter, who, with his wife, was one of the most dedicated abolitionists in the Rochester community. Although Porter's letter is missing, we know from Douglass's reply that Porter told of "scandalous reports implicating" Douglass and Julia Griffiths circulating all over Rochester.

In keeping with his indefatigable lifelong campaign to be treated as an individual and equal human person, Douglass's first reaction was that he had "individual . . . rights" and was not disposed to bow to someone else's claims on his behavior. Similarly, Julia Griffiths was a "free woman" with "free will" and could live where she pleased.

Anyway, Douglass concluded, he was not going to answer anonymous accusations. When someone showed the courage to come forward and own the charges of impropriety, he would dignify them with an answer. Douglass would soon get an open accusation. His life would be altered forever by it.

Garrison Stays the Course

In the years while Weston Chapman and Douglass were reorganizing their personal lives, Garrison suffered a genuine tragedy. The second of his seven children, beloved six-year-old son Charlie, died. Juvenile mortality in 1849 was common. Still, the death of the Garrisons' "beautiful, affectionate" boy was a terrible loss.

The Garrisons'—and *The Liberator*'s—money troubles continued to plague them as well. But they were never in peril like Douglass was. A publishing group was responsible for *The Liberator*, with Garrison as an employee. When subscriptions did not cover the costs, the business fell behind in paying Garrison's salary, which was a difficult burden on him to be sure. The sad, miserable family came back from Garrison's water cure to the nasty Boston boardinghouse where they could barely afford to live.

But while the upstate New Yorkers left Douglass mostly to his own devices, Garrison's backers had already planned a rescue. Garrison's board organized to set up the company as a printing enterprise under its accomplished printer James Yerrinton, who could then use *The Liberator*'s printing press for other work, much the way Richard Webb did in Dublin and other Boston printers had done for decades. To be fair, the leaders of the Western New York Anti-Slavery Society had started to organize a rescue for *The North Star* too, but Douglass would not hear of submitting his financial records or his decisions to anyone's supervision. Only Julia Griffiths managed to slip into that role with Douglass. Garrison's somewhat erratic attention to business, by contrast, had the advantage of allowing others to take some control and to help him, and his Boston backers did just that.

Francis Jackson, a real estate entrepreneur, found a house for the Garrisons to rent in a new block of buildings he was putting up, and the group started assembling a small trust fund for Garrison's personal support. Here again by contrast, it was Julia Griffiths and her sister who took on the burden of rescuing Douglass's family home for him by assuming his mortgage. There is no evidence that anyone in the abolition community in Rochester ever said a word about helping him with his mortgage as he tried to keep *The North Star* afloat.

22

(1848–1850)

Compromise Makes Conflict Worse

IN 1848, THE COALITION FREE SOIL PARTY had won ten percent of the ballots cast for president, and the Whig candidate, plantation owner Zachary Taylor, went to the White House.

Modern abolition was not even two decades old. As slave power fire-brand John C. Calhoun foresaw in the 1850 census, if northern antislavery ever realized its political power, the whole wicked system would collapse. Demography was destiny.

But it was a big "if." Free Soil had a limited agenda—stopping the spread of slavery while mostly leaving the existing slave states alone. When the Free Soil campaign ended in 1848, Garrison was harshly critical of the venture as having sold out and failed anyway. Since Garrison believed political action was doomed, he at least had the satisfaction of having been prophetic. In his rejection of any middle ground, Garrison strangely re-sembled his chief adversary, Gerrit Smith. Smith, the loudest voice for po-litical action, contended that the only valid political position was complete and immediate abolition everywhere. Rather than reject politics, Smith was irreversibly committed to ever more perfect political vehicles, moving from the Liberty Party when it joined the Free Soil alliance to the Liberty League. When the League failed, he started the aptly named Radical Ab-olition Party.

Garrison and Smith were both too dogmatic to take full advantage of the political opportunity that unfolded in the next few years. But Doug-lass would, he pledged, "speak in any meeting where freedom of speech is allowed and I may do anything toward exposing the bloody system of slavery."

Fruits of the Election Returns

As we have seen, after 1848 the status of slavery could not be cordoned off from politics. California, taken from Mexico, was waiting at the door of Congress for entry as a free state. The northern states had passed a raft of Latimer laws and were no longer willing to have their law enforcement serve at the behest of some planter who wanted to catch or recapture a fugitive. The cadre of antislavery representatives had demonstrated their willingness to disrupt the people's house.

Henry Clay thought he could finesse the issue of slavery and the treatment of the new territory. His proposals would admit California and abolish the slave trade in the District of Columbia for the northern faction. It would leave the rest of the Mexican territory up to local control. For the South, he offered a rigorous, federally enforced Fugitive Slave law that gave Black people in the North essentially no defense against capture and enslavement if an enslaver, real or fraudulent, decided to pursue them.

Every piece of legislation he proposed involved a rejection of the extreme positions each side had taken, off and on, since the Missouri Compromise. First, California. Massachusetts's Timothy Fuller had contended in 1819 that Congress should not allow slavery in any new state, because the Constitution explicitly guarantees to the states a "republican form of government." On the other side, southern Congressmen had laid down the argument that slaves were property, protected by the constitutional guarantees against deprivation of property without due process of law. So there could be no such thing as a free state — in Missouri or anywhere else. The 1820 Congress ducked the debate and admitted slave Missouri with the free state of Maine, a process later called pairing. Now, thirty years later, Clay proposed to duck again. California would join the union free.

If California was admitted, as Clay proposed, that still left Congress with the rest of the huge lands acquired from Mexico, just as the 1820 Congress had to assign the rest of the Louisiana Purchase to one or the other of the contending sides. In the run-up to the Missouri Compromise and after, proslavery forces had intermittently argued that Congress did not have the power to prohibit or abolish slavery in the territories. The territories, they argued, belonged to all the people, and the federal government could not exclude anyone with his lawful property from its own territorial possessions. (By implication, this position also included the District of Columbia.) Now Clay proposed a solution that was more proslavery than the Missouri Compromise. The rest of the Mexican territories would be consigned to a kind of limbo without any pro- or antislavery proviso; they'd be decided by the local people settling them. He did, however, offer the North one thing: abolishing not slavery but the unseemly slave trade in Washington, D.C.

Moving the slave auctions to nearby Virginia wasn't such a sacrifice to the southerners. It was the legal theory they feared. Such an act implied that the common territories, such as the lands taken from Mexico and the District of Columbia, were not, constitutionally, the property of all states in common, immune from federal laws against slavery. Who knew what an aroused abolitionist movement, turned away from Garrison and toward politics, might do?

But Clay offered the southerners a weapon aimed right at the heart of the North and its abolitionists: a new, stunningly aggressive Fugitive Slave Act to force the North to participate in returning the runaways. It was a dangerous move. Fugitive slaves were always the stress point in the uneasy legal agreement after the Missouri debate to leave the free states free and slave states to slavery. The Supreme Court had ruled in 1842 in *Prigg* that the North had sold its birthright to protect the slaves running from the South in exchange for the union in 1789. In the years after *Prigg*, northern states pushed back as hard as they could, enacting the Latimer laws to withhold their support from returning the fugitives.

Congress, which was still mostly Whig or Democrat, passed Clay's legislation piecemeal. Whigs from the upper South voted with the North to pass the law admitting California as a freestanding law. Antislavery Democrats from the North joined their southern Democratic brethren to get the measures for the South. Some northerners actually left the chamber to avoid having to commit when the Fugitive Slave Act was being considered. But it still got enough votes to became law.

The suite of legislation is called the Compromise of 1850. It was the most potent act to date to force the North to live out the worst aspects of the document it had signed in 1789 to get the union in the first place. The two-party proslavery system just barely held.

Across the abolitionist movement, the Compromise of 1850 was received as a wrenching defeat, a victory for slavery. Almost immediately it became clear how Pyrrhic the enslavers' victory was. Thomas Jefferson had called the 1820 Missouri debate the "death knell of the Union." He was not wrong, just thirty years premature.

The Cost of Compromise

Clay's master plan failed on a strategic level because it demonstrated the power of politics when it came to the future of abolition, a message the abolitionists were bound to pick up. Abandoning constitutional restraint, the badly divided Congress had legislated on every aspect of the peculiar institution. Although the substance of the laws was mostly horrific, confirming that Congress could govern the issue also confirmed that, going forward, politics was the field of battle for abolition.

Clay's plan was a tactical failure too. It was bound—in a mechanism Garrison had always understood—to mobilize the force of the printing press. For some years leading up to 1850, independent national newspapers had sprung up, and after Horace Greeley went to New York to start the *Tribune*, abolition had indeed gone mainstream. By 1850 there was also the power of the telegraph. Beginning in 1844, the telegraph had started carrying the news at the speed of electricity. In 1846, private investors ran a telegraph line from Washington to New York. After that, in a New York minute, news from Congress flashed all over the country, to the web of newspapers serving the Washington denizens' constituents back home —across the populous North.

Thanks to political abolition, there were eloquent spokesmen for abolition and antislavery in Congress: William Seward, Samuel P. Chase, John P. Hale, the great Joshua Reed Giddings. So when the lions of the Congress—Clay, Webster, Calhoun—began debating the bills constituting the Compromise of 1850, they produced an instantaneous national teach-in over the legality and morality of slavery. Abolition, which always held the moral and rhetorical high ground, began to run on the enriched fuel of telegraphy.

The high point of the campaign to change public opinion had to be New York abolitionist Senator William Seward's speech of March 11, 1850. Although he started out on a somewhat technical point—was it fair to ask free California to wait for the stability of statehood—he soon moved to the abolitionists' moral redoubt. Conscript Northerners into helping the South chase its fleeing slaves? "Has any government," Seward asked, "ever succeeded in changing the moral convictions of its subjects by force?" He demanded the enslavers stop telling the North to violate its morality for the Constitution. "There is a higher law than the Constitution," Seward concluded, "which regulates our authority over the domain."

The higher law argument stood in direct opposition to the South's legal claims. Starting with *Somerset v. Stewart* in 1772, slavery's essential evil always tainted the slaveholders' appeal to positive law. Even if white superiority exists, Seward continued in another stemwinding speech in July, it would still not justify such "oppression": "Slavery and freedom are conflicting systems brought together by the union of the States, not neutralized, nor even harmonized. Their antagonism is radical and therefore perpetual." How long would such arguments be confined to the contemporary squabbling over the margins—Washington, D.C., the territories—before it moved to the question of enslavement everywhere?

With this ringing abolition oration in the United States Senate, the telegraph and the steam printing press swung into action. Within three weeks, the Tappan brothers' vaunted pamphlet machine took up the cause, and more than one hundred thousand pamphlet copies of Seward's speech were distributed, with a roughly equal number reprinted in newspapers throughout the country. Garrison devoted nearly an entire page of the four-page edition of the July *Liberator* to reproducing Seward's text. When there was a moral battle to be fought, he would always be on the front lines.

The editor of the *Green-Mountain Freeman* reveled in the pleasure the old "Liberty Men" must be taking in their newfound prominence on the floor of Congress. Once derided, the paper recalled, for a "'night of years' through which they almost hopelessly labored to awaken the public mind to a sense of the wrong of slavery . . . and behold a host coming forward to proclaim the doctrines they then preached unheeded and unheard . . . Why should they not feel proud of what they have done?"

The northern press spread the word of the immorality of slavery. Then the Fugitive Slave Law rubbed the northerners' noses in it. The law, presented at first as merely a shoring up of the existing mechanisms of capture and return, was the charter of a machine of legal oppression unprecedented in American history. Any slaveholder or hunter could arrest an accused fugitive, bring the captive before any federal judge, and get an order of return. Judges being the busy men they were, the law called upon the formerly small staff of informal "commissioners" working for the judge to create a corps of informal decision makers to seal each fugitive's fate. (Commissioners got ten dollars for each person renditioned to the South but only five dollars if they set someone free.) No rights—habeas corpus, jury trial—applied to the accused Black defendants. The states having proved themselves reluctant to chase the southerners' slaves, the federal government would do it itself. In addition, the state Latimer laws provoked the southern congressmen to the self-destructive strategy of conscripting their northern countrymen into the hunt. Under the law, the commissioners could call northern bystanders to assist in capturing a fugitive. Anyone helping the fugitive would be fined a thousand dollars.

The Fugitive Slave Drama Becomes Actual Theater

On June 5, 1851, eight months after the passage of the Fugitive Slave Law, the magazine *The National Era* published episode one of Harriet Beecher Stowe's novel *Uncle Tom's Cabin*. A month later, readers met the fugitive slave Eliza and her baby boy scrambling off the last ice floe in the Ohio River from slave Kentucky to free Ohio. A kind neighbor she knew from her slave days helps her up the bank on the Ohio side. "There's nowhar I can take ye," he tells her, but he directs her to a house where she might hope for help. Her enslaver won't be happy, he muses, as she disappears into the distance, but "I don't see no kind of 'casion for me to be hunter and catcher for other folks, neither." With each installment, the ranks of readers swelled. Soon the book was made into a play. Productions of *Uncle Tom's Cabin* proliferated across the North.

The stories were not limited to fiction. Within weeks of the Fugitive Slave Act's passage in September 1850, the first victim caught, one James Hamlet of Brooklyn, was taken before a "commissioner" and sent back to Baltimore. When his co-religionists at the A.M.E. Church bought his freedom, a crowd of thousands gathered to greet him. But that was nothing compared to what transpired in Boston.

Just a few months after Hamlet's capture, slave catchers grabbed a fu-

Black slave rescuer Lewis Hayden. *Courtesy of the New York Public Library.*

gitive slave, Shadrach Minkins, a couple of years out of Virginia, at his job in Boston. Minkins was represented by one of the first Black lawyers in American history, Robert Morris, and white abolitionist Boston lawyers, including Little Med's lawyer, Ellis Gray Loring. Stymied everywhere by the sweeping language of the Fugitive Slave Act, the best the lawyers could do was get a continuance. While Minkins was in the courthouse, however, a rescue squad led by another Black fugitive, Lewis Hayden, stormed in and hustled him out to a waiting, mostly Black crowd. Within weeks he was in Canada. The slave rendition machine had to content itself with pursuing the rescuers, including Lewis Hayden and the white abolitionists who were supposed to be guarding Minkins. None of the actions against the rescuers succeeded, but the victories were on simple matters of fact or jury refusal to convict. The Fugitive Slave Act was untouched.

Southerners, bent on bringing abolitionists to heel, foolishly sought more confrontation on the streets of Boston. One of the next victims of their zeal, Georgia fugitive Thomas Sims, made the mistake of contacting his free Black wife in Savannah. His owner, all too willing to make an example of him, sent slave catchers to the white-hot center of abolition sentiment to execute a Georgia warrant. The usual lawyers made the usual appeal to state justice Shaw and met with an order refusing to interfere in federal proceedings. After fifteen long years of wrestling with his conscience, Shaw laid out the rotten bargain his state and the rest of the North had made. Slavery, he wrote, was so terrible that nothing could possibly justify it other than a sovereign's positive law. You did it, he said, when you sold your soul to the South to get a union under the Constitution. There would never have been a union if slaves could flee to free soil. Interestingly, Shaw compared the northern and southern states to two foreign countries living under international law. Some union.

Sims's abolitionist lawyers then tried Alvan Stewart's move, invoking the pure language of the Constitution against the enslavers. If the Constitution applies to slaves, then slavery law must live by the Constitution. Sims didn't have a lawyer when the Georgia court issued the warrant. The commissioners were not neutral, and anyway they were illegal judges because not constitutionally protected with life tenure by Article III, which created the federal judicial branch. So Sims didn't get due process, and therefore the whole charge was unconstitutional. Lemuel Shaw's decision in *Sims* neatly sidesteps all these issues. Renditioning a slave isn't a full judicial act; it's just a teensy ministerial act that low-level federal employees can take care of. As to Sims's absence when the warrant was issued, Shaw argued, he ran away, so his absence was his own fault. The court argued that it was not deciding his status but merely sending him to Georgia to decide his fate, just as America would extradite a foreigner if it had a treaty with the foreigner's home country. And if you don't like the procedures Georgia uses, well, that's slavery. Sims was dragged back to Georgia. He finally found his freedom, escaping during the Civil War.

Garrison did a robust I-told-you-so: the Constitution that justified the

Fugitive Slave Act was a slave document, and free people should withdraw from the union it made. He had believed this since the hated Supreme Court decision in *Prigg v. Pennsylvania* in 1842. "We owe it," Garrison's Massachusetts Anti-Slavery Society resolved at its 1851 convention, "as a sacred duty to God and man to seek the dissolution of a Union that in its very nature is bound to extend equal protection to the slaveholders and the friends of freedom."

Even Garrison could not short-circuit the argument. If the Constitution shut the door to any restraints on slavery, political action was useless, and only extreme measures like Garrison's disunion were left. But if the Constitution empowered the national government to act against slavery, or even if it just allowed the states to take such measures, political action was a reasonable strategy. With new supporters flocking to abolition every day courtesy of the Pyrrhic victory of the Compromise of 1850, the central question of the movement—politics or no politics—was the most important matter the movement had to decide.

23

(1850–1853)

Douglass Recruits the Constitution

As FREDERICK DOUGLASS, AIDED BY THE ENERGETIC Julia Griffiths, was trying to keep *The North Star* afloat the events of the 1850s opened the crucial last phase of the movement. From the moment he left Massachusetts in 1849, a chorus of voices rose to turn Douglass away from Garrisonian nonresistance to a political activist position. One of his neighbors in Rochester, a "C. H. Chase," opened the campaign, challenging Douglass to a debate over whether the Constitution was antislavery in all of its provisions.

Douglass was hardly a blank slate. By 1849 he'd been out of slavery for a decade, and active in the movement for eight years. Even when a loyal follower of Garrison and his faction, Douglass had revealed a deeper loyalty: to "do anything toward exposing the bloody system of slavery."

Fortunately for Douglass's relationship with the Boston wing, Garrison's ultraism had always left some wiggle room. Garrison was probably most rigid about his opposition to physical resistance to slavery. But as to disunion and the futility of political action under the Constitution, Garrison had not started out as a complete nonresistant. He had supported the early petitions and made an exception to his nonrecognition of slavery when it was Douglass who wanted to buy his freedom. Fighting in the state legislature for the Latimer laws, to prohibit Massachusetts public servants from assisting slave catchers, the New England abolitionists were engaging in political action to exploit the little loophole that Justice Story had left in *Prigg*. It is possible to trace Garrison's increasing insistence that the Constitution shut down politics to *Prigg* and the judiciary's ensuing increasingly extreme reading of the document, which left the abolitionists less and less room for meaningful political action.

Competing for Douglass's Allegiance

Douglass answered C. H. Chase very briefly: "On a close examination of the Constitution, I am satisfied that if strictly 'construed according to its reading,' it is not a pro-slavery instrument."

As soon as Douglass's exchange with Chase appeared in *The North Star*, he heard from Gerrit Smith. Douglass was a supporter worth winning for the political faction. "With you and your paper on the right side," Smith wrote to Douglass, "something more can be done for Liberty than has been done."

You admitted in your recent letters in *The North Star* that the Constitution is capable of an antislavery interpretation, Smith wrote. If that is true, then the rest follows naturally. Why would anyone with abolition in mind choose to read the Constitution as a slaveholder would? Let's figure this out. Come on over to my house, he concluded, and spend some time with me.

Douglass published Smith's letter in *The North Star*, which elicited a somewhat unhappy reaction from the writer. "It would have been written more carefully if I supposed you would print it," he said. But unless Douglass could convince Smith that, under the Constitution, the federal government lacked the power to affect slavery, Smith concluded, then Douglass had to admit that he could vote in federal elections. Politics would matter.

Smith was overreaching. What Douglass had said was that the *text* of the Constitution, standing alone without reference to the intention of the Framers, was not proslavery. Douglass then wrote a long, very careful essay on the subject. His statement "has excited some interest," he noted. "Each class of opinion and feeling is represented in the letters" from both sides that he placed in the issue of *The North Star*. "Of one thing . . . we can assure our readers," he continued: "that we bring to the consideration of this subject no partisan feelings, nor the slightest wish to make ourselves consistent with the creed of either." Since, as Smith's first letter reflects, Douglass's and *The North Star*'s endorsement were exceedingly valuable to the political movement, his refusal to swear loyalty to either the Garrison or the Gerrit Smith creed as he worked it through was portentous.

He first rejected the higher law argument. The Constitution is "human," he reasoned, "and must be explained in the light of those maxims and principles which human beings have laid down." Not coming from heaven, where there is no slavery, but rather from a land where slavery already existed, "we find no difficulty in ascertaining its meaning in all the parts which we allege to relate to slavery . . . [I]t was made in view of the existence of slavery, and in a manner well calculated to aid and strengthen that heaven-daring crime." Legal abolitionist thinkers like Lysander Spooner, Douglass noted, offer readings that deny the slave orientation of the document. But Douglass then recited the many places where the Constitution talks about the conditions of slavery—ending the international trade, returning fleeing persons. "We might just here drop the pen," he concluded, but out of respect for the contending parties, he declared himself "prepared to hear all sides and to give the arguments of our opponents a candid consideration." As late as January 1850, however, Douglass still forcefully defended the full Garrisonian position on the proslavery Constitution, including in a debate over the subject with Gerrit Smith.

Smith was undeterred. He went right back to his original position: the Constitution can be interpreted on its face. That being the case, he did not need to refer to the context of enslavement and North-South bargaining to understand it. Instead, Smith wrote a long essay-letter for *The North Star,* reiterating the arguments for an antislavery Constitution. It must be read on its face without reference to the Founders' proslavery intentions, and if that fails, if the Constitution is proslavery, it must be abandoned. Douglass's answer is revealing. He rejects all of Smith's arguments save one, that the Constitution must be read on its face. "Such rules [of interpretation] may exist," Douglass responded, "but we have not yet seen them." The back-and-forth about this crucial issue of constitutional meaning, carried on in public view in the pages of *The North Star,* is detailed, painstaking, and sophisticated on both sides. It is therefore the more surprising that the Garrisonians would later blame Gerrit Smith for turning Douglass's head.

In truth, Smith did deploy every social asset in establishing a relationship with the most powerful Black man in America. Come on out to Peterboro, he wrote Douglass, before they had ever met in person, and spend a week at the house talking constitutional theory. Gerrit's wife, Nancy, made friends with Anna Douglass through their shared love of gardening. When Smith heard of the attack on Douglass and Julia Griffiths in New York in 1850, he wrote Douglass an outraged letter. It was a reflection of Smith's clear understanding of Douglass that he comforted his "Outraged and Afflicted Brother" by telling him he suffered because he presumed "to demean [himself] as a man . . . a shining mark that cannot escape the notice . . . of a people educated to despise and hate the colored race." And he supported *The North Star* in the most important way, asking in the middle of their debates over law and politics if the paper was "well supported." Douglass's account books are full of the records of Smith's financial backing.

But long before he ever laid eyes on Gerrit Smith, or received a penny from him, Douglass had warned Weston Chapman and all the Garrisonians that he would do anything he thought would advance the goal of abolition. In pondering the debate about the Constitution and slavery from this vantage point in 1850, Douglass asked, "Who is right in this contest?" and could not find an answer. "So far as the Constitution is concerned," he wrote, "all are wrong."

Could the Races Ever Be Brought Together?

Salmon P. Chase and the Free Soilers thought they had found solid ground in the constitutional argument that slavery was protected only in the slave states. This position on the legal question allowed political animals like Chase, the former Whig who had finagled a Senate seat as the parties unraveled, to pursue political action in Congress to limit slavery in the territories and everywhere else outside the South. Chase did just that, of course, trying to pass the Wilmot Proviso and fighting the Compromise of 1850. Douglass could have settled on the Chase position; he had, after all, briefly supported Free Soil in 1848, and Chase's position was at least not directly in conflict with the proslavery history of the Constitution. But Douglass understood all too well that the limited goals of Free Soil politics were not the same as the abolition of slavery in the slave states and equality for Black Americans everywhere.

Douglass cultivated Senator Chase, just as he had wished the Free Soil Party Godspeed, as better than the alternatives. As Douglass was casting about for supporters of *The North Star*, he got a letter from the senator. Chase opened by donating a "mite" to the paper. Then he moved on to his real agenda: asking Douglass if he thought Black people weren't physically more suited to live somewhere else. Chase pledged he had been "utterly opposed to any discrimination," but still, he looked forward to the day when the races were again separated, perhaps by America's "Black Race" moving to the West Indies and South America.

Funniest thing, Douglass replied to the insulting proposal. "On the subject on which you have done me the honor to ask my views, I have taken the liberty to enclose two articles from my pen originally published in my paper, the *North Star*." This Black man, who had risen to be a writer of articles and the editor of his own paper, proposed that "the black man's constitution as readily adapts itself to one climate as another." Douglass thought the issues affecting Black people's destiny were "political" and "moral," not climatological. And he thought the moral and political prospects for their destiny had never been more favorable than they were that day in 1850.

Chase and the rest of the politicos' half-baked thinking about justice for Douglass's "Black Race" was never going to satisfy Douglass. If it was a slave Constitution, nothing would do but to face it head-on, either by leaving the union, as Garrison implied, or by subjecting the deal to a higher law, as Seward said. After the abolitionists' so-called allies in Congress voted for or absented themselves from passage of the Compromise of 1850 and its murderous Fugitive Slave Act, there was no alternative but to face the whole rotten order head-on. And events would not wait.

"The fullest liberty to plunder, burn and kill"

In August 1850, right before the Senate passed the Fugitive Slave Act, Smith called an anti–Fugitive Slave Act convention in Cazenovia, New York. So many thousands of people arrived that the meeting had to be moved outdoors, to an apple orchard. There, Douglass got a blast of real radicalism. In the guise of a fugitive slave, the convention generated a letter "To the American Slaves" endorsing a slave rebellion. "You are prisoners of war in an enemy's country," the letter asserted, "and therefore," it continued, "by all the rules of war, you have the fullest liberty to plunder, burn and kill." A local history buff on the scene at the convention recorded

Anti–Fugitive Slave Act convention. *Courtesy of the Madison County, N.Y., Historical Society.*

that Smith was the author of the letter and that Douglass, not about to let a white man use a pseudonym to present a fugitive slave's position, made Smith put the letter to a vote of the largely Black attendees. He may have been wrong; the published letter is unsigned, and a version appears in Douglass's paper. After a full discussion, the convention endorsed the letter.

Upon his return to Rochester, Frederick Douglass devoted most of the September 5 *North Star* to what had transpired: "THE SLAVE WAS HERE REGARDED AS A MAN!" which was always Douglass's touchstone. "The laws of slavery were esteemed but the infernal edicts of pirates — the religion of slaveholders was held to be a horrid and revolting blasphemy against the majesty of Heaven, and a moral war was declared against the law and the religion thus specified." In sum, "the ground was distinctly taken in the Convention, that slave laws should be held in perfect contempt."

Douglass was by no means the only Black activist organizing for self-defense. When the new law unleashed an army of southern hunters into the cities of the North, all communities of color were at risk and saw themselves as at risk. Speaking to a mixed-race meeting at Faneuil Hall that October of 1850, Douglass claimed his role: "Lawfully authorized by the colored portion of [Boston's] citizens to declare their sentiments and feelings to the meeting, after the fullest deliberation we one and all— without the slightest hope of making successful resistance—are resolved rather to die than to go back." He predicted the attendees would soon "see the streets of Boston flowing with innocent blood." Three months later, Douglass reiterated his position that the Fugitive Slave Act had changed the terms of resistance. If the enslavers were, like bloodhounds, going to chase the fugitives into the North, then the slaves should draw their blood. If enough of the hunting southerners died, he continued, sounding like anything but a Garrisonian nonresistant, that should deter them from continuing. As Douglass predicted, slavery's resisters began to do just that, starting with the dramatic rescue of Shadrach Minkins from the Boston courthouse.

Garrison and some of the white Garrisonians acknowledged they were trapped. In a meeting of "coloured citizens of Boston," after decades of attending so many such meetings, Garrison declared he would be nonresistant until he died. He recognized that this was one area where he could not prescribe for his vulnerable brethren. Strangely for a nonresistant, he invoked the examples of William Tell and George Washington, but concluded that the moral power of public sentiment would be more potent than physical resistance. As one Black activist-led rescue after another took center stage on the streets of Boston, the ranks of the white abolitionists embracing violent resistance swelled. The Reverend Theodore Parker, an influential Boston figure, became substantially more radical; even someone who called himself "E.Q."(who could be no other than Edmund Quincy) praised "the disinclination of the colored people to being restored to the bosom of the patriarchs!"

"She does not regard me with a friendly eye"

As the Fugitive Slave Act pulled Douglass, and all the Black activists, away from Garrison and his nonpolitical nonresistance, the ever present Richard

Webb wrote Douglass a nasty letter from Ireland. Stop sending free copies of *The North Star* to your British women supporters, Webb wrote. I'm so sorry, Douglass wrote back. "I never expected them to pay for it but sent it merely to keep up communications with friends who cheered me when a stranger in your land." The women's fondness for Douglass would not have been news to Webb, who, a year earlier, had written to Weston Chapman's sister Anne about how the two faithless women were followers of Douglass and partisans of the Liberty Party faction.

While Douglass had Webb's attention, he stuck in the shiv. "My Dear Friend Richard," he continued, "I have ... wronged you somwhat in my mind." It was "that unfortunate letter of Mrs. Chapman's to you ... which struck me at the time [now five years in the past] as wholly uncalled for." Even now, Douglass continued, "I have reason to know that She does not regard me with a friendly eye. Well let all pass. I've been to England and am now in America and was not seduced by British gold." After a little news of mutual friends, Douglass finished, "Of Boston you are I am sure as well informed as myself—for in addition to the *Standard* and the *Liberator*—you doubtless enjoy the keenist private out pourings of E. Q.'s pen." Edmund Quincy no doubt had used the same pen with which he wrote to Caroline Weston of Douglass: "wooly," and the "unconscionable [n-word]." We don't know if Douglass knew of those specific letters, but he surely knew that E.Q. was no friend.

It is impossible to read this letter as anything but Douglass's declaration of independence from the whole poisonous bunch. Webb told him that people he thought were friends did not even want free copies of his newspaper, and in turn, Douglass let Webb know what he thought about him and his friend Mrs. Chapman.

"Sick and tired of arguing on the slaveholders' side"

Douglass might have thought Garrison was right about the Constitution, but after the 1850 letter to Webb, whatever position he took on any other critical matter would not be driven by personal ties to the Bostonians. Three months later, he abandoned ship.

He wrote to Gerrit Smith on January 21, 1851: "I am so much impressed by your reasoning that I have about decided to let Slaveholders and their Northern abbettors have the Labouring *oar* in putting a proslavery interpretation upon the constitution. I am sick and tired of argueing on the slaveholders' side of the question, although they are doubtless right so far as the intentions of the framers of the Constitution are concerned."

He could never completely silence the voice of reason. "Is it good morality," he asked Smith, to interpret a legal document the opposite of how its Framers intended? Well, in any case, he, Douglass, had "ceased to affirm it." But he quickly moved from his limited endorsement to full-throated support. I said that, he told Smith, only because I was still worried about the Framers' intentions. But now, I have made up my mind that "I am only in reason and in conscience bound to learn the intentions of those who framed the Constitution — *in the Constitution itself.*"

As early as March 1851, when Douglass went out to lecture with Garrisonian Stephen Foster and saw Samuel May, he told them that he no longer believed in Garrison's no-voting theory. The Garrisonians wasted no time in reacting. Two months later, at the annual American Anti-Slavery Society convention in May, they moved to withdraw the support of the Society from any paper that did not treat the Constitution as proslavery.

In the next *North Star,* Douglass came right out with it in a long article, which Garrison then reprinted in *The Liberator:* "Change of Opinion Announced." In his frank announcement, Douglass admitted, "We have arrived at the firm conviction that the Constitution ... might be made consistent ... with the noble purposes avowed in its preamble ... and that hereafter we should ... demand that it be wielded in behalf of emancipation." He now refused to "go behind the letter of the Constitution" to the slavery-embracing history that supported the assertion that the Constitution was proslavery. He even credited the rival faction with changing his mind: "[T]he writings of] Lysander Spooner, of Gerrit Smith, and of William Goodell have brought us to our conclusion." But of course, he continued, he was now taking heat from the Garrisonians for his new position; when he went public with his change of opinion at the 1851 annual meeting, Garrison said, "There is roguery somewhere." But Douglass "can easily forgive this ... imputation," Garrison continued piously, because "we shall never cease to be grateful."

Well, maybe not never.

Ironically, the 1851 meeting where Douglass and the Garrisonians clashed openly over the role of the Constitution had taken place in Syracuse, New York, in the belly of the Gerrit Smith organization. Typical of his generous character, when anti-abolition fury had thwarted the Garrison faction's attempts to meet in New York City, Smith had made accommodations for the Boston-led group in his territory upstate. Their audience was filled with Liberty Party political types, including William Goodell, one of the leading Liberty Party legal thinkers. The mixed meeting at Syracuse shows that there was not a complete breach between the Liberty faction and the Garrisonians even then. For a year Douglass continued to lecture occasionally on the American Anti-Slavery Society circuit, and even attended their 1852 annual meeting.

Then Gerrit Smith made him an offer he could not refuse. The Smith-financed *Liberty Party Paper* was a useless mess, incompetently run and suffering from the inability to focus on the cause that mattered. After a month of negotiation, Douglass (or Smith behind the scenes) managed to extract the Syracuse paper from its editor, and the *Liberty Party Paper* and *The North Star* merged. The new journal was to be called, openly, *Frederick Douglass' Paper*. From June 1851 on, Gerrit Smith would be underwriting *Frederick Douglass' Paper*.

It was almost ten years to the day since its eponymous editor had stood up at the Nantucket meeting and haltingly told his story. Smith now could scarcely contain his delight. Most of all, he was happy that Douglass had come to believe that "slavery is incapable of legalization." Smith was not alone. Douglass got letters from supporters as diverse as Chicago free Black abolitionist (and Underground Railroad activist) Henry O. Wagoner and Boston's George W. F. Mellen, white theorist of abolition jurisprudence, "rejoicing," in Mellen's word, at Douglass's change of mind.

Douglass's colleagues in Boston did not share the excitement. After the angry exchange between Douglass and the Garrisonians at the 1851 Society meeting, the arguments got louder and broader. When the British abolitionist George Thompson visited in late 1851, the various factions hosted him at lectures and the like, but, unknown to the hospitable Liberty Party, he was writing a steady stream of criticism of their disagreement with Garrison's faction. Douglass's ever watchful adversary Richard D. Webb lost no time in sharing Thompson's low opinion of Douglass's apostasy in a piece in the Garrisonian *National Anti-Slavery Standard*. Douglass was furious, and he printed a long angry criticism of Webb—and Thompson for his ingratitude—in his own outlet. Webb responded promptly, unloading on Douglass for his error on the matter of the Constitution and his intolerance of criticism. A mutual acquaintance, Emma Mitchell, gleefully informed Weston Chapman in Paris that the latest *Frederick Douglass' Paper* included an attack on Webb and Thompson—"He [Douglass] is evidently stung to the quick." But, she added, Douglass's attack was not explicitly aimed at Garrison himself.

At the next annual meeting, in May 1852, Douglass, as he reported in his long article in the paper the following week, was regarded "as little better than an enemy." He bitterly recited every charge laid against him— that he was adverse to the American Anti-Slavery Society, that he hadn't refined his position in the year he'd had to clarify his thinking, that he had taken a bribe from a colonizationist, and so on.

The lineup of people who now rose to speak against him was more moving than the details of the quarrel: Abby Kelley Foster, who had defended him so fiercely in 1843 when John Collins tried to hijack the speaking tour for his latest idealistic cause. Her husband and colleague, Stephen Foster (they had found time to marry in 1845). Charles Remond, who scolded the assembly for treating Douglass "with kid gloves," had been his only Black colleague on the speaking tour for so many years and had stood side by side with Douglass against Collins and all attempts to hijack abolition for other causes. Wendell Phillips, who had written the beautiful letter introducing Douglass's memoir in 1845, said Douglass had exiled himself from their society. Even Garrison accused Douglass of palling around with some of the many activists who had fallen from his favor.

Two months later, Douglass went to the Free Soil Party convention for the election of 1852. There, with the nomination of Lewis Tappan, of the New York City faction, he was elected secretary of the convention. The party, called alternatively Free Soil and Free Democracy, was a weakened version of the coalition assembled in 1848. Most of the malcontents had returned to the Democratic Party in the interim. But the smaller third party ventured further along the path to abolition legal theory, enacting a platform that dropped the 1848 concession that there were places where Congress lacked the power to regulate slavery. Smaller but more threatening, the new third party appealed to Secretary Douglass, who, for a while, embraced it in his paper. But Gerrit Smith was hard to satisfy and remained adamant in support of the disappearing—but thoroughly abolitionist—Liberty Party. In that very same election of 1852, Douglass briefly abandoned Free Democracy for Smith's side again. As Douglass's great biographer David Blight describes it, he was on a roller coaster. But he never gave up his radicalism. It was always two steps toward politics even with one step back.

PART V

◆

DOUGLASS AND GARRISON DIVIDE

24
(1852–1854)
The Political Divorce

MUCH INK HAS BEEN SPILLED OVER WHY Douglass and Garrison finally split up. The breach is the final, most compelling example of the strengths and weakness of the interracial alliance. Weston Chapman was gone, and the drama played out with the two actors remaining onstage. Was Garrison ultimately unable to accept a Black man's full independence of his tutelage? Too bad, Garrison wrote, that *Frederick Douglass' Paper* doesn't have a proper name. Or, indeed, was Garrison unable to credit anyone who disagreed with him? Was Douglass's sensitivity to criticism at fault? Were they just fundamentally different characters, one moral and the other political at heart? Or in the end, was Garrison's commitment to utopian secession from the slave nation just a white man's fantasy, destined to fall short of emancipating the enslaved, while formerly enslaved Frederick Douglass never took his eye off the ball?

The Phony War

After the harsh scene at the 1852 meeting, each of the men backed off briefly. Garrison gave a patently ridiculous explanation for his "roguery" outburst, and the Anti-Slavery Society withdrew its threat to disestablish *Frederick Douglass' Paper* for its heretical views.

The Liberator was uncharacteristically silent. A survey of its references to Douglass — and to Gerrit Smith — during the year after the 1852 meeting reveals little but formal coverage: the Free Democrats naming Douglass a secretary, Douglass denied service at an Ohio hotel, Douglass's *Life and Times* for sale, and the like. Here and there, however, the underlying argument surfaces. Boston's Wendell Phillips debated the Liberty faction about the Constitution. *The Liberator* reprinted Douglass's criticism of its coverage of the dispute and then criticized Douglass for criticizing *The Liberator.*

But the Boston faction was simmering. Right before the 1852 annual meeting, Abby Kelley Foster wrote Garrison an incendiary letter accusing Douglass of "playing a double part in order to get aid from all parties" by starting a Rochester Anti-Slavery Society separate from the existing network. She and husband Stephen maneuvered to get him to reveal his "true spirit," and he erupted in such wrath as Kelley Foster had never seen. Got to keep an eye on Douglass, she concluded, especially since "that miserable Julia Griffiths is doing all in her power to make trouble on both sides of the Atlantic."

Then who should emerge but of all people Maria Weston Chapman, who had been hearing about Griffiths from her sisters. Carrying on her usual extensive correspondence, now from Paris, she shared with British Garrisonians John Bishop Estlin and his daughter Mary Anne that Frederick Douglass had always been "untrustworthy," and especially now because of his "disreputable connection with that wretched English woman who has brought so much trouble into his family & disgrace upon himself." Weston Chapman's phrase "trouble into his family" would soon take on a life of its own as the Boston faction's attention turned to the private, rather than the public, aspect of Douglass's doings.

Anne Weston was retailing the details of Douglass's and Griffiths's daily routine not just to sister Maria but all around her transatlantic web of correspondents. Letters passed from her to her many sisters, to British colleagues, and to local abolitionists, who began pressuring Douglass to end the gossip-inducing situation. Finally, Julia Griffiths moved out of the Douglass home. Douglass wrote to local critic Samuel Porter: "Now we are separate and only meet at my office at business and for business purposes." Can we let this go now? Susan B. Anthony, the famous suffragist and a Rochester neighbor, wrote to Garrison in December, swearing that Douglass's wife, Anna, had thrown Julia Griffiths out.

Miraculously, the 1853 annual American Anti-Slavery Society meeting passed uneventfully, with Douglass speaking at both the Garrisonian meeting and the Tappan brothers' faction (the American and Foreign

Anti-Slavery Society, also meeting in New York). *The Liberator* reported Douglass's appearance as reflecting the many paths to a common goal.

But in May, within weeks of the meeting, Douglass unloaded on old Garrisonian comrades Henry Wright and his now vocal opponent Stephen Foster. These Garrisonians had to absent themselves from the May 1853 meeting, Douglass claimed, because they wanted to protect their group against the charge that the Society was anti-Christian, as they cozied up to the conservative abolitionists who were always worried about the clergy. I don't care if the Garrisonians are infidels or not, he continued. We should not be excluding anyone from antislavery because of anything except not being against slavery. The cause, Douglass stressed, is too important to turn down help from anyone. As Douglass said in his next salvo in the escalating conflict in August, Foster, Wright, and Garrison associate Parker Pillsbury were unbelievers, but he still thought they should not be separated from the main cause—"to give liberty to the enslaved people of this country." In August, Wendell Phillips spoke at a meeting in Framingham, Massachusetts, to celebrate the anniversary of British abolition and, spotting Douglass in the audience, proceeded to attack him for the May article. And then Douglass answered Phillips's attack in the August paper.

Why Douglass was so outspoken about his adversaries' treatment by his other adversaries seems incomprehensible. But clearly here, Douglass is talking about himself and the other believers in the antislavery Constitution and political abolition. The American Anti-Slavery Society had threatened, in 1852, to strike political abolitionist newspapers from the approved list, and Stephen and Abby Kelley Foster had recently appeared at Douglass's new New York society to denounce his followers for not joining the Boston-based network. The whole argument about Foster and the rest is a proxy for Douglass's resistance to being read out of the Boston branch.

But Douglass already knew that the Garrisonians were pushing him out. What had happened to make matters so much worse between May and August of 1853? A close look at the August issue of *Frederick Douglass' Paper* reveals that he'd been royally snubbed by his old colleagues. The American Anti-Slavery Society, having finally procured a place for its 1853 meeting in New York City for the first time in three years, had sent special invitations to its old adversaries on the Tappan side of the blanket. "Sundry gentlemen not in sympathy with the distinctive peculiarities of the Society, and who have not acted with it for the last dozen years, were especially invited to be present," Douglass reported. "It is true," Douglass admitted, "I got no special circular." By April 1853, Douglass was no doubt tired of being controlled—from his early years of enslavement, to the later years of being "managed" by Maria Weston Chapman, trying to keep his paper afloat without the Garrisonians' support. But it does not take a genius to figure out that you don't leave off the invitation list someone you're trying to keep inside the tent.

On September 16, Garrison published extracts from his old colleague Douglass's editorial on the escalating quarrel in the dungeon of *The Liberator*, the "Refuge of Oppression" column.

The Personal Is Political

"With Douglass," Garrison wrote to his old friend Samuel May on September 23, "the die seems to be cast," adding, "I lament the schism, but it is unavoidable."

Poor May had invited Garrison to come to Syracuse and speak at the second celebration of the rescue of fugitive slave "Jerry" by a mass of two thousand liberators in Syracuse in 1851. The annual "Jerry Rescue" festivities commemorating an act of outright resistance had become a brilliant abolitionist strategy to keep people's hopes up during the dark days of the Fugitive Slave Act. Before he realized that the die was cast, May told Garrison he would be sharing the stage with other "orators" such as Gerrit Smith and Frederick Douglass, should he choose to join them in Syracuse. So many cats to wash, Garrison responded, with an elaborate recitation of his travel schedule. And also, the die was cast.

Garrison revealed the personal character the die had taken on. With Douglass now painted as the traitor, Garrison described Gerrit Smith of the Liberty Party as his "noble friend." At that moment, Smith was engaged in prolonged litigation defending Jerry's rescuers and pursuing the federal marshal who had arrested him. A big part of Smith's litigation strategy was to challenge the constitutionality of the Fugitive Slave Act. Smith's legal argument was a direct violation of the Garrisonian orthodoxy at the center of Garrison's first break with Douglass—that the Constitution protected slavery. Nonetheless, by November of 1853, Smith was, in

The Liberator, "the great apostle of American abolition," and Douglass was in the "Refuge of Oppression." Douglass, the star orator and literary lion —not Gerrit Smith—was at that point probably the greatest threat to the beleaguered Garrison position. Yet it is impossible to avoid thinking, given the contrast between the Garrisonians' treatment of Douglass and of their white opponent, that these white managers had actually never accepted the full humanity of Frederick Douglass.

25

(1853–1854)

The Personal Divorce

ON SEPTEMBER 24, 1853, THE GARRISONIAN *NATIONAL Anti-Slavery Standard* came right out and attacked Douglass personally. We do not hate him for his views, the new editor Oliver Johnson wrote; after all, we do not hate Gerrit Smith, whose views are equally deviant. But Smith is still "in every respect friendly while ... the former [Douglass] is at heart [the Garrisonians'] enemy, and has been endeavouring, for years, in an underhand way, to build himself up by pulling them down."

"In this work," the *Standard* continued in its attack, Douglass "has had the aid of a *Jezebel*, whose capacity for making mischief between friends it would be difficult to match."

Thoroughly Modern Julia

In the Bible, Jezebel is the wicked wife of wicked King Ahab, who promotes the worship of the wrong god, Baal. So evil is she that after she's thrown from a window, her body is left to be consumed by dogs before burial. Luckily for Julia Griffiths, the Boston clique was not in control of the state. So no defenestration for her.

In 1853, Julia Griffiths, in her fourth year of living in Rochester and working on Douglass's cause, might seem to us now, over a century and a half later, like a familiar figure—the independent woman. In 1850, however, her unvarnished claim to full humanity made her exotic even to the reformers of the abolition movement.

Griffiths arrived in America at the age of thirty-eight, one of two daughters of a British reform family. Somehow, even though she lived with an aunt for some part of her childhood as the family fortunes gyrated, she acquired a good education, as well as substantial skills in the publishing business her father was sometimes in.

Griffiths was skilled. When she came to Douglass's assistance, in addition to taking over fundraising and spiffing up the technical standards of the publication and managing the account books, she worked marketing wonders. Griffiths offered free subscriptions as incentives for subscribers to pay dues, and established a rich donors' fund to form a kind of endowment (one hundred donors of ten dollars each). She was herself a good writer, contributing a variety of columns, and her book reviews are to this day a wonderful example of the form.

She was political. When Griffiths came from England, she was coming from the establishment tradition of the British and Foreign Anti-Slavery Society, which had been on the New York side of the American schism from the beginning. She later described herself as a "Wilberforce" abolitionist, someone who believed in political action, with all the compromises it involved. She certainly did not rise up out of the crucible of fire — the social alienation, the physical danger — that had shaped the Garrisonians and tied them to Garrison, for all his dogmatism and insistence on ideological conformity to nonresistance and political abstinence.

She was robustly comfortable in her own self-image. As soon as she moved to town, the Garrisonians started reporting back and forth to one another about her showy and eccentric appearance. Predictably, Anne Weston quickly let her sister Maria in on Rochester sightings of Griffiths in her unconventional outfits. With a weakness for artsy clothes and flamboyant jewelry, Julia Griffiths was never going to satisfy the peculiarly conventional individuals drawn to Boston's radical abolition movement.

She was immune to shame. She pounded on Douglass's rich backers, demanding that they make pledges to support him, buy more subscriptions, pay their pledges. She wrote repeatedly to Senator William Seward, reminding him of his relatively minor five-dollar pledge and noting that he was receiving his paper. She was so relentless with Douglass's main sponsor, Gerrit Smith, that Douglass found himself apologizing to Smith for how often she shook the cup in front of him, writing, "I fear she is too urgent on my behalf." She called herself the paper's "banker," and fretted constantly over the state of its "treasury."

For someone so clear about her place in the world, oddly, she was not interested in Rochester neighbor Susan B. Anthony's feminist movement (and, as we have seen, Anthony wasn't a fan of Griffiths either). She was always and only interested in the abolition of slavery. But she understood clearly the power that women wielded in the movement. They were the golden geese. Griffiths knew that the women's antislavery societies made money through a whole variety of fundraising devices, but most of all through their antislavery fairs; she was in London when Douglass's Rochester friend Amy Post started vying with the Weston sisters for the moneymaking items from Europe to sell at their competing fairs.

When Griffiths arrived in Rochester, she didn't have to reinvent the wheel. She just did everything Weston Chapman had done. First, she started a Douglass-friendly women's society, the Rochester Ladies Anti-Slavery Sewing Society. Then she had the new group start a "festival." It was Griffiths's work that Stephen and Abby Kelley Foster were trying to derail, when they "popped" in on that inaugural festival meeting in 1852. Griffiths's fair, bolstered by the goods she solicited from her large group of contacts in the U.K., raised a trove of money. The Garrisonians were apoplectic. But the worst was yet to come.

"A sectarian Delilah"

To Garrisonian Oliver Johnson of the *National Anti-Slavery Standard,* Julia Griffiths's Jezebel was a troublemaker. But to Garrison, Douglass's companion did more than make trouble: she, in terms Garrison got from Maria Weston Chapman ("trouble in his family"), had "caus[ed] much unhappiness in his household." As his letters in the two prior rounds with the Boston clique—in 1843 and 1847—reflect, Douglass was prepared to argue about almost anything: Was he politically faithful? Could he be bought? What gratitude did he owe to the Boston establishment? Now that he had his own paper, he was so deep in the weeds of the dispute with the Garrisonians that even his admiring biographer David Blight approvingly quotes a critic calling Douglass "a whine of persecution." But he had already told his Rochester neighbor Samuel D. Porter what he would do if someone criticized his private behavior: I'm a free man, and she's a free and independent woman. Douglass refused to have the argument.

Charged up, as always, by the censorious Weston Chapman, Garrison used her words to accuse Douglass of wronging his family. Almost immediately, the founder received a letter purportedly from Anna Douglass (who, as we know, could not write): "SIR:—It is not true, that the presence of a certain person in the office of Frederick Douglass causes unhappiness in his family.—Please insert this in your next paper." Garrison published Anna Douglass's letter in *The Liberator*, but with an introduction that made clear he did not believe her.

Douglass, however, stuck to his refusal to argue. "The charge of unhappiness in my household," he informed Garrison in the same issue, "is one which I refuse to answer in this place, or in any public journal, unless required to do by some proper and competent tribunal known to the law of the land." Here's why you don't settle a political dispute by attacking my role in my family, Douglass elaborated:

1. Because it involves considerations wholly foreign to the present controversy.
2. Because the public have not been called upon by my household to pass upon its affairs, its happiness or its unhappiness or upon the cause of either.
3. Because to deny the charge would be an ex parte denial.
4. Because in matters of this sort, ex parte denials are worthless.
5. Because such denial would satisfy nobody who was before dissatisfied.
6. Because the precedent of dragging a man's domestic affairs before the public with a view to damage him in public estimation, is bad.
7. Because a man's wife and children should be spared the mortification involved in public discussion of matter so entirely private and which can come to no issue in such a Court.
8. Because the stake I hold in the happiness of my household is greater than that of any other person.

In one short exchange, Douglass asserts the foundation of his lifelong politics, regardless of the changes in his affiliations and tactics. Was he not a MAN? as Garrison, who posed the question at their first meeting in 1841, had asked. As a man, he was not going to submit his conduct to any closer scrutiny than any other man, Black or white, should take. He was engaged in a political argument with the Garrisonians; what could justify their dragging in his wife and children? Only if he was so inferior to full adulthood that random outsiders should take a hand in caring for his wife and children, their happiness, their domestic affairs.

From the beginning of her association with him, Douglass went further and applied to Julia Griffiths the same human claim to dignity and freedom of action he claimed for himself. She was not some Jezebel; she was his "adviser," and "as to whether my 'adviser' is the best or 'the worst' is a matter of different opinions. I am, at any rate, profoundly grateful for the eminent services of that 'adviser' in opening my eyes to many things."

Garrison, the "dear friend" of so many reams of letters among the abolitionists, the father figure, the moralist, would not let it go. First, he answered Mrs. Douglass's denial in the same issue of *The Liberator* by arguing with her about verb tenses. Griffiths had long since moved out. Garrison contended that while she might not be causing unhappiness in your household *now*, that's not to say she didn't in the past. The unhappiness business "was not meant unkindly, nor intended to imply any thing immoral." Like Weston Chapman, who accused Douglass of betrayal all those years ago, Garrison purported not to understand why Douglass was offended. His comments were not intended to be unkind. (After all, even Jesus was imperfect, Weston Chapman had pointed out, in defense of her accusations against Douglass in the 1847 conflict. Of course, by that standard, they could level any accusation at their colleague. They were just treating him like Jesus.)

Garrison at last conceded that maybe it was a mistake to say Douglass was causing unhappiness in his family, because "it had no relevancy." But, he could not resist adding, we could prove it easily through "a score of unimpeachable witnesses in Rochester." In 1854, unimpeachable witness Amy Post tried to help Douglass out with his family life when Griffiths's landlords moved away, reopening the issue of where she should live. We know from an exchange of letters between Post and her cousin Sarah Thayer how Douglass responded to her efforts. With "base impudence!!" How could he be so ungrateful, the cousins wondered? Post was just exerting herself for his happiness. Thayer wished Douglass were white, so she could make his behavior public. But she "dared[ed] not say a word as I knew the reply would be 'that is the Nigger of it.'"

But even without the help of the Rochester ladies, who wished they could meddle in Douglass's family life without raising the specter of racism, the Bostonians thought they had all the evidence they wanted. Douglass had admitted, Garrison wrote, "all we care to extort" when he said Griffiths opened his eyes. "In what condition his vision now is — and whether in slumbering in the lap of a prejudiced, sectarian Delilah, he has not at last enabled the pro-slavery Philistines to ascertain the secret of his strength, cut off his locks, and rejoice over his downfall — we leave to our readers ... to judge." What secret did the enslavers learn from Douglass's association with Julia Griffiths? That he thought the Constitution might allow for political action against slavery? The Garrisonians were fine with Gerrit Smith taking the identical position. But when Douglass asserted it, Garrison equated his politics with a biblical-level downfall.

For years after 1853, Parker Pillsbury referred to Griffiths as "Miss Jezebel Griffiths." There are times when a powerful person's sexual behavior is indeed fair game in politics. But this was not one of them. Douglass is not accused of taking advantage of a subordinate or, as Harriet Beecher Stowe's brother, white preacher Henry Ward Beecher, would be accused of, preaching sexual purity while hypocritically bedding a married parishioner. Garrison and Douglass were supposed to be arguing about the Constitution, not about the Ten Commandments.

Twelve years after crying out the manhood of the fugitive slave at Nantucket and breaking off with the New York faction over female abolitionist Abby Kelley's presence, Garrisonians tagged Douglass as the n-word and his adviser as Miss Jezebel.

Right after the Delilah affair, historian John Stauffer's brilliant book *The Black Hearts of Men* reveals, Douglass's close Black friend the political abolition activist James McCune Smith had an uncanny insight into the shameful denouement of the always fragile alliance. There are few Blacks in Garrison's organization, McCune Smith charged, because of the racism of its members. There is no evidence that Smith had any idea of the existence of the n-word correspondence that had tainted the principles of the white Boston group since Maria Weston Chapman complained in 1843 that her Black speakers didn't like to work. But, like Douglass, this proud and brilliant Black man figured it out anyway.

The quarrel broke into the open when McCune Smith accused the old organization in the pages of *Frederick Douglass' Paper* of favoring white speakers over Black. Oliver Johnson, writing for the combative *National Anti-Slavery Standard* on December 23, answered the charge by saying the organization certainly wouldn't fire their white friends to make room for people like Frederick Douglass and McCune Smith himself. Maybe there aren't a lot of Black abolitionists, Johnson continued, because Black people are in favor of or indifferent to slavery. McCune Smith wrote an extraordinary editorial in response. We have been resisting slavery since at least 1813, he wrote, when Black men tried to stave off Pennsylvania's Black registration law. Resisting colonization was a Black idea, he argued, and Garrison got it from us. And we were there for Garrison, he continued, when no one would send him a dime to get *The Liberator* launched. It was free Black men who sold the paper, McCune Smith elaborated, and Garrison who lauded them with praises and expressions of esteem.

McCune Smith dated the breakdown of the Black and white alliance as far back as 1835, when, he asserted, *The Liberator* replaced its Black agent corps with white general agents. Nevertheless, Douglass had a long and productive career with the Garrisonians after he escaped from slavery in 1841; nor was he the only Black lecturer in those later years. As we have seen, the unraveling of the Garrison–Douglas–Weston Chapman alliance was a much longer story.

Publishing Well Is the Best Revenge

With superhuman concentration, as David Blight observes, Douglass and Griffiths managed, at that same time they were under personal attack, to assemble a gift book, *Autographs for Freedom*, under the auspices of the Griffiths-founded Rochester Ladies' Anti-Slavery Society. The book was of course an unacknowledged homage to yet another brilliant Weston Chapman institution, the gift book *The Liberty Bell*. The collection of writings in the first of the two annual volumes included Douglass's only work of fiction, "The Heroic Slave." Contributors signed their pieces, adding the value of their autographs to the content of the book.

Autographs for Freedom is a testament to the value of Frederick Douglass's support for the new political abolitionist movement he now embraced. The table of contents of volume one is a who's who of political abolition. William Seward, the abolitionist senator from New York, wrote the first piece, "Be Up and Doing." Other contributors included Harriet Beecher Stowe, the little woman whose book "started" the great war; Charles Sumner, senator from Massachusetts, the heart of the Radical Republicans; and Horace Greeley, the newspaperman and, briefly, congressman who is credited with naming the Republican Party.

To Have Douglass on Your Side

It is impossible to calculate how valuable Douglass was to the emerging political movement. Douglass was America's best-known Black man, and one of the most prominent Americans of any color. His second volume of memoir, *My Bondage and My Freedom*, published in 1855, sold eighteen thousand copies in the five years before the war. When the Democrats wanted to wound the emerging Republican Party with the dread charge of racial equality, it was Douglass they invoked. On the other side, people kept suggesting the Democrats, including the legendary orator Illinois senator Stephen Douglas, debate their great orator. It made the racist Stephen Douglas insane. Historians speculate that more people knew who Frederick Douglass was than knew Abraham Lincoln.

He had stood, trembling, before an all-white audience on Nantucket three years after fleeing slavery. He had told his Boston managers in no uncertain terms several times that they must never set themselves up as his overseers. And when they appointed themselves the guardians of his family's happiness, he had told them to mind their own business. They rejected him, and seven years later, Douglass's candidate, Abraham Lincoln, was elected the sixteenth president of the United States.

The South seceded. Almost immediately after Fort Sumter, Maria Weston Chapman started calling for the dissolution of the American Anti-Slavery Society. Although the remnants of the original movement engaged in a lively fight over whether to dissolve, Weston Chapman was gone. In 1865, after passage of the Thirteenth Amendment abolishing slavery, Garrison joined in the movement to dissolve, and when the motion failed, he resigned. On December 29, 1865, he published the last issue of *The Liberator*. Douglass fought on for another generation for the equality of Black Americans.

EPILOGUE: THREE MEETINGS AND A FUNERAL

"I SHALL NEVER FORGET MY FIRST INTERVIEW with this great man," Douglass wrote in his 1892 autobiography after he met the president.

Free and Equal (August 1863)

In August 1863, it was uncertain whether the "ex-slave, identified with a despised race," as he described himself, would even be admitted to the White House. Frederick Douglass had struggled for years to be recognized for his value to the white man's movement. His rhetorical genius, his charisma and fame, his untiring toil—nothing gained him the place in the movement to which he was so unambiguously entitled. He had to break with the Bostonians, move out of town, and abandon his colleagues of decades—effectively go on strike—to realize his dream of publishing a newspaper. But by 1863, as the most important Black person in America, he had some demands to make of the president of the United States.

And there was reason for the president to see him. Douglass had just gone on strike again.

After Lincoln issued the Emancipation Proclamation on January 1, 1863, Douglass had thrown himself into gathering American Black men, both free and fugitive, to join the Union Army and lead the charge for their own freedom. Douglass, as usual, saw the big picture. As in his battle with slave breaker Edward Covey thirty years before, armed resistance to the enslavers would now mark the Black soldiers as equal American citizens and free human beings, he thought. In his classic article in his magazine *Douglass' Monthly*, "Another Word to the Black Man," in April 1863, he laid out his vision: "The white man's soul was tried in 1776. The black man's soul is tried in 1863. The first stood the test, and is received as genuine — so may the last." Douglass listed the reasons to enlist: "1st. You are a man, although a colored man," and "manhood requires you to take sides . . . 2d. You are, however, not only a man, but an American citizen . . . and you have hitherto expressed in various ways not only your willingness but your earnest desire to fulfil any and every obligation which the relation of citizenship imposes." And finally, "the only way open to any race to make their rights respected is to learn how to defend them." Ten years of using politics to abolish slavery had taught Douglass that in the republic white men had created in 1776, freedom was just a stop along the way. The goal was full citizenship.

But the Union was refusing to receive the Black soldiers as "genuine," to treat them as men and citizens, and to respect them. Despite Douglass's unstinting efforts, the Lincoln administration had refused to pay the Black recruits more than half what whites earned. Worse, when Confederate president Jefferson Davis announced that Black Union soldiers would be murdered or enslaved if caught, Lincoln had resisted all efforts to announce retaliatory measures against the white Confederate prisoners of war. After the Proclamation, they might be free, but they were not equal. And so Frederick Douglass went on strike.

An old Boston Brahmin Douglass had worked with on recruitment urged him to take his case to the commander in chief and wrote a letter of introduction. But Douglass thought his associates from all his decades in abolition politics would open more doors than his single white Boston sponsor would. After all, it was political abolition that had paved the way for Lincoln to be in office in the first place. "I might be told to go home and mind my business," he speculated, but "my acquaintance with Senators Charles Sumner, Henry Wilson, Samuel Pomeroy, Secretary Salmon P. Chase, Secretary William H. Seward, and . . . Charles A. Dana encouraged me to hope for at least a civil reception." Douglass's invocation was a virtual list of the contributors to his and Julia Griffiths's 1854 essay collection.

He set out for D.C., touching, for the first time in twenty-five years, the slave soil of Maryland on his way. His first morning, he reached out to his friend Senator Pomeroy, who agreed to take him around. Technically, the doors to the White House were always open to anyone in those days, and when Douglass arrived, he found throngs of petitioners lining up. Douglass and his senatorial companion were admitted at once.

As Douglass relayed during a speech to a rapt audience at the Anti-Slavery Society a few months after the visit, when he walked into the president's office, Lincoln was sitting with his feet splayed well out into the room, and when he rose to greet Douglass, he seemed to rise and rise. "He impressed me as being just what every one of you have been in the habit of calling him — an honest man," Douglass continued, now serious.

By the time he arrived at the White House, Douglass was better disposed toward Lincoln than when he had set out from Rochester to demand action on the treatment of Black prisoners of war. He had learned in the interim that Lincoln had issued an order to kill or put to hard labor one Confederate captive for every Union soldier killed or enslaved as Jefferson Davis had ordered.

That leaves only two issues between us, Douglass told the president of the United States: equal pay for the Black soldiers, and promotions. After all, it was equality as men and citizens that they had enlisted for. That's where Lincoln drew the line. The country was not ready to treat "the colored man" as equal. He would think, he continued, that the Black soldiers were enlisting to fight for emancipation and be grateful for the opportunity to defend their freedom regardless of what they were paid. Just as the Boston clique had thought Frederick Douglass should be grateful for the opportunity to lecture against slavery regardless of what his other ambitions were. The payoff to an alliance with the most powerful man in the country might be greater, but the perils were little altered.

He was honest, Douglass later concluded, speaking to his Anti-Slavery Society audience, more important than wise or great. It wasn't Lincoln who had created the Republican Party or grown a northern constituency for reining in slavery. By the time war came, Douglass reminded the abolitionists, people had come to hate the old order, with its disproportionate representation of the slave power and its Fugitive Slave Act, turning northerners into bloodhounds. They had left the national proslavery parties and voted Lincoln in. If we are to be saved, he told his audience at the meeting that December, the captain cannot save our ship. We will have to save ourselves.

As for Lincoln, the president was imperfect, Douglass concluded, but had come far enough so that Douglass would go back to work gathering soldiers for his forces.

Even Freedom Is in Peril (August 1864)

A year later, Lincoln was the one seeking a meeting.

More than a year had passed since the supposedly decisive defeat of the South at Gettysburg, and still the war ground on. Lincoln's newest military savior, General Ulysses S. Grant, fought the dwindling and ill-supplied Rebel army without success in Virginia for four months, from the Wilderness in May 1864, through the siege of Petersburg starting in June. The fighting was constant, the casualties staggering, and the outcome a deadlock. Richmond was still secure, and in those months in 1864, the Union had taken more than sixty percent of the total casualties to the Army of the Potomac since the war began. On July 9, 1864, a tiny unit of Lee's army broke off into a dead run and managed to attack D.C. itself. In the absolute nick of time, Grant sent a corps to defend the capital and turned the attackers back. Grant, the redeemer, had raised the nation's hopes for a triumphant end to war. One disaster followed another. The election was four months away. Everyone, North and South, knew the election would decide the war.

Lincoln was beset from the left, as the radical Republicans threatened to break from the new political party. In the established tradition of political abolition, they called for a convention. Ominously for Lincoln, Douglass joined the call for the radical convention. Douglass had been outraged when Lincoln's Union general, who was governing conquered Louisiana, took the first step in reconstructing the nation by instituting all-white elections. For more than ten years Douglass had been part of a political movement based on voting. Douglass meant for the war to establish "perfect equality for the black man in every state before the law, in the jury box, at the ballot box and on the battlefield." In May the radicals nominated 1856 Republican candidate John C. Frémont to challenge Lincoln for president.

The nation waited to see if the Democrats really would nominate George B. McClellan, the cowardly failed general Lincoln had fired. If the Democrats won the election under McClellan, Lincoln believed, they would offer the South the chance to undo emancipation and return to the union. Stripped of their essential Black allies, the North didn't stand a chance and would soon sue for peace. The ragged old men and youths— all who were left of Lee's Army of Northern Virginia—would have won the war. As the Civil War historian S. C. Gwynne put it, "So half a century of bitter political fighting had come down to an election, and the main goal of both armies along the Rapidan [River] was to affect its outcome."

The contemporaneous records of that momentous summer reveal a president racked with worry about his newly emancipated human allies as free people and equally concerned about their utility as fighting men. And they were fighters. Frederick Douglass had thought that if Black people took up arms, they would be stepping into their birthright as citizens. They fought like tigers in combat at the siege of Port Hudson in 1863 and then defending their white brothers' retreat at Olustee, Florida, a year later. As the election loomed, Lincoln reaffirmed his faith. "There have been men who have proposed to me to return to slavery the black warriors of Port Hudson & Olustee to their masters to conciliate the South," Lincoln told a friend and ally, Wisconsin Governor Alexander Randall. "I should be damned in time & in eternity for so doing. The world shall know that I will keep my faith to friends & enemies, come what will."

As always, Lincoln was focused on utility as well as justice. "Freedom has given us the control of 200 000 able bodied men, born & raised on southern soil," he continued, "My enemies condemn my emancipation policy. Let them prove by the history of this war, that we can restore the Union without it." The hundreds of thousands of emancipated Black Americans were not all in the army. They were scattered all over the South, wherever Union troops had prevailed. They lived, effectively, in refugee camps. Worse, there were huge numbers of people who had not moved toward freedom because they were afraid, or they didn't know about the Proclamation, or they were in territory beyond Union Army lines. What to do?

Lincoln believed he had earned Douglass's support. He had already started considering suffrage for "worthy" Black citizens, Lincoln defended himself indignantly to a high-ranking abolitionist in Grant's command. He was evolving; Douglass should be patient. Douglass's hard-won strategy of skeptical cooperation with his powerful white allies—his under-standing that his standoffishness could win concession—was having an effect.

In August, Lincoln reached out directly. Douglass went, of course, at once. It was August 19, 1864. Almost immediately, the president told the ex–fugitive slave what he wanted. He was worried, he said, about the cries for peace and the still-enslaved people who would be left behind. He wanted Douglass to do what the martyred John Brown had planned five years before—and been hanged for: "Go into the rebel States, beyond the lines of our armies, and carry the news of emancipation and urge the slaves to come within our boundaries." Douglass noticed immediately that Lincoln, who had once said that he would save the union with slavery or without, "showed a deeper moral conviction against slavery than I had ever seen before." Maybe Douglass's conviction that the "black warriors" of the Union Army, many recruited by Douglass and including his two sons, had done the work he predicted of becoming "American citizens."

Douglass started organizing the rescue mission. He proposed that the president make him a general agent and give him a budget for subordi-nates to send behind the Union lines. But more importantly, he left the White House heartened by the prospect that the Emancipation Procla-mation now meant something more to President Lincoln than just getting additional cannon fodder for the faltering northern armies.

We will never know what Lincoln really had in mind, because Douglass never had to make his rescue plan operational. On September 2, 1864, the Democrats did nominate McClellan. But that same day, after two months of fighting, Union troops led by General William Sherman finally took Atlanta. Frémont withdrew from Lincoln's left flank, and the threat to his reelection receded. Frederick Douglass did not have to spend the last months of the war trying to rescue hundreds of thousands of fugitives from slavery from the rollback of emancipation.

After their momentous planning meeting, Lincoln invited Douglass to come for tea before he left Washington to start his mission. Douglass re-gretfully declined the president's invitation. He had committed to a speak-ing engagement that day. The two men would have many opportunities, Douglass thought, to meet and to work together. It may have been frail, but the Lincoln-Douglass alliance was the highest a Black man would reach for a hundred years.

No One Whose Opinion Matters More (March 1865)

On March 4, 1865, Abraham Lincoln was inaugurated for the second time. David Blight tells the story of how Frederick Douglass journeyed to Washington to witness the occasion. In a symbol of how the world had changed, abolition lawyer and politician Salmon P. Chase had replaced the author of *Dred Scott v. Sandford*, Roger Taney, on the Supreme Court. Douglass, as we know, had met Chase years before on the abolition lecture circuit. And so Frederick Douglass, a Black man who Taney said had no rights that white America needed to respect, went to Chase's chambers to help him try on the robe he would wear to swear in Lincoln. Then he went to the Capitol to watch the ceremony.

Douglass later said that Lincoln's Second Inaugural contained "more vital substance than I have ever seen compressed in a space so narrow." After Lincoln's journey from his infatuation with colonization all the way to the desperate plot to stage a John Brown raid on the Confederacy, the president had finally come around to recognizing that slavery was a sin. He hoped the scourge of war would pass away. But, as he put it in his im- mortal text, "if God wills that it continue until all the wealth piled by the bondman's two hundred and fifty years of unrequited toil shall be sunk, and until every drop of blood drawn with the lash shall be paid for by another drawn with the sword . . . the judgments of the Lord are true and righteous altogether."

After the ceremony, Douglass determined to "present himself" at the traditional reception, "though no colored person had ever ventured" to do so. After all, he thought, freedom had become the law of the land, and "colored men were on the battle-field mingling their blood with that of white men in one common effort to save the country."

No one "of his own color" would go. They were unwilling to risk the unhappiness of rejection. As usual Douglass would have to lead the way. As usual too, he held up his decision to his lifelong standard: Did going to the White House for the inaugural reception fit his self-image as a man? "I had for some time looked upon myself as a man," he reminisced later, "but now in this multitude of the elite of the land, I felt myself a man among men." Wherever Frederick Douglass went in the elite white society that was America, he would present the issue of whether a Black man could be a "man among men."

Soon enough America reminded him of how fragile his feeling was. Two policemen at the door roughly turned him away. But as the other people of color who had pushed him to go first may have foreseen, he was not just some man; he was *Frederick Douglass*. Someone recognized him and took the word to Lincoln. Next thing Douglass knew, he was standing in the East Room with the president. Lincoln wanted to know what the other great orator thought about his speech. When Douglass demurred at taking so much of the president's time, Lincoln answered: "There is no man in the country whose opinion I value more than yours. I want to know what you think of it?"

"It was a sacred effort," Douglass answered. "I am glad you liked it," said Lincoln. Any man distinguished by such regard from the president, Douglass thought, would have been honored.

It must have seemed so hopeful. Received at the White House in full view of the public, told that his opinion mattered more than anyone else's, the cause of his life reinforced by a newly reelected president who had recognized at last the central sinfulness of slavery. Douglass wrote, looking back, words that we often associate with a much later leader, Martin Luther King Jr. When he broke tradition by going places as he did, white men found him presumptuous and Black condemned him for going where he was not wanted. "The conditions of human association are founded upon character rather than color," Douglass replied, and so people equal in "mind and morals" should meet "on the plane of civil or social rights."

The End

On April 15, 1865, Abraham Lincoln was assassinated. In 1870 the country ratified the Fifteenth Amendment, giving Black men the vote. The American Anti-Slavery Society dissolved. Its work was done.

Douglass lived another quarter century after the abolitionists dissolved their society. Lincoln dead, the nation soon bent to the job of undoing his great work of emancipation. The fragile hope of a Black and white movement toward equality, resting on these two extraordinary men, would have to wait. Nonetheless, Douglass persisted. When he died, on February 20, 1895, he was in the middle of his campaign against lynching.

ACKNOWLEDGMENTS

Again to editor Deanne Urmy, for extraordinary editing and support.

Thank you, Elie Mystal and Keli Goff, for frankness and friendship. Thanks to Eric Foner and David Blight for unselfish encouragement.

To David Kuhn, Becky Sweren, and Nate Muscato at Aevitas Creative for your advocacy of and confidence in my work. Thanks to Ben Kalin for heroic fact-checking.

A NOTE ON SOURCES

Anyone who writes about this central drama of the American past stands on so many shoulders you could mount a cheer team from the modern historians alone.

The iconic works of David B. Davis, Eric Foner, and David Blight of course form the backdrop of any foray into the subject of abolition. There are the comprehensive biographies of the two men in my story, including Henry Mayer's massive biography of Garrison, *All on Fire,* and, late in my labors but critical, David Blight's poetic *Frederick Douglass: Prophet of Freedom.* Manisha Sinha has chronicled the story of the transnational, interracial, and gender-integrated long movement in her comprehensive book *The Slave's Cause: A History of Abolition.*

Less obvious were the works that helped me frame my new approach to the subject, through the lens of interracial and gender cooperation and the daily work of movement building. Biographers of either Garrison or Douglass touch on the breach, which is central to my story, and there are a few excellent but short articles about the breakup, starting with the legendary Black historian Benjamin Quarles's essay "The Breach Between Douglass and Garrison," in the *Journal of Negro History* in 1938. Quarles is also the author of the invaluable *Black Abolitionists* from 1969. Lawrence J. Friedman's *Gregarious Saints: Self and Community in American Abolitionism, 1830-1870* revealed the ties of class and culture that go so far to explain the fragility of Douglass's place in Garrisonian abolition and to reveal the snobbishness and insularity of the social radicals.

Historian and women's studies scholar Lee V. Chambers highlights the underreported Maria Weston Chapman in her book *The Weston Sisters: An*

Abolitionist Family. Of course a feminist scholar would be among the first to recognize Weston Chapman's significance.

I could not have understood the importance of the breakup for the history of abolition without the revisionist histories that revived the political action behind its ultimate success. Starting, of course, with Foner's *Free Soil, Free Men, Free Labor: The Ideology of the Republican Party Before the Civil War,* I also owe an immense debt to Richard Sewell, *Ballots for Freedom: Antislavery Politics in the United States;* Corey M. Brooks, *Liberty Power: Antislavery Third Parties and the Transformation of American Politics;* and Joanne B. Freeman, *The Fields of Blood: Violence in Congress and the Road to Civil War.*

Much of what I saw in the book is the view from the top of the pyramid. If my insight into the meaning and limits of the alliance and the addition of the portrait of a woman substantially overlooked — and critical — adds a bit to the pile, I will consider my work done.

NOTES

Introduction: Meeting on Nantucket, August 11, 1841

page

xiii *"Accustomed to consider":* Frederick Douglass, "A Few Facts and Personal Observations of Slavery: An Address Delivered in Ayr, Scotland, on March 24, 1846," *Ayr (Scotland) Advertiser,* March 26, 1846; *The Frederick Douglass Papers,* series 1, *Speeches, Debates, and Interviews,* ed. John Blassingame et al. (New Haven: Yale University Press, 1979), 195.

"There is no spot": Douglass, "A Few Facts and Personal Observations."

xiv *"Tell your story, Frederick":* Frederick Douglass. *My Bondage and My Freedom* (London: Partridge and Oakey, 1855).

"Flinty hearts were pierced": Lydia Maria Child, *National Anti-Slavery Standard,* August 26, 1841.

"Come saints and sinners": For this account, see Parker Pillsbury, *Acts of Anti-Slavery Apostles* (Rochester, N.Y.: Clague, Wegman, Schlicht, & Co., 1883), 326–28, remembering the events.

xvi *"the Contessa":* Henry Mayer, *All on Fire: William Lloyd Garrison and the Abolition of Slavery* (New York: St. Martin's Press, 1998), 353; Robert Vincent Sparks, "Abolition in Silver Slippers: A Biography of Edmund Quincy" (Ph.D. diss., Boston College, 1978), 113, 209–16.

"movement literature of abolition": Manisha Sinha, *The Slave's Cause: A History of Abolition* (New York: Penguin Classics, 2003), 421.

"Messrs. Bradburn, Collins": The Liberator, August 20, 1841.

xvii *Garrison's foundational abolitionist:* C. Peter Ripley, ed., *Black Abolitionist Papers,* vol. 4. (Chapel Hill: University of North Carolina Press, 1991), 259–60.

Douglass had subscribed: Frederick Douglass, *My Bondage and My Freedom* (New York and Auburn, 1855) 354.

all over the North: David D. Blight, *Frederick Douglass, Prophet of Freedom* (New York: Simon & Schuster, 2018), 94.

1. Printer Garrison Learns His Trade

3 *during the Napoleonic Wars:* Mayer, *All on Fire,* 12.

boardinghouse of exemplary piety: Wendell Phillips Garrison and Francis Jackson Garrison, *William Lloyd Garrison, 1805–1879: The Story of His Life, Told by His Children,* vol. 1, *1805–1835* (New York: The Century Co., 1885), 24–26. There are family papers at

Smith College and the University of Wichita for original documentation of this information.

a drinker, stuck around: Lee V. Chambers: *The Weston Sisters: An American Abolitionist Family* (Chapel Hill: University of North Carolina Press, 2014), 47–48.

4   *on American history:* Mayer, *All on Fire,* 5–7.

she married him: Mayer, *All on Fire,* 23.

5   *grew from 106 to 491:* Sydney E. Ahlstrom, *Religious History of the American People* (New Haven: Yale University Press, 2004), 442–43. Much of this section comes from Ahlstrom's foundational work.

part of their message: Ahlstrom, *Religious History,* 422–23.

competitive Methodists and Baptists: Ahlstrom, *Religious History,* 421–22.

6   *evangelical Second Great Awakening:* Charles I. Foster, *An Errand of Mercy: The Evangelical United Front, 1790–1837* (Chapel Hill, University of North Carolina Press, 1960).

copies of the Bible: Foster, *An Errand of Mercy,* 108.

their planned destination: Foster, *An Errand of Mercy,* 105–8.

ten percent of Kentucky's population: Douglas Allen Foster et al., *The Encyclopedia of the Stone–Campbell Movement: Christian Church (Disciples of Christ), Christian Churches/ Churches of Christ, Churches of Christ* (Grand Rapids: Wm. B. Eerdmans Publishing, 2004), 165–66.

particularly the enslaved: Henry Smith, *Recollections and Reflections of an Old Itinerant. A Series of Letters Originally Published in the "Christian Advocate and Journal" and the "Western Christian Advocate"* (Sydney: Wentworth Press, 2016).

preachers and "exhorters": Nancy Bullock Woolridge, "The Slave Preacher—Portrait of a Leader," *Journal of Negro Education* 14, no. 1 (1945): 28–37.

7   *including its enslaved population:* Ahlstrom, *Religious History,* 701–4.

worshippers in the pews: Ahlstrom, *Religious History,* 701–2.

participants of color: Sylvia R. Frey, *Come Shouting to Zion* (Chapel Hill: University of North Carolina Press, 1998), 140–41.

150 yards from the whites: Paul K. Conkin, *Cane Ridge: America's Pentecost* (Madison: University of Wisconsin Press, 1990), 96.

8   *"Thoughts upon Slavery":* John Wesley A.M., *Thoughts upon Slavery* (Philadelphia: Joseph Crukshank, 1776).

beginning of Western abolitionism: Dee E. Andrews, *The Methodists and Revolutionary America, 1760–1800* (Princeton: Princeton University Press, 2000), 23.

along sectional lines: Ahlstrom, *Religious History,* 662.

to buy his freedom: Ashley McCullough, "Richard Allen," Pennsylvania Center for the Book, College Park, Fall 2005; Andrews, *The Methodists and Revolutionary America,* 141.

start their own church: Richard S. Newman, *Freedom's Prophet: Bishop Richard Allen, the AME Church, and the Black Founding Fathers* (New York: NYU Press, 2008), 64.

in the Methodist denomination: Ahlstrom, *Religious History,* 708.

9   *Baptist hymns together:* Garrison and Garrison, *William Lloyd Garrison,* 1:29.

fortitude it could get: Mayer, *All on Fire,* 19–22.

10   *found decent work:* Mayer, *All on Fire,* 20.

semi-weekly Newburyport Herald: Garrison and Garrison, *William Lloyd Garrison,* 1:35.

by her white master: Frederick Douglass, *Narrative of the Life of Frederick Douglass, an American Slave* (Boston: The Anti-Slavery Office, 1845), 2.

11   *mass-producing the Bible: The history of printing: published under the direction of the Committee of General Literature and Education Appointed by the Society for Promoting Christian Knowledge* (London: Society for Promoting Christian Knowledge, 1855), 82.

sixteen presses working: An Abstract of the American Bible Society (Daniel Fanshaw, 1830).

12   *speed of the old:* D. J. R. Bruckner, "How the Earlier Media Achieved Critical Mass: Printing Press; Yelling 'Stop the Presses!' Didn't Happen Overnight," *New York Times,* November 20, 1995.

print an hour: Denis Brennan, *The Making of an Abolitionist: William Lloyd Garrison's Path to Publishing "The Liberator"* (Jefferson, N.C.: McFarland, 2014), 31.

several thousand pages an hour: Robert Hoe, *A Short History of the Printing Press and of the Improvements in Printing Machinery from the Time of Gutenberg Up to the Present Day* (New York: Robert Hoe, 1902).

in his apprenticeship: Brennan, *The Making of an Abolitionist,* tells the story in detail.

a missionary in Liberia: Garrison and Garrison, *William Lloyd Garrison,* 1:56.

political discussion: Garrison and Garrison, *William Lloyd Garrison,* 1:41, 55.

13   *maiden submission:* Garrison and Garrison, *William Lloyd Garrison,* 1:42.

"cannot decay or sever": Garrison and Garrison, *William Lloyd Garrison,* 1:47.

"opinion into silence": Free Press (Newburyport), March 22, 1826.

14   *candidate for Congress:* Brennan, *The Making of an Abolitionist,* 62–63.

afford his own rooms: Brennan, *The Making of an Abolitionist,* 65.

"good sense of the audience": An Old Bachelor [William Lloyd Garrison], to the *Boston Courier,* December 1826.

"painfully upon the ear": The Letters of William Lloyd Garrison, vol. 1, *I Will Be Heard! 1822–1835,* ed. Walter M. Merrill (Cambridge: Belknap Press of Harvard University Press, 1971), 38, hereafter cited as *Letters.*

his friend's place: Brennan, *The Making of an Abolitionist,* 31–33.

15   *committed to temperance:* William Buell Sprague, *Annals of the American Pulpit: Baptist* (New York: Robert Carter & Brothers, 1860).

the nation's borders: Foster, *An Errand of Mercy,* 121–22.

into national societies: Foster, *An Errand of Mercy,* 108.

on internal improvements: Foster, *An Errand of Mercy,* 121; *Quarterly Register of the American Education Society* 3 (1830–31): 63.

around New York: Foster, *An Errand of Mercy,* 188.

16   *satisfied with the results: The National Philanthropist,* March 2, 1828.

morally reprehensible: The National Philanthropist, March 21, 1828.

"most intemperately": The National Philanthropist, May 2, 1828.

"probably there": The National Philanthropist, May 9, 1828.

Against Slavery, in 1688: Brycchan Carey and Geoffrey Plank, eds., *Quakers and Abolition* (Champaign: University of Illinois Press, 2014).

17   *"chain of oppression":* Benjamin Lundy, *Genius of Universal Emancipation,* November 1832.

Slavery Irreconcilable: Andrew E. Murray, "'The Book and Slavery Irreconcilable,' by George Bourne," *American Presbyterians* 66, no. 4 (1988): 229–33.

southern intransigence: David W. Blight, "Perceptions of Southern Intransigence and the Rise of Radical Antislavery Thought, 1816–1830," *Journal of the Early Republic* 3, no. 2 (Summer 1983): 141.

placid years: Kate Masur, *Until Justice Be Done: America's First Civil Rights Movement, from the Revolution to Reconstruction* (New York: W. W. Norton, 2021).

18   *such "citizens"?:* Masur, *Until Justice Be Done,* 48–50.

antislavery activists: Merton L. Dillon, *Benjamin Lundy and the Struggle for Negro Freedom* (Champaign: University of Illinois Press, 1966), 30.

natural talent: Dillon, *Benjamin Lundy,* 48.

filled the partisan void: Masur, *Until Justice Be Done,* 47.

"republican form of government": W. O. Blake, *The History of Slavery and the Slave Trade, Ancient and Modern* (Columbus: H. Miller, 1861), 402.

19 *Senate refused:* The vote was 87–76: 86–10 among the northern states and 66–1 in the southern.

"knell of the Union": Thomas Jefferson to John Holmes, April 22, 1820, Library of Congress.

in the Genius: Benjamin Lundy, *Genius of Universal Emancipation,* February 1823. The words are from Corinthians 6:17, which he was most likely quoting.

General Assembly: Dillon, *Benjamin Lundy,* 114.

set sail for Haiti: Dillon, *Benjamin Lundy,* 118.

20 *rhetorical battle over slavery:* Ford Risley, *Abolition and the Press: The Moral Struggle Against Slavery* (Evanston: Northwestern University Press, 2008).

his former property: Genius of Universal Emancipation, January 1827.

petitioning Congress: Dillon, *Benjamin Lundy,* 123.

subscriptions to the paper: Dillon, *Benjamin Lundy,* 127.

enough to end slavery: Dillon, *Benjamin Lundy,* 133.

lead to civil war: Dillon, *Benjamin Lundy* 132; William Ellery Channing to Daniel Webster, May 14, 1828, in *Works of Daniel Webster,* vol. 5 (Boston: Little, Brown and Co., 1872), 366–67.

2. Manager Weston Chapman Comes of Age

21 *sailing master Abijah Garrison:* Lee V. Chambers, *The Weston Sisters: An American Abolitionist Family* (Chapel Hill: University of North Carolina Press, 2014), 46–48.

prosperous extended families: Chambers, *Weston Sisters,* 64–67.

supposedly for farming: Chambers, *Weston Sisters,* 47.

22 *alcoholic husband:* Chambers, *Weston Sisters,* 47.

the children's school: Chambers, *Weston Sisters,* 65.

to read and write: Joel Perlmann, Silvana R. Siddali, and Keith Whitescarver, "Literacy, Schooling, and Teaching Among New England Women, 1730–1820," *History of Education Quarterly* 37, no. 2, Special Issue on Education in Early America (Summer 1997): 117–39.

wave of support: Kathryn Kish Sklar, "The Schooling of Girls and Changing Community Values in Massachusetts Towns, 1750–1820," *History of Education Quarterly* 33, no. 4 (Winter 1993): 511–42.

legendary teachers: Chambers, *Weston Sisters,* 67.

for girls as well: Robert A. McCaughey, *Josiah Quincy, 1772–1864: The Last Federalist* (Cambridge: Harvard University Press, 1974), 123.

new high school: McCaughey, *Josiah Quincy,* 132–36.

girls who were Irish: Justin Winsor, ed., *The Memorial History of Boston Including Suffolk County, Massachusetts, 1630–1880,* vol. 4 (Boston: James R. Osgood & Company, 1883), 344.

the mayor's side argued: McCaughey, *Josiah Quincy,* 129.

fought Mayor Quincy fiercely: Justin Winsor, *The Memorial History of Boston: The Hundred Years,* pt. 2, *Special Topics* (Boston: James R. Osgood & Company, 1881), 251–52.

23 *"feverish anticipation":* Maria Weston Chapman to her sisters, October 22, 1840s (exact year not known). The Weston sisters' letters are available from the Boston Public Library

archives, www.bpl.org/blogs/post/notable-women-notable-manuscripts-maria-weston
-chapman.

a daughter, ten: Tribute of Boston Merchants to the Memory of Joshua Bates (Boston: John
Wilson and Son, 1864).

"should be quite happy": Maria Weston Chapman to Anne and Debora Weston, ca. 1825–
1828. (Although the sisters wrote constantly and at length, and saved everything, there
is but one surviving missive from Maria in London. In that letter she refers to writing at
other times, so there was obviously other correspondence.)

"bright as the Methodists": Maria Weston Chapman to her sisters, October 22, ca. 1825–
1828. This remark is a reflection of the potent role of the Methodist Church in promoting education in nineteenth-century America. John T. Smith, *Methodism and Education,
1849–1902: J. H. Rigg, Romanism, and Wesleyan School* (Oxford: Clarendon Press, 1998).

"and deep blue eyes": Maria Weston Chapman, ed., *Harriet Martineau's Autobiography,* vol.
1 (Boston: James R. Osgood, 1877), 215.

young educator in 1830: Chambers, *Weston Sisters,* 53.

from its earliest days: Chambers, *Weston Sisters,* 226.

24 *all American exports:* Sven Beckert, *Empire of Cotton: A Global History* (New York: Vintage Books, 2014), 243.

the growing network: Beckert, *Empire of Cotton,* 220.

not tainted by slavery: Chambers, *Weston Sisters,* 67.

25 *seventy thousand slaves:* Beckert, *Empire of Cotton,* 215.

increasingly massive riches: Joshua Bates diary, 1830–1834, Baring Archive, baringarchive.
org.uk. Copy on file with the author.

3. Garrison Will Be Heard

26 *a crusading editor:* Mayer, *All on Fire,* 135–36.

27 *in New York, Freedom's Journal:* Jacqueline Bacon, "The History of *Freedom's Journal*: A
Study in Empowerment and Community," *Journal of African American History* 88, no. 1
(Winter 2003): 1–20.

became more combative: Dillon, *Benjamin Lundy,* 145–46.

the "Black List": Garrison and Garrison, *William Lloyd Garrison,* 1:163.

devices in American history: Garrison and Garrison, *William Lloyd Garrison,* 1:453.

areas of the New South: Sinha, *Slave's Cause,* 92–93.

28 *seen in the North:* Dillon, *Benjamin Lundy,* 127–39.

"highway robbers and murderers": William Lloyd Garrison, *A brief sketch of the trial of
William Lloyd Garrison, for an alleged libel on Francis Todd, of Newburyport, Mass.* (Boston:
Printed by Garrison and Knapp, 1834).

the criminal prosecution: Mayer, *All on Fire,* 85.

29 *"applying the torch":* William Lloyd Garrison to the *Newburyport Herald,* June 1, 1830.

30 *walls of his cell:* Garrison and Garrison, *William Lloyd Garrison,* 1:178.

"burst of general indignation": Garrison and Garrison, *William Lloyd Garrison,* 1:183.

"Association of Gentlemen": Gilbert Hobbes Barnes, *The Anti-Slavery Impulse: 1830–1844*
(Gloucester, MA: Peter Smith, 1964), 20.

Tappan bailed him out: Arthur Tappan to Benjamin Lundy, May 29, 1830, Anti-Slavery
Collection, Boston Public Library.

new cotton states: Mayer, *All on Fire,* 92.

to read and write: Douglass, *Narrative.*

4. The Enslaved Write Their History

31 *occasionally for — slavery:* Amanda Brickell Bellows, "Author! Author!," *New York Times,* March 16, 2012.

32 *"the land is fertile":* Venture Smith, *Narrative of the Life and Adventures of Venture, a Native of Africa* (New London: C. Holt, at the Bee-office, 1798), 7.

33 Grimes, the Runaway Slave: William Grimes, *Life of William Grimes, the Runaway Slave* (New York: W. Grimes, 1825).

34 *only to please his master:* Grimes, *Life,* 18.
    little children, imposed: Frederick Douglass, *My Bondage and My Freedom* (New York: Miller, Orton & Mulligan, 1855), 37.

35 *"the way of presents":* Douglass, *My Bondage and My Freedom,* 35–36.
    dripping to the floor: Douglass, *Narrative,* 7.

36 *"a man-stealer":* Douglass, *Narrative,* 122.
    "Liberty and Equality": Grimes, *Life,* 5.
    "charter of American Liberty": Grimes, *Life,* 68.

5. Frederick Douglass's History in Slavery

37 *"at a very early age":* Douglass, *Narrative,* 2–4. Much of the information about Douglass's life before his escape is drawn from his first memoir. Where I rely on another version, I add a new citation. Where I move from one episode in his life to another, I add a citation for the new material.

38 *"unmotherly indifference":* Douglass, *My Bondage,* 52–54.

39 *"laid in the gashes":* Douglass, *Narrative,* 27.
    off Aliceanna Street: Jacques Kelly, "2 Neighborhoods Show City's Gems of Black History," *Baltimore Sun,* February 19, 1993.
    "mistress, Sophia Auld": Douglass, *Narrative,* 30.
    "from slavery to freedom": Douglass, *Narrative,* 33.

40 "a slave for life!": Douglass, *Narrative,* 38–39.

41 *him to rural slavery:* Douglass, *Narrative,* 57.
    "a slave in fact": Douglass, *Narrative,* 73.
    "the Easter holidays": Douglass, *Narrative,* 83–87.

42 *"'got you, haven't we?'":* Douglass, *Narrative,* 92.
    "reward of this toil": Douglass, *Narrative,* 93–99.
    whole story of his escape: Douglass, *Narrative,* 100–117; and Douglass, *My Bondage,* 321–35.
    details of his escape: Frederick Douglass, *The Life and Times of Frederick Douglass* (Hartford: Park Publishing Co., 1881), 177–201.

6. Frederick Douglass's Escape

43 *revised in 1892:* Frederick Douglass, *Life and Times of Frederick Douglass* (Boston: De Wolfe & Fiske Co., 1892).
    he left the South: Frederick Douglass to Wilbur Siebert, March 27, 1893, Wilbur H. Siebert Underground Railroad Collection, Ohio History Center Archives/Library.
    as early as 1838: Robert Clemens Smedley, *History of the Underground Railroad in Chester and the Neighboring Counties of Pennsylvania* (Lancaster, Pa.: The Office of the Journal, 1883), 355.

passed in 1793: Herbert Aptheker, *A Documentary History of the Negro People in the United States: Colonial Times Through the Civil War* (New York: Citadel Press, 1968), 39–44.

a separate congregation: Newman, *Freedom's Prophet,* 173.

founder of Allen's group: Elmer P. Martin and Joanne M. Martin, "Daniel Coker, Community Leader," *Baltimore Sun,* February 19, 1998.

44 *their human property?:* Daniel Coker, *A Dialogue Between a Virginian and an African Minister* (Boston: Benjamin Edes, 1810).

going back to Africa: Sinha, *Slave's Cause,* 131.

who would be expelled: "The African-American Mosaic: Colonization," Library of Congress.

"elevate the Blacks": Vincent P. Franklin, "Education for Colonization: Attempts to Educate Free Blacks in the United States for Emigration to Africa, 1823–1833," *Journal of Negro Education* (Winter 1974): 91–103.

45 *bring the building down:* Benjamin Quarles, *Black Abolitionists* (Oxford: Oxford University Press, 1969), 14.

brethren to freedom: Quarles, *Black Abolitionists,* 4–5.

roll off the press: Jacqueline Bacon, "The History of *Freedom's Journal:* A Study in Empowerment and Community," *Journal of African American History* (Winter 2003): 1–20.

the fugitive's papers: This account is drawn from Douglass, *Life and Times* (1881), 233–49.

nautical-looking outfit: William S. McFeely, *Frederick Douglass* (New York: W. W. Norton & Co., 1991), 70.

46 *"den of hungry lions.":* Douglass, *Narrative,* 107.

Underground Railroad in New York: We have no way of knowing whether Douglass had been told to look for Ruggles by the well-established Baltimore Black community. Ruggles was one of the most effective and prominent Black players in the New York escape route. It strains credulity to think he fell into Ruggles's hands by a chance meeting on the streets of New York.

7. David Walker Appeals and Garrison Hears

51 *September of 1829:* David Walker, *Walker's Appeal, in Four Articles; Together with a Preamble, to the Coloured Citizens of the World, but in Particular, and Very Expressly, to Those of the United States of America* (Boston: David Walker, September 28, 1829).

52 *increasingly competitive economy:* "Free Blacks in the North," *Encyclopedia of the New American Nation,* Encyclopedia.com, April 15, 2021.

discrimination in the North: Nina Mjagkij, *Organizing Black America: An Encyclopedia of African American Associations* (London: Routledge, 2001), 282.

"our miserable condition": Peter P. Hinks, *To Awaken My Afflicted Brethren: David Walker and the Problem of Antebellum Slave Resistance* (University Park, Pa.: Penn State University Press, 2006), 93.

its brief lifespan: Bacon, "The History of *Freedom's Journal,*" 50.

Garrison's writing as well: Marcy J. Dinius, "'Look!!! Look!!! Look!!! at This!!!': The Radical Typography of David Walker's 'Appeal,'" *PMLA* (January 2011): 55–72.

53 *moment in any movement:* Walker, *Appeal,* 9–21.

"advantage of us": Walker, *Appeal,* 30.

54 *effrontery of practicing Christianity:* Walker, *Appeal,* 41.

slaves were men: Walker, *Appeal,* 52.

"a slave to a tyrant?": Walker, *Appeal,* 30.

predictably, had fits: Horace Seldon, "Decision, Dilemma and Doubt: The Death of David Walker," David Walker Memorial Project, davidwalkermemorial.org.

Genius of Universal Emancipation: Mayer, *All on Fire,* 83. Mayer describes the process by which Garrison gravitated away from the timid Lundy, under the logic of Walker's *Appeal.*

55 *Edwin Garrison Walker:* Hinks, *To Awaken,* 270.

56 *out of jail:* Mayer, *All on Fire,* 101.

friend James Forten: Julie Winch, *A Gentleman of Color: The Life of James Forten* (Oxford: Oxford University Press, 2002), 240.

from Little Women: Anne K. Phillips and Gregory Eiselein, eds., *The Louisa May Alcott Encyclopedia* (Westport, Conn.: Greenwood Press, 2001), 20.

57 *issues of Garrison's newspaper:* Paul Goodman, *Of One Blood: Abolitionism and the Origins of Racial Equality* (Berkeley: University of California Press, 1998), 38.

"colored people" of Boston: Letter from James George Barbadoes, *The Liberator,* February 12, 1831.

"beneficial to our color": William Lloyd Garrison to James G. Barbadoes, December 10, 1830, *The Liberator,* February 12, 1831.

Despotism of Freedom: David Lee Child, "The Despotism of Freedom, Or, The Tyranny and Cruelty of American Republican slave-masters, shown to be the worst in the world; in a speech, delivered at the first anniversary of the New England Anti-Slavery Society, 1833," Library of Congress.

58 *begging for money:* James Forten to William Lloyd Garrison, December 31, 1830.

"I WILL BE HEARD": The Liberator, January 1, 1831.

59 *"sufferings I participate":* William Lloyd Garrison, *An Address Delivered Before the Free People of Color in Philadelphia and Other Cities* (Boston: Stephen Foster, 1831). Garrison arranged for his speech to be bound in a little pamphlet, explaining that his Black supporters had asked for a copy.

abolished in 1843: Amber D. Moulton, *The Fight for Interracial Marriage Rights in Antebellum Massachusetts* (Cambridge: Harvard University Press, 2015), 2.

before Allen's death: Newman, *Freedom's Prophet,* 269.

convention — in 1831: "Minutes and Proceedings of the First Annual Convention of the People of Colour, held by adjournments in the city of Philadelphia, from the sixth to the eleventh of June, 1831," omeka.coloredconventions.org.

location in Delaware: Gail Arlene Ito, "Abraham Doras Shadd (1801–1882)," *Black Past,* February 24, 2009.

"firmly to resist it": "Minutes and Proceedings of the First Annual Convention of the People of Colour," 4.

60 The Liberator *asked: The Liberator,* January 8, 1831.

characteristic all caps: The Liberator, April 23, 1831.

broadside against colonization: William Lloyd Garrison, *Thoughts on African Colonization* (Boston: Garrison and Knapp, 1832).

"as their advocate": John Hilton to William Lloyd Garrison, *The Liberator,* February 12, 1831.

uprising in Virginia: Thomas R. Gray, *The Confessions of Nat Turner* (Richmond: Thomas R. Gray, 1831).

61 *"Was not Christ crucified?":* Gray, *Confessions of Nat Turner.*

sympathetic to the cause: Mayer, *All on Fire,* 120.

defending the enslaved: Sinha, *Slave's Cause,* 212; Mayer, *All on Fire,* 123.

distributing incendiary matter: Mayer, *All on Fire,* 122.

its editor's rendition: Mayer, *All on Fire,* 123.

suppress its publication: National Intelligencer, September 15, 1831.
tear the union apart: Robert N. Elliott, "Gales, Joseph," *NCPedia,* 1986.
Garrison the exposure: Mayer, *All on Fire,* 220.
62 *his life, years later:* Douglass, *Narrative,* 41.

8. Starting the Black and White Antislavery Societies

63 *and a pittance:* Arthur Tappan to William Lloyd Garrison, August 9, 1830.
the eastern seaboard: Beckert, *Empire of Cotton,* 204.
64 *support Garrison's cause:* Arthur Tappan to William Lloyd Garrison, October 12, 1831.
65 *those founding days:* Oliver Johnson, *William Lloyd Garrison and His Times; or, Sketches of the Anti-Slavery Movement in America, and of the Man Who Was Its Founder and Moral Leader* (Boston: Houghton, Mifflin and Company, 1885).
"N—r Hill": Johnson, *William Lloyd Garrison,* 85.
talk of colonization banished: Anne Morrow Lindbergh, *Against Wind and Tide: Letters and Journals, 1947–1986* (New York: Pantheon Books, 2012), 60–61.
Black names, including James Barbadoes: Mayer, *All on Fire,* 646.
Garrison's antislavery group: William Cooper Nell, *William Cooper Nell: Nineteenth Century Abolitionist, Historian, Integrationist* (Baltimore: Black Classic Press, 2002), 12.
in Lynn, Massachusetts: William Lloyd Garrison to Alonzo Lewis, March 13, 1832.
66 *for the new group: Second Annual Report of the New England Anti-Slavery Society* (Boston, 1834), 11–12.
first Female Anti-Slavery Society: Dorothy Sterling, *We Are Your Sisters: Black Women in the Nineteenth Century* (New York: W. W. Norton & Company, 1996), xvii.
more worldly preachers: Roger Joseph Green, "Charles Grandison Finney: The Social Implications of His Ministry," *Asbury Theological Journal* 48, no. 2 (1993): 5–26. Finney was no advocate for racial equality either, excluding Black church members from office, and pursuing a centrist line for most of the antebellum period.
go into the field: Mayer, *All on Fire,* 170.
"Quaker hatter": Mayer, *All on Fire,* 139.
shoemakers, cordwainers: Edward Magdol, *The Antislavery Rank and File* (Westport, Conn.: Praeger, 1986), 46–50.
67 *African Colonization, in 1832:* Mayer, *All on Fire,* 135. The title is a full Garrison: *Thoughts on African Colonization: or an Impartial Exhibition of the Doctrines, Principles and Purposes of the American Colonization Society. Together with the Resolutions, Addresses and Remonstrances of the Free People of Color.*
around the Benevolent Empire: Goodman, *Of One Blood,* 56.
Maine's Colby College: Mayer, *All on Fire,* 140.
Western Reserve College in Ohio: Beriah Green, Western Reserve College, to William Lloyd Garrison, March 8, 1833.
for antislavery spread: Goodman, *All on Fire,* 57.
68 *part of each school year:* Barnes, *The Antislavery Impulse,* 38.
some of its power: Edwin A. Miles, "The Old South and the Classical World," *North Carolina Historical Review* 48, no. 3 (July 1971): 258–75.
the manual labor school: Beriah Green, *The Miscellaneous Writings of Beriah Green* (Whitesboro, N.Y.: Oneida Institute, 1841), 396.
society for immediate abolition: Milton C. Sernett, *North Star Country: Upstate New York and the Crusade for African American Freedom* (Syracuse: Syracuse University Press, 1986), 30.

dignity of manual labor: Barnes, *Antislavery Impulse,* 38.

abolitionist Charles Stuart: Owen W. Muelder, *Theodore Dwight Weld and the American Anti-Slavery Society* (Jefferson, N.C.: McFarland & Company, 2011), 52–53.

to find a location: Muelder, *Weld,* 202.

teach-in on abolition: Muelder, *Weld,* 36–37.

69   *who had settled in Cincinnati:* Sernett, *North Star Country,* 28.

stop the discussion of abolition: Barnes, *Antislavery Impulse,* 70–71.

for lack of funds: Muelder, *Weld,* 37.

around the region: Jon Miltimore, "What America's First Student-Led Rebellion Looked Like," *Intellectual Takeout,* October 11, 2016.

with stunning results: Ron Gorman, "William T. Allan—Lane Rebel from the South," *Oberlin Heritage Center Blog,* August 12, 2013.

throughout the North: Barnes, *Antislavery Impulse,* 38–41.

paid much of the freight: Quarles, *Black Abolitionists,* 20–21.

new, interracial movement: Sinha, *Slave's Cause,* 221.

70   *Garrisonian immediatists:* Mayer, *All on Fire,* 157.

"determined to be off": Douglass, *Narrative,* 49–50.

9. A National Movement Emerges

71   *New York from Europe:* Barnes, *Anti-Slavery Impulse,* 34–35; Mayer, *All on Fire,* 166–68.

incite the mob: Garrison and Garrison, *William Lloyd Garrison,* 1:380–419.

when he stayed late: Quarles, *Black Abolitionists,* 21.

drove the abolitionists out: Mayer, *All on Fire,* 167.

72   *flee their own homes:* Dorceta E. Taylor, *The Environment and People in American Cities, 1600–1900s: Disorder, Inequality, and Social Change* (Durham: Duke University Press, 2009), 63.

ransacked Lewis Tappan's home: Taylor, *Environment and People,* 62.

his own protection: The Liberator, October 24, 1835.

73   *witnessing that event:* Mayer, *All on Fire,* 208.

ink by the barrel: The saying "Never argue with a man who buys ink by the barrel" is sometimes attributed to Mark Twain but also to Indiana congressman Charles Brownson; see Fred Shapiro, "Ink by the Barrel," *Freakonomics,* May 12, 2011.

"political religion of the nation": Paul Simon, *Freedom's Champion: Elijah Lovejoy* (Carbondale: Southern Illinois University Press, 1994), 163.

meeting immediately anyway: Mayer, *All on Fire,* 177.

benevolent society, the Adelphi: Mayer, *All on Fire,* 171.

74   *fifteen percent of the population:* Clerk of the House of Representatives, *Returns of the Fifth Census* (Washington, D.C.: Duff Green, 1832).

were held in slavery: W. S. Rossiter, Chief Clerk of the Bureau of the Census, *A Century of Population Growth (1790–1900),* National Archives, Records of the Bureau of the Census, 132–41.

people in American history: Goodman, *Of One Blood,* 16.

all other southern crops: Knut Oyangen, "The Cotton Economy of the Old South: American Agricultural History Primer," Iowa State University Center for Agricultural History and Rural Studies.

mills wove the cloth: Anne Farrow, Joel Lang, and Jenifer Frank, *Complicity: How the North Promoted, Prolonged, and Profited from Slavery* (New York: Ballantine Books, 2005), 13–16.

"lords of the loom": Charles Sumner, speech at Worcester, Mass., June 28, 1848, in *Charles Sumner, His Complete Works*, vol. 2 (Boston: Lee and Shepard, 1900), 233.

75 *the North and the South:* Michael F. Holt, *Political Parties and American Political Development from the Age of Jackson to the Age of Lincoln* (Baton Rouge: Louisiana State University Press, 1992), 36–37.

Historians dispute: The two poles of this dispute are represented by Michael F. Holt in, among other works, *Political Parties; Forging a Majority: The Formation of the Republican Party in Pittsburgh, 1848–1860* (Pittsburgh University of Pittsburgh Press, 1990); and *The Fate of Their Country: Politicians, Slavery Extension, and the Coming of the Civil War* (New York: Hill and Wang, 2004) on the one hand and, on the other, Eric Foner, *Free Soil, Free Labor, Free Men: The Ideology of the Republican Party Before the Civil War* (Oxford: Oxford University Press, 1970), and the astonishing body of work inspired since Foner first produced it in 1970.

causes of the Civil War: This is not the place to weigh in on that dispute, nor am I the one to do it. This book has been heavily shaped by Foner's work and, before him, the work of my teacher David B. Davis, which focuses on the central role of slavery. The purpose of this chapter is to share with my readers how politics became central to the goal of abolition, which makes Douglass's ultimate move to political abolition so weighty.

mutually assured destruction: Patrick Rael, *Eighty-Eight Years: The Long Death of Slavery in the United States, 1777–1865* (Athens: University of Georgia Press, 2015), 189.

"perplexing and agitating": The Liberator, August 11, 1837.

abolition within the church: Lewis M. Purifoy, "The Southern Methodist Church and the Proslavery Argument," *Journal of Southern History* 32, no. 3 (August 1966): 325–41.

76 *humans in his power:* Douglass, *Narrative*, 53–54.

State House in Boston: Mayer, *All on Fire*, 137–40.

fact of Black inferiority: Leon Littwack, *North of Slavery: The Negro in the Free States, 1790–1860* (Chicago: University of Chicago Press, 1965), 64–66.

in courts of law: An amateur historian, Douglas Harper, has gathered a survey of the legal status of Black people in the antebellum North, "Slavery in the North," slavenorth.com. The whole issue is the subject of the important recent book by Kate Masur, *Until Justice Be Done;* see x–xi and passim.

race riots in 1834: Littwack, *North of Slavery*, 219.

10. The Liberator *Will Be Read*

78 *the spoken word:* Muelder, *Weld*, 23.

led the movement: Muelder, *Weld*, 36.

in precarious straits: Mayer, *All on Fire*, 229.

most beautiful Benson daughter: Garrison, *Letters*, 84–85.

"token of my esteem": William Lloyd Garrison to Helen Eliza Benson, January 18, 1834, Garrison Family Archives, Houghton Library, Harvard University.

79 *would be "inefficient":* Helen Eliza Benson to William Lloyd Garrison, February 18, 1834.

and exposed position: Garrison and Garrison, *William Lloyd Garrison*, 423.

incendiary founding statement: The Liberator, December 14, 1833.

80 *cruel and dangerous:* The statement is condensed minimally here for clarity.

"Refuge of Oppression": The Liberator, January 11, 1834.

81 *"men and measures":* The Liberator, January 2, 1835.

11. Maria Weston Chapman Takes the Reins

83   *"cause of emancipation";* The Liberator, January 7, 1832.
     confined to white women: Julie Roy Jeffrey, *The Great Silent Army of Abolitionism: Ordinary Women in the Antislavery Movement* (Chapel Hill: University of North Carolina Press, 1998), 41–43.
     Maria's: I occasionally use "Maria" to distinguish Weston Chapman from her Weston sisters.
     Boston Female Anti-Slavery Society: The Liberator, September 13, 1834.
     joined quickly in 1834: Jeffrey, *Great Silent Army,* 43–44.
     she was a spy: Debra Gold Hansen, *Strained Sisterhood: Gender and Class in the Boston Female Anti-Slavery Society* (Amherst: University of Massachusetts Press, 2009), 104.
84   *raised little money:* Chambers, *Weston Sisters,* 42–43.
     "sell for a fortune!": Maria Weston Chapman to unknown recipient, ca. 1835.
     antislavery society's debt: Hansen, *Strained Sisterhood,* 127.
     announcement every year: Debora Weston to Anne Warren Weston, December 1840.
     "few others of that sort": Anne Warren Weston to Debora Weston, December 21, 1836.
85   *upcoming antislavery fair:* Hansen, *Strained Sisterhood,* 128.
     several to a bed: Chambers, *Weston Sisters,* 146.
     in effectiveness: Hansen, *Strained Sisterhood,* 128.
     Garrison personally: Hansen, *Strained Sisterhood,* 127.
     the Female Society: The date is unclear. Biographer Lee Chambers cites a July 21, 1835, letter written by Anne Warren Weston as secretary from the papers of the Boston Female Anti-Slavery Society at Memorial Hall Library, Andover, Mass. (*Weston Sisters,* 210), while in her essay "Maria Weston Chapman," in *Portraits of American Women: From Settlement to the Present,* ed. G. J. Barker-Benfield and Catherine Clinton (New York: Oxford University Press, 1998), 137–46, Catherine Clinton assigns the post at that date to Maria Weston Chapman. The first letter cited here is dated July 1835 in the Weston papers at the Boston Public Library and certainly sounds like the executive speaking.
     youthful American movement: Mayer, *All on Fire,* 200.
     critics charged: C. Duncan Rice, "The Antislavery Mission of George Thompson to the United States, 1834–1835," *Journal of American Studies* (April 1968): 25.
86   *"you please of this letter":* Maria Weston Chapman to unknown recipient, October 17, 1835.
     "subject of Freedom": Maria Weston Chapman to Debora Weston, September 6, 1839.
     "moonstruck and unsexed": Maria Weston Chapman to Mary Ann Estlin, March 24, 1853.
     "never lost it": Maria Weston Chapman to unknown recipient, 1855, cited in Clinton, "Maria Weston Chapman," 150.
     be put in danger: Mayer, *All on Fire,* 200.
     "die here as anywhere": Janet L. Coryell, "The Weston Sisters: An American Abolitionist Family," *Civil War Book Review* (Summer 2015), digitalcommons.isu.edu.
     "them to leave?": Mayer, *All on Fire,* 202.
     trouble for the mayor: Mayer, *All on Fire,* 202.
87   *the Chapman house:* Lawrence Friedman, *Gregarious Saints: Self and Community in Antebellum American Abolitionism, 1830–1870* (Cambridge: Cambridge University Press, 2010), 54–55.
     (and her unruly sisters): Chambers, *Weston Sisters,* 160.
     nature of the enterprise: Friedman, *Gregarious Saints,* 55.
     "give their opinion": Anne Warren Weston to Mary Weston, April 15, 1836.
     born in 1837: Chambers, *Weston Sisters,* 82.

88 *her secret weapon:* Chambers has told the social history in her book *The Weston Sisters,*
from which much material in this paragraph is drawn.
the more political: Chambers, *Weston Sisters,* 81–84.
"District of Columbia?": The Liberator, August 10, 1833.
on people's doors: Chambers, *Weston Sisters,* 25.
talking at all: Susan Zaeske, *Signatures of Citizenship: Petitioning, Antislavery, and Wom-
en's Political Identity* (Chapel Hill: University of North Carolina Press, 2003), 47.
89 *to be known, "gagged":* Zaeske, *Signatures,* 11.
twice that number: Zaeske, *Signatures,* 119.
between the states: Douglass, *Narrative,* 41–42.
two million signatures: Jeffrey, *Great Silent Army,* 88.
90 *six-year-old "Little Med":* Hansen, *Strained Sisterhood,* 17. The report of the Boston Female Anti-Slavery Society from 1836 says merely that the vice president of the Society
brought Med's existence and place of residence to their attention. Although many sec-
ondary sources relate the story of the tea, no primary source gets any closer.
"or freedom principle": Joseph T. Murphy, "Neither a Slave nor a King: The Antislavery
Project and the Origins of the American Sectional Crisis, 1820–1848" (Ph.D. diss., City
University of New York, 2016).
against the British: Paul Finkelman, *An Imperfect Union: Slavery, Federalism, and Comity*
(Clark, N.J.: The Lawbook Exchange, 2000).
nothing to argue about: Masur, *Until Justice Be Done,* 2–3, 5, 9, 10; Finkelman, *Imperfect
Union,* 21–23. See also "American Slavery and the Conflict of Laws," *Columbia Law
Review* 71 (January 1971): 74–79.
91 *southern jurisdictions:* Murphy, "Neither a Slave," 57.
"but for our own": "Reports of the arguments of counsel and of the opinion of the court,
in the case of Commonwealth vs. Aves" (Boston: Isaac Knapp, 1836).
92 *not an obligation:* Joseph Story, *Commentaries on the Conflicts of Laws, Foreign and Domestic* (Boston: Billiard, Gray and Company, 1834).
93 *Boston Anti-Slavery Society:* Finkelman, *Imperfect Union,* 87–88.
Seward, in 1839: Finkelman, *Imperfect Union,* 109–12.
all over the state: Finkelman, *Imperfect Union,* 79–80.
"actually confiscated?": The Liberator, October 15, 1836.
free soil in 1772: Leonard Levy, *The Law of the Commonwealth and Chief Justice Shaw*
(New York: Oxford University Press, 1957), 62–68.
paste them on: Zaeske, *Signatures,* 50.
94 *convention in New York:* Ira V. Brown, "'Am I Not a Woman and a Sister?' The Anti-Slavery Convention of American Women, 1837–1839," *Pennsylvania History: A Journal of
Mid-Atlantic Studies* (January 1983): 1–19.
not an accident: Darlene Clark Hine, "Lifting the Veil," in *The State of Afro-American
History: Past, Present and Future* (Baton Rouge: Louisiana State University Press, 1986),
231–32.
and interracial, gathering: Zaeske, *Signatures,* 82.
Grimké's resolution: Ira V. Brown, "Cradle of Feminism: The Philadelphia Female Anti-Slavery Society, 1833–1840," *Pennsylvania Magazine of History and Biography* (April
1978): 143–66.

12. Antislavery on the March

95 *of his first child:* Mayer, *All on Fire,* 220–27.
he was a hypochondriac: William Lloyd Garrison to George Benson, May 25, 1838.

some of her creations: Maria Weston Chapman, *Songs of the Free and Hymns of Christian Freedom* (Boston: Isaac Knapp, 1836).

abolition and women's rights: Maria Weston Chapman, *Right and Wrong in Boston* (Boston: Dow & Jackson's Anti-Slavery Press, 1839).

Massachusetts Anti-Slavery Society: Jane H. Pease and William H. Pease, "The Role of Women in the Antislavery Movement," *Historical Papers* 2, no. 1 (1967):167–83.

96   *the 1835 rioting:* Chambers, *Weston Sisters,* 145; William Lloyd Garrison to Helen Benson Garrison, March 5, 1836.

even in self-defense: Elizabeth Forest, "William Lloyd Garrison and the Problem of Non-Resistance," *Ex Post Facto* 7 (1998).

97   *with the immediatist movement:* Mayer, *All on Fire,* 216.

from times past: Mayer, *All on Fire,* 195.

his status, Garrison: Nancy Pope, "America's First Direct Mail Campaign," Smithsonian National Postal Museum blog, July 29, 2010.

charismatic Theodore Weld: Muelder, *Weld,* 38–39.

98   *"Weld's Seventy":* Muelder, *Weld,* 38–39.

Seventy in New York: Muelder, *Weld,* 60.

power of the word: John Lytle Myers, "The Agency System of the Anti-Slavery Movement, 1832–1837, and Its Antecedents in Other Benevolent and Reform Societies" (Ph.D. diss., University of Michigan, 1960), 413–20.

"Gradualism": William Lloyd Garrison to Henry E. Benson, December 3, 1836.

silence his instrument: Muelder, *Weld,* 39.

across the North: John L. Myers, "Organization of 'The Seventy': To Arouse the North Against Slavery," in *History of the American Abolitionist Movement: A Bibliography of Scholarly Articles,* ed. John R. McKivigan (New York: Garland Publishing, 1999), 287–88.

college teach-ins: Muelder, *Weld,* 68–98.

99   *first recorded Black agent:* Les Wallace, "Charles Lenox Remond: The Lost Prince of Abolitionism," *Negro History Bulletin* (May–June 1977): 696–701.

created around New England: John L. Myers, "The Anti-Slavery Agency System in Maine, 1836–1838," *Maine History* (1983): 57–58.

its southern members: Myers, "The Anti-Slavery Agency System in Maine," 69–70.

"on my head injured": Muelder, *Weld,* 56–57.

"orator of his time": Myers, "The Agency System of the Anti-Slavery Movement," 166.

"great tact and power": William Birney, *James G. Birney and His Times* (New York: D. Appleton and Company, 1890), 152.

100   *"familiar illustrations":* Birney, *James G. Birney and His Times,* 152.

by local merchants: Myers, "The Agency System of the Anti-Slavery Movement," 392–93.

family to attend: Myers, "The Agency System of the Anti-Slavery Movement," 385.

"issue of temperance": Myers, "The Agency System of the Anti-Slavery Movement," 385, citing Henry B. Stanton, *Random Reflections.*

101   *from slave Kentucky:* Birney, *James G. Birney,* 207.

an estimated 150,000: Muelder, *Weld,* 146.

was twice that: Sinha, *Slave's Cause,* 252.

13. Moral Garrison Splits with the Politicos

102   *Park Street Church:* "We are all alike guilty. Slavery is strictly a national sin." William Lloyd Garrison, address at Park Street Church, Boston, July 4, 1829.

among religious scholars: Caroline L. Shanks, "The Biblical Anti-Slavery Argument of the Decade 1830–1840," *Journal of Negro History* 16, no. 2 (April 1931): 132–57.

from their pulpits: Mayer, *All on Fire,* 226; William Goodell, *Slavery and Antislavery: A History of the Great Struggle in Both Hemispheres, with a View of the Slavery Question in the United States* (Arkose Press, 2015), 430.

103 *"whoredom and adultery": The Liberator,* July 23, 1836.

"colored people": William E. Channing, *Slavery* (Boston: James Munroe and Company, 1835), 82.

directed at Beecher: The Liberator, February 7, 1836.

"is against us": The Liberator, February 27, 1836.

104 *Boston every Sunday:* Chambers, *Weston Sisters,* 26.

listen to the Grimkés: Anne Warren Weston to Caroline Weston, August 7, 1837.

"Pastoral Letter": The Liberator, August 11, 1837.

"permanent injury": Weston Chapman, *Right and Wrong.*

on Boston churches: Wendell Phillips Garrison and Francis Jackson Garrison, *William Lloyd Garrison, 1805–1879: The Story of His Life, Told by His Children,* vol. 2, *1835–1840* (New York: The Century Co., 1885), 137–38.

sister Debora Weston: Anne Warren Weston to Debora Weston, September 15, 1837.

105 *silent in church:* 1 Corinthians 14:34–35.

most exigent member: Mayer, *All on Fire,* 233–36; clergy letter reprinted in *The Liberator,* August 11, 1837.

106 *training camp in 1836:* Mayer *All on Fire,* 232; Katharine Du Pre Lumpkin, *The Emancipation of Angelina Grimké* (Chapel Hill: University of North Carolina Press, 2014), 109–12.

"identical with men": Fourth Annual Report of the Boston Female Anti-Slavery Society (Boston: Isaac Knapp, 1837), 42–44.

"Try Men's Souls": "Proceedings of the Woman's Rights Convention, Held at the Unitarian Church, Rochester, N.Y.," August 2, 1848 (New York: Robert J. Johnston, 1870).

manufacturing and commerce: Hansen, *Strained Sisterhood,* 72–73. Hansen did extraordinary work identifying the members from names on petitions and lists of convention delegates and reconstructing their social identity. In chapter 4 and its notes, Hansen details the research.

107 *flourishing alternative path:* Hansen, *Strained Sisterhood* 109. The story as told in Hansen's 1993 book heavily favors the Weston Chapman version of who did better after the breakup. A generation later, the historian Julie Roy Jeffrey found previously scattered archival material reflecting a robust and competitive life for the breakaway Massachusetts Female Emancipation Society. Julie Roy Jeffrey, "The Liberty Women of Boston: Evangelicalism and Antislavery Politics," *New England Quarterly* 85, no. 1 (March 2012): 38–77.

deference to the ministers: Juliana Tappan letter to Anne Warren Weston, July 21, 1837.

their critics did: Chambers, *Weston Sisters,* 31.

Ralph Waldo Emerson: Maria Weston Chapman to William Lloyd Garrison, August 30, 1838.

108 *one in Cleveland:* Sinha, *Slave's Cause,* 262; Richard H. Sewell, *Ballots for Freedom: Antislavery Politics in the United States, 1837–1860* (New York: Oxford University Press, 1976), 52.

to a key committee: Chambers, *Weston Sisters,* 33.

The Non-Resistant: Jane H. Pease and William H. Pease, *Bound with Them in Chains: A Biographical History of the Antislavery Movement* (Westport, Conn.: Praeger, 1972),

50; Kim Reynolds, "Notable Women, Notable Manuscripts: Maria Weston Chapman,"
Boston Public Library blogs.

109 *could refuse to vote:* The proceedings were reported in the *Seventh Annual Report of the
Board of Managers of the Massachusetts Anti-Slavery Society, Presented January 24, 1839*
(Boston, 1839); *The Liberator,* February 1, 1839.
"every abolitionist a voter?": Chambers, *Weston Sisters,* 34.
breakaway societies: Hansen, *Strained Sisterhood,* 113.
New York society's Emancipator: Mayer, *All on Fire,* 268–69; *The Emancipator,* March 12,
1840; *The Liberator,* June 19, 1840.
no human government: Birney's charge was reprinted in *The Liberator,* April 5, 1839.
"influencing Church and State": William Lloyd Garrison, "The Anti Slavery Organization," *The Liberator,* April 5, 1839.

110 *New England chapters:* Aileen S. Kraditor, *Means and Ends in American Abolitionism:
Garrison and His Critics on Strategy and Tactics, 1834–1850* (New York: Pantheon Books,
1969), 120–23.
written and leaked: Mayer, *All on Fire,* 276–77.
"exploded the society": John Greenleaf Whittier to Benjamin Jones, July 1840, in Dorothy
Sterling, *Ahead of Her Time: Abby Kelley and the Politics of Antislavery* (New York: W. W.
Norton, 1991), 384; Mayer, *All on Fire,* 282.
for twenty years: "Who Was Abby Kelley Foster?" Worcester Women's History Project,
www.wwhp.org.
committee with her: Mayer, *All on Fire,* 281.

111 *racial segregation policy: The Liberator,* July 9, 1841.
feeling quite empowered: National Anti-Slavery Standard, August 26, 1841.

14. Douglass Joins Garrison

115 *from a border state:* Sinha, *Slave's Cause,* 382.
plight in freedom: Quarles, *Black Abolitionist,* 49.
advocates of equality: Quarles, *Black Abolitionist,* 46–49.

116 *Pennington had served:* Quarles, *Black Abolitionist,* 46; Herbert Aptheker, "The Negro in
the Abolitionist Movement," *Science & Society* 5, no. 2 (Spring, 1941): 148–72.
important relationship: Blight, *Frederick Douglass,* 117.
weakened and marginalized: Barnes, *Anti-Slavery Impulse,* 161–62.

117 *attending national meetings:* Quarles, *Black Abolitionist,* 54.
white-run organizations: Quarles, *Black Abolitionist,* 55–56.
away to safety: Sinha, *Slave's Cause,* 385.
in any year before: J. Blaine Hudson, *Fugitive Slaves and the Underground Railroad in the
Kentucky Borderland* (Jefferson, N.C.: McFarland, 2011).

118 *touching free soil:* Sinha, *Slave's Cause,* 384–85; Paul Stewart, "Underground Railroad
History: Vigilance Committees," *New York Almanack,* August 25, 2014.

119 *lose the legal proceedings:* Bruce A. Ragsdale, "Amistad: The Federal Courts and the Challenge to Slavery," Federal Judicial Center, 2002, 4.

120 *importation of slaves:* "An Act Prohibiting the Importation of Slaves" (1808), National
Archives.
"property in men": Howard Jones, *Mutiny on the Amistad: The Saga of a Slave Revolt and Its
Impact on American Abolition, Law, and Diplomacy* (New York: Oxford University Press,
1987), loc. 1965.

model of a firebrand: James Oakes, *The Crooked Path to Abolition: Abraham Lincoln and the Antislavery Constitution* (New York: W. W. Norton & Company, 2021), 35–36.

121 *duties as a congressman:* Jones, *Mutiny,* loc. 2104.

try out his theories: "Argument of John Quincy Adams, Before the Supreme Court of the United States, in the Case of the United States, Appellants, vs. Cinque, and Others, Africans, Captured in the Schooner Amistad, by Lieut. Gedney, Delivered on the 24th of February and 1st of March, 1841," Library of Congress.

"this case is decided": "Argument of John Quincy Adams."

122 *"to be deemed free":* United States v. The Amistad, 40 U.S. 518.

123 *jails for two years:* Sinha, *Slave's Cause,* 407–10.

funding the defense: Mayer, *All on Fire,* 308; Sinha, *Slave's Cause,* 406–11.

articles about the case: Maggie Montesinos Sale, *The Slumbering Volcano: American Slave Ship Revolts and the Production of Rebellious Masculinity* (Durham: Duke University Press, 1997), 227.

125 *"wrongs he had endured":* The Pennsylvania Freeman, October 20, 1841.

"like a heavy weight": Frederick Douglass, "I Have Come to Tell You Something About Slavery," in Blassingame et al., *Frederick Douglass Papers,* 1:5.

"to the south": Frederick Douglass, "The Union, Slavery, and Abolitionist Petitions," in Blassingame et al., *Frederick Douglass Papers,* 1:5.

clutching his train seat: John A. Collins, "Eastern Railroad — Colorphobia — Lynch Law–Robbery — Quakerism," *The Liberator,* October 15, 1841.

staying on for days: Blight, *Frederick Douglass,* 106–7.

126 *"pathos and humor":* Elizabeth Cady Stanton, "An 1895 Public Letter from Elizabeth Cady Stanton on the Occasion of Frederick Douglass's Death," in *In Memoriam: Frederick Douglass,* ed. Helen Douglass (West Bloomfield, Mich.: Franklin Classics, 2018).

"talk so well?": Blight, *Frederick Douglass,* 113.

"the American Lyceum": Carl Bode, *The American Lyceum: Town Meeting of the Mind* (New York: Oxford University Press, 1965).

127 *"conscious intellectual production":* Donald M. Scott, "The Popular Lecture and the Creation of a Public in Mid-Nineteenth Century America," *Journal of American History* 66, no. 4 (March 1980): 791–809.

"web of national civilization": Thomas Wentworth Higginson, "The American Lecture System," *MacMillan's Magazine,* May–October 1848, 49.

a collective culture: Scott, "Popular Lecture," 808.

the Middle West: Angela G. Ray, *The Lyceum and Public Culture in the Nineteenth-Century United States* (East Lansing: Michigan State University Press, 2005), 627; Scott, "Popular Lecture," 809.

breakup of the union: Foner, *Free Soil.* In 1995, Foner wrote a new introduction to the 1970 book, in which he modestly described its impact a product of a changed intellectual environment. It was a "threshold," as he puts it. But his work carried the field over the threshold, and its impact cannot be overstated.

northern middle class: Jeffrey C. Benton, *Respectable and Disreputable: Leisure Time in Antebellum Montgomery* (Montgomery, Ala.: New South Books, 2011), 31–33.

more than ten years: Tom F. Wright, *Lecturing the Atlantic: Speech, Print, and an Anglo-American Commons, 1830–1870* (Oxford: Oxford University Press, 2017).

128 *amplify his voice:* Angela G. Ray, "Frederick Douglass on the Lyceum Circuit: Social Assimilation, Social Transformation?," *Rhetoric and Public Affairs* 5, no. 4 (2002): 625–47.

matter of moral uplift: Ray, "Frederick Douglass on the Lyceum Circuit," 630–34.

15. The Façade and the Cracks in the Alliance

129 *where Douglass spoke:* Gregory P. Lampe, *Frederick Douglass: Freedom's Voice* (Lansing: Michigan State University Press, 1998), 73.
only in the North: Lampe, *Freedom's Voice,* 72–74.
"was then passed": Lampe, *Freedom's Voice,* 75; "Proceedings of the Plymouth Co. Antislavery Society at Hingham," *The Liberator,* December 3, 1841.
his pacifist philosophy: The Liberator, July 1, 1842.

130 *"streamed to the ground":* Lampe, *Freedom's Voice,* 81.
bits of good news: "Proceedings of the Plymouth Co. Antislavery Society Hingham," *The Liberator,* December 3, 1841.
"and all sides free": Frederick Douglass to William Lloyd Garrison, November 8, 1842. He was, of course, well advised to take note, as much of the antebellum North routinely segregated the races, even in church.
freedom of his family: Lampe, *Freedom's Voice,* 75.

131 *role of political action:* Lampe, *Freedom's Voice,* 100.
then refuting it: Lampe, *Freedom's Voice,* 101.
political abolitionists' ways: Lampe, *Freedom's Voice,* 100–101.

132 *"pile up proofs against":* Lampe, *Freedom's Voice,* 103; *The Liberator,* February 11, 1842.
faction of antislavery: Lampe, *Freedom's Voice,* 161.
and Garrison himself: Lampe, *Freedom's Voice,* 158.
"reading" and thinking: Douglass, *My Bondage,* 361.

133 Prigg v. Pennsylvania: *Prigg v. Pennsylvania,* 41 U.S. (16n Pet.) 539.
or enslaving them: William R. Leslie, "The Pennsylvania Fugitive Slave Act of 1826," *Journal of Southern History* (November 1952): 434–35.
Pennsylvania in 1832: Prigg v. Pennsylvania, 41 U.S. 539 (1842).

134 *claim his property:* Lampe, *Freedom's Voice,* 145; Robert Cover, *Justice Accused: Antislavery and the Judicial Process* (New Haven: Yale University Press, 1984), 216; Andrew Delbanco, *The War Before the War: Fugitive Slaves and the Struggle for America's Soul from the Revolution to the Civil War* (New York: Penguin Press, 2018), 180–84.
North Star: Delbanco, *The War Before the War,* 182–83.

135 *doing just that:* Delbanco, *The War Before the War,* 181–83.
born into slavery: Lampe, *Freedom's Voice,* 146.

16. Political Abolition Pulls on Garrisonians

137 *"No Union with Slaveholders":* William Lloyd Garrison to Rev. Samuel J. May, July 17, 1845; *The Liberator,* May 6, 1842.
enslavement in the South: Robert Pierce Forbes, *The Missouri Compromise and Its Aftermath: Slavery and the Meaning of America* (Chapel Hill: University of North Carolina Press, 2007), Kindle loc. 1999-2004.

138 *fugitives away to safety:* Thomas D. Morris, *Free Men All: The Personal Liberty Laws of the North, 1780-1861* (Baltimore: Johns Hopkins University Press, 1974), 10, 11, 23–41.
positions on enslavement: Sewell, *Ballots for Freedom,* 17–18.
their own free soil: Morris, *Free Men All,* 42.
pursue the runaways: Delbanco, *The War Before the War,* quotes slavery's spokesman John C. Calhoun calling runaway slaves "the gravest and most vital of all questions." *Congressional Globe,* 30th Cong., 1st sess., April 20, 1848, 501–4.
union with them: Friedman, *Gregarious Saints,* 115.

139 *suspicious of politics:* Friedman, *Gregarious Saints,* 104–12.

had different ideas: Friedman, *Gregarious Saints,* 96.

New York household: There is speculation that Gerrit's father, Peter, held slaves before abolition in New York State. The Gerrit Smith Estate National Historic Landmark biography says "perhaps" (www.gerritsmith.org/origins/gerrit-smith); Norman K. Dann, *Practical Dreamer: Gerrit Smith and the Crusade for Social Reform* (Hamilton, N.Y.: Log Cabin Books, 2009).

when in college: Dann, *Practical Dreamer,* 17–19.

becoming a lawyer: Dann, *Practical Dreamer,* 21.

the Benevolent Empire: Dann, *Practical Dreamer,* 228–29, 239.

path into colonization: Dann, *Practical Dreamer,* 406.

to Garrisonian immediatism: Dann, *Practical Dreamer,* 408.

140 *a good breakfast:* Dann, *Practical Dreamer,* 418–19.

largest donors: Friedman, *Gregarious Saints,* 100.

rich, well-educated men: Friedman, *Gregarious Saints,* 98.

"Jamestown in 1620": Alvan Stewart, *Writings and Speeches of Alvan Stewart, on Slavery* (New York: Haskell House Publishers, 1860), 10.

"by nature equally free": Cover, *Justice Accused,* 43.

regulate commerce: Alvan Stewart, *Writings and Speeches,* 86; William Wiecek, *The Sources of Anti-Slavery Constitutionalism in America, 1760–1848* (Ithaca: Cornell University Press, 1977), 218, 271, 273.

141 *outlawed slavery everywhere:* State v. Van Beuren and State v. Post, writ of habeas corpus, Supreme Court of New Jersey, May 1845; Stewart, "A Constitutional Argument on the Subject of Slavery," *Friend of Man,* October 18, 1837, conveniently reprinted in Jacobus tenBroek, *Equal Under Law* (New York: Macmillan, 1965), appendix B, 28 1–295.

Stewart was wrong: Friedman, *Gregarious Saints,* 114.

slavery was unconstitutional: George W. F. Mellen, *An Argument on the Unconstitutionality of Slavery: Embracing an Abstract of the Proceedings of the National and State Conventions on This Subject* (Boston: Saxton & Pierce, 1841).

"free and independent": Cover, *Justice Accused,* 43.

gradual emancipation law: Geneva Smith, "Legislating Slavery in New Jersey," Princeton & Slavery, Princeton University, slavery.princeton.edu/stories.

cannot also be enslaved: Cover, *Justice Accused,* 55.

development of his argument: Cover, *Justice Accused,* 55–61.

142 *against natural law:* Cover, *Justice Accused,* 158; Lysander Spooner, *The Unconstitutionality of Slavery* (Boston: Bela Marsh, 1860), 152.

to love in religion: Dann, *Practical Dreamer,* 238–40.

"what to do to others": Dann, *Practical Dreamer,* 600, citing letter from Gerrit Smith to Henry Ward Beecher, May 20,1863.

enabling the domination: Dann, *Practical Dreamer,* 309.

143 *passionately in voluntarism:* Dann, *Practical Dreamer,* 318–19.

"place on record": The Liberator, April 10, 1840.

New York vote: Dann, *Practical Dreamer,* 327.

"April fools": Dann, *Practical Dreamer,* 323, citing Gerrit Smith, "A Report from the County of Madison to Abolitionists," November 13,1843, Madison County, N.Y., Historical Society.

silver-tongued Theodore Weld: Douglas Montagna, "Ohio, Evangelical Religion, and the Merging of the Antislavery Movement: Joshua R. Giddings, Salmon P. Chase, and Their Remarkable Crusades Against Slavery," *Studies in Midwestern History* 5, no. 1 (May 2019), passim.

144 *at Lane Seminary:* Stanton is listed as a contributor to the pamphlet *Debate at the Lane*

Seminary, Cincinnati: Speech of James A. Thome, of Kentucky, Delivered at the Annual Meeting of the American Anti-Slavery Society, May 6, 1834 (Boston: Garrison & Knapp, 1834).

openly abolitionist congressman: Reinhard O. Johnson, *The Liberty Party, 1840–1848: Antislavery Third-Party Politics in the United States* (Baton Rouge: Louisiana State University Press, 2009); Sewell, *Ballots for Freedom,* 47.

most numerous denomination: Holt, *Forging a Majority,* 54.

Weld showed up: See the introduction by Arthur W. Thompson in Joshua R. Giddings, *The Exiles of Florida* (Paderborn: Outlook Verlag, 2020); Montagna, "Ohio, Evangelical Religion," 9–12.

where to focus: Montagna, "Ohio, Evangelical Religion," 9–12.

145 *became abolition central:* Sean Wilentz, *The Rise of American Democracy* (New York: W. W. Norton, 2006), 550; Corey M. Brooks, *Liberty Power: Antislavery Third Parties and the Transformation of American Politics* (Chicago: University of Chicago Press, 2016), 55.

the gag rule: Montagna, *Ohio,* "Evangelical Religion," 17.

hour to restore order: Brooks, *Liberty Power,* 55; Montagna, "Ohio, Evangelical Religion," 17.

did not back down: Joanne B. Freeman, *The Field of Blood: Violence in Congress and the Road to Civil War* (London: Picador, 2019), 66–69, 115–16. Freeman's history expounds in detail on the way the southerners used the threat and manifestation of violence to silence the representatives from less bellicose regions of the North and how the northerners suffered from their humiliation in a culture dominated by notions of honor.

146 *returned to the fold:* Montagna, "Ohio, Evangelical Religion," 18.

abolitionists should not vote: Montagna, "Ohio, Evangelical Religion," 19.

an actual political party: Sewell, *Ballots for Freedom,* 107–12.

Liberty Party was consistent: Sewell, *Ballots for Freedom,* 99–100.

survival and political freedoms: Sewell, *Ballots for Freedom,* 101.

147 *rest of the states:* Foner, *Free Soil,* 9.

was a sectional party: Brooks, *Liberty Power,* 79.

Democrat James K. Polk: Daniel Walker Howe, *What Hath God Wrought: The Transformation of America, 1815–1848* (Oxford: Oxford University Press, 2007).

17. The Cracks Widen

148 *Remond, or both:* Lampe, *Freedom's Voice,* 108–9.

"tyrants unto blood": The Liberator, July 1, 1842.

"truly eloquent in delivery": The Liberator, July 8, 1842.

149 *behind the scenes:* Blight, *Frederick Douglass,* 119.

a critical word: Blight, *Frederick Douglass,* 119.

"but not large": Lampe, *Freedom's Voice,* 119–21.

Garrison readily acknowledged: The Liberator, July 15, 1842.

upstate New York: Lampe, *Freedom's Voice,* 140–43.

even to "arms": Lampe, *Freedom's Voice,* 140.

argue with their competitors: Lampe, *Freedom's Voice,* 143.

attend their meetings: Lampe, *Freedom's Voice,* 143.

150 *Garrisonian purist:* Peter Hughes, "George Bradburn," *Dictionary of Unitarian & Universalist Biography,* www.uudb.org.

unrelated to abolition: Mitchell K. Jones, "Hunting for Harmony: The Skaneateles Community and Communitism in Upstate New York, 1825–1853" (master's thesis, SUNY Brockport, 2020), 4–6.

an anti-property meeting: Lampe, *Freedom's Voice,* 176–77.

152   *not yield the stage:* Lampe, *Freedom's Voice,* 176–77.
153   *campaign and resign:* Lampe, *Freedom's Voice,* 177.
      wrote to Maria Weston Chapman: Friedman, *Gregarious Saints,* 6.
      *informal Society meetings: Proceedings of the American Anti-Slavery Society at Its Second
      Decade* (New York: American Anti-Slavery Society, 1854), 31.
      "could untie a garter": McFeely, *Frederick Douglass,* 107; Pease and Pease, *Bound with
      Them in Chains,* 29, citing a letter from Lewis Tappan to Gamaliel Bailey, October 26,
      1843.
      postage for private letters: Richard R. John Jr., "Private Mail Delivery in the United States
      During the Nineteenth Century: A Sketch," *Business and Economic History* 15 (1986):
      135–47.
      "from everyone?" she wondered: Maria Chapman Weston to William Lloyd Garrison, Au-
      gust 4, 1843.
      comfort his friend: Edmund Quincy to Maria Weston Chapman, June 20, 1842.
154   *Collins, "Cor. Secretary":* John Anderson Collins to Maria Weston Chapman and Caro-
      line Weston, February 28, 1842.
      well worth taking: Edmund Quincy to Maria Weston Chapman, June 20, 1842.
      utopian collective community: William Hinds, *American Communities and Co-Operative
      Colonies* (Chicago: Charles Kerr & Company, 1908), 293–94; McFeely, *Frederick Doug-
      lass,* 104–5.
155   *"everything in its place":* Abby Kelley Foster to Maria Weston Chapman, June 28, 1843.
      "the agents sky high": Abby Kelley Foster to Maria Weston Chapman, August 2, 1843.
      "like slavery": Abby Kelley Foster to Maria Weston Chapman, August 12, 1843.
      "and to himself": Eunice Messenger Collins to Maria Weston Chapman, August 15,
      1843.
      Douglass on August 19: Frederick Douglass to Maria Weston Chapman, September 10,
      1843.
156   *another white abolitionist:* Maria Weston Chapman to Francis Jackson, August 31, 1843.
      "approved of every word": Weston Chapman says she wrote to "Douglass and Remond,"
      so there may have been two letters, which are lost to history.
      gentle admonition: Frederick Douglass to Maria Weston Chapman, September 10, 1843.
      money for his wife: Blight, *Frederick Douglass,* 129.
      "he had been appointed": Abby Kelley Foster to Maria Weston Chapman, August 28,
      1843.
157   *"very sorry for it":* Maria Weston Chapman to David Lee Child, August 24, 1843.
      Kelley on September 3: Maria Weston Chapman to Abby Kelley Foster, September 3,
      1843.
158   *replied on September 10:* Frederick Douglass to Maria Weston Chapman, September 10,
      1843.
159   *"I think so still":* Douglass, *Life and Times* (1881), 282–83.
      his brother-in-law: Mayer, *All on Fire,* 323.
      Boston antislavery operation: William Lloyd Garrison to Maria Weston Chapman, July 7,
      1843.
      mother-in-law's leg: Mayer, *All on Fire,* 323–24.
160   *"side of the story":* William Lloyd Garrison to Maria Weston Chapman, September 9,
      1843.
      to visit his family: Lampe, *Freedom's Voice,* 180.
      lecturers in the park: Lampe, *Freedom's Voice,* 180–81.
      Liberty Party faction: Sinha, *Slave's Cause,* 319.
161   *"than live . . . slaves":* Blight, *Frederick Douglass,* 132; Henry Highland Garnet, "An Ad-
      dress to the Slaves of the United States of America," 1843, www.blackpast.org.

officially from the convention: Blight, *Frederick Douglass,* 133.
Indiana with George Bradburn: Blight, *Frederick Douglass,* 135.
"here in the West": Abraham Brooke to Maria Weston Chapman, October 5, 1843.
to different gatherings: Abraham Brooke to Maria Weston Chapman, October 10, 1843.

18. Douglass Writes and Garrison Publishes

162　*nine such stories:* "North American Slave Narratives," *Documenting the American South,* accessed April 27, 2015.
their fourth baby: Blight, *Frederick Douglass,* 137.
to the slave catchers: Henry David Thoreau to *The Liberator,* March 28, 1845, reporting on Phillips's speech.
his enslavers, altered: James Williams, *Narrative of James Williams, an American Slave, Who Was for Several Years a Driver on a Cotton Plantation in Alabama* (New York: American Anti-Slavery Society; Boston: Isaac Knapp, 1838); James G. Birney and Lewis Tappan, "Alabama Beacon Versus James Williams," *The Emancipator,* August 30, 1838; Lara Langer Cohen, *The Fabrication of American Literature: Fraudulence and Antebellum Print Culture* (Philadelphia: University of Pennsylvania Press, 2012), 118–21; Hank Trent, *Narrative of James Williams, an American Slave* (Baton Rouge: Louisiana State University Press, 2013). Cohen tells the story from the assumption that the book was a fabrication; Trent purports to have validated the essentials of Williams's story. For our purposes, it does not matter if it was true or false or partially true and partially false. The controversy meant that Douglass dared to reveal the real names of his enslavers, risking his kidnapping and return to slavery.

163　*world of the slave narrative:* Trent, *Narrative of James Williams,* Kindle loc. 678–84; Cohen, *Fabrication of American Literature,* 118–19, relates that suspicion was almost ubiquitous, including suspicion of Douglass.
Whittier was also boarding: Trent, *Narrative of James Williams,* Kindle loc. 109–86.
by John Greenleaf Whittier: Trent, *Narrative of James Williams,* Kindle loc. 703.
in the abolition press: Trent, *Narrative of James Williams,* Kindle loc. 206, citing Birney and Tappan, "Alabama Beacon Versus James Williams."

164　*impeach Rittenhouse's source:* Trent, *Narrative of James Williams,* Kindle loc. 265–323.
"sale of the work": Birney and Tappan, "Alabama Beacon Versus James Williams"; Statement, *The Emancipator,* reprinted in the *African Repository and Colonial Journal* (June 1839): 163.
Abolition, a Sedition: Calvin Colton, *Abolition a Sedition, by a Northern Man* (Philadelphia: Geo. Donahue, 1839).
letter by Wendell Phillips: McFeely, *Frederick Douglass,* 117.
preface to Douglass's book: The Liberator, May 9, 1845.

165　*"No. 25 Cornhill, 1845":* Douglass, *Narrative,* title page.
"through the press": Mayer, *All on Fire,* 350.
"his own production": Douglass, *Narrative,* x.

166　*daily in New York:* Adam Tuchinsky, *Horace Greeley's "New York Tribune": Civil War–Era Socialism and the Crisis of Free Labor* (Ithaca: Cornell University Press, 2009).
"Where is thy brother?": New York Tribune, June 10, 1945.
age of emancipation: David Brion Davis, *The Problem of Slavery in the Age of Emancipation* (New York: Vintage, 2015).

167　*concluded, "a slave":* Douglass, *Narrative,* 2.
"but dangerously so": Douglass, *Narrative,* 47.
"bound to respect": Dred Scott v. Sandford, 60 U.S. (9 How.) 393.

some cases learn Christianity: Dickson D. Bruce Jr., "Politics and Political Philosophy in the Slave Narrative," in *The Cambridge Companion to the African American Slave Narrative* (Cambridge: Cambridge University Press, 2007), 28–43.

horrific physical torture: Bruce, "Politics and Political Philosophy," 29–31.

168 *"hell of slavery":* Douglass, *Narrative,* 6.

his lecturing career: Blight, *Frederick Douglass,* 114.

"you are to fulfill": Frederick Douglass, "The Southern Style of Preaching to Slaves," January 28, 1842.

"he stuffed them": Douglass, *Narrative,* 44.

169 *"his whole life-time":* Foner, *Free Soil,* xxiii.

service by brute force: Bruce, "Politics and Political Philosophy," 28.

"whom we were ranked": Douglass, *Narrative,* 38.

the "slaveocracy": Foner, *Free Soil,* 90.

the rest of America: Foner, *Free Soil,* 90.

copies in four months: "An 1845 Review of Narrative of the Life of Frederick Douglass," *Book Marks,* February 20, 2019.

19. Frederick Douglass, International Superstar and Publisher

170 *two days later:* Lampe, *Freedom's Voice,* 254–55.

"that gentleman's clerk": Lampe, *Freedom's Voice,* 264.

plan a trip abroad: Lampe, *Freedom's Voice,* 276; Douglass, *My Bondage,* 363–64.

171 *at his presence:* The basic facts of Frederick Douglass's journey can be found in Blight, *Frederick Douglass;* McFeely, *Frederick Douglass;* and *The Life and Writings of Frederick Douglass,* 5 vols., ed. Philip S. Foner, vol. 1, *Early Years* (New York: International Publishers, 1950).

an economical measure: McFeely, *Frederick Douglass,* 126.

"was being circulated": Frederick Douglass to William Lloyd Garrison, September 1, 1845.

scene to Garrison: Frederick Douglass to William Lloyd Garrison, September 1, 1845.

free soil of England: Frederick Douglass to William Lloyd Garrison, January 1, 1846.

172 *his British tour:* Frederick Douglass to William Lloyd Garrison, September 1, 1845.

of the marketplace: Tom Chaffin, *Giant's Causeway: Frederick Douglass's Irish Odyssey and the Making of an American Visionary* (Charlottesville: University of Virginia Press, 2014), 101.

his own printshop: Chaffin, *Giant's Causeway,* 99–100.

delegate Lucretia Mott: Chaffin, *Giant's Causeway,* 102–3.

173 *"immoral and inauthentic":* Richard Davis Webb to Maria Weston Chapman, ca. 1842–1844.

Ireland for his health: William Lloyd Garrison to Richard Davis Webb, February 1842.

"tell me about him": Richard Davis Webb to Maria Weston Chapman, ca. 1842–1844.

Foreign Anti-Slavery Association: Clare Midgley, *Women Against Slavery: The British Campaigns, 1780–1870* (New York: Routledge, 1995), 122.

sorry he was not well: Mrs. Mary Welsh, Edinburgh [Scotland], to Maria Weston Chapman, October 30, 1843.

"greatness of his design": Richard Davis Webb to Maria Weston Chapman, September 2, 1844.

174 *"unworthy of him":* Richard Davis Webb to Maria Weston Chapman, September 17, 1844.

"expenses of his journey": Richard Davis Webb to Maria Weston Chapman, June 2, 1845.

"philanthropic enterprise": This discussion is drawn from Maria Weston Chapman to Richard Davis Webb, June 29, 1845–May 1, 1846.

"strong enough to endure it": Maria Weston Chapman to Richard Davis Webb, June 29, 1845–May 1, 1846.

"telling him myself": Maria Weston Chapman to Richard Davis Webb, fragment dated June 29, 1845.

175 *"friends of my own":* Leigh Fought, *Women in the World of Frederick Douglass* (Oxford: Oxford University Press, 2017), 78.

"true blue": Richard Davis Webb to Maria Weston Chapman, September 16, 1845.

176 *Webb mused:* Richard Davis Webb to Maria Weston Chapman, September 30, 1845.

"in jest or correct": Richard Davis Webb to Maria Weston Chapman, October 12, 1845.

177 *hoping he would return:* Jane Jennings to Maria Weston Chapman, November 25, 1845.

"has ever visited": Isabel Jennings to Maria Weston Chapman, undated.

family and friends: Frederick Douglass to Isabel Jennings, September 22, 1846.

"of benevolent objects": Frederick Douglass to Richard Dowden, November 11, 1845.

Irish movement politics: A good short analysis of the backdrop to Frederick Douglass's Irish tour appears in Chaffin, *Giant's Causeway,* passim.

178 *"a heart of iron":* Frederick Douglass to William Lloyd Garrison, February 26, 1846.

"had joined together": Chaffin, *Giant's Causeway,* loc. 2249–50, citing *Limerick Reporter,* November 11, 1845.

star orator advice: Richard Davis Webb to Maria Weston Chapman, November 16, 1845.

leg of his tour: Chaffin, *Giant's Causeway,* loc. 2361, citing a November 1845 letter from Richard Webb to Frederick Douglass which is not located.

Douglass refused: Frederick Douglass to Richard Webb, November 10, 1845.

"man of one idea": Frederick Douglass to Richard Webb, November 10, 1845.

refused to accommodate: Chaffin, *Giant's Causeway,* loc. 321.

179 *"all will go well":* Extracts from three letters from Maria Weston Chapman to Richard Davis Webb, June 29, 1845. Excerpts sent to abolitionist Samuel May include a supposed letter from Weston Chapman to Webb, June 29, 1846.

"the way of temptation": Maria Weston Chapman to Richard Davis Webb, February 24, 1846.

to Weston Chapman himself: Frederick Douglass to Maria Weston Chapman, March 29, 1846.

180 *clever little missive:* Edmund Quincy to Caroline Weston, August 14, 1842.

181 *breach of "confidence":* Richard Davis Webb to Maria Weston Chapman, May 16, 1846.

"his best friends": Chaffin, *Giant's Causeway,* loc. 1434–35; Blight, *Frederick Douglass,* 146–49. The voluminous correspondence among the principals is maddeningly opaque at the time, but Douglass's visit in December might have been the time when Richard Webb decided to share with Douglass what his Boston managers really thought about him. Webb says he dropped the news on Douglass as soon as he and Buffum arrived in Ireland; Richard Davis Webb to Maria Weston Chapman, May 16, 1846. But Webb's version seems unlikely, as no one said a word about it until nine months later, in February 1847. In February and March, however, letters flew fast and furiously. Douglass was capable of holding his fire, as we saw when he clashed with Collins, but it's doubtful he waited nine months to express himself when offended.

182 *harm their friendship:* Frederick Douglass to Maria Weston Chapman, August 18, 1846.

not once but twice: Frederick Douglass to William Lloyd Garrison, May 23, 1846.

had good reason: Sinha, *Slave's Cause,* 290.

slaveholding American branches: Frederick Douglass to William Lloyd Garrison, May 23, 1846.

Joseph Sturge in Birmingham: Chaffin, *Giant's Causeway,* 169.

183 *"SEND BACK THE MONEY":* Frederick Douglass to William Lloyd Garrison, April 16, 1846.

"North Buxton, Bart.": Frederick Douglass to William Lloyd Garrison, May 23, 1846.

184 *"bloody system of slavery":* Frederick Douglass to Maria Weston Chapman, August 18, 1846.

early in his career: Frederick Douglass to William A. White, July 30, 1846.

intent on recapturing him: Boston Journal, September 13, 1886.

vulnerable to being seized: Douglass, *My Bondage,* 363–64.

a sitting duck: Frederick Douglass to William A. White, July 30, 1846.

option for Douglass: Much of what follows comes from Leigh Fought, "Anna Murray, Mrs. Frederick Douglass 1810–1848," chap. 2 of *Women in the World of Frederick Douglass.*

185 *any public record:* Rosetta Douglass Sprague, "Anna Murray Douglass—As I Recall Her," *Journal of Negro History* 8, no. 1 (January 1923): 93–101.

his family's doings: Blight, *Frederick Douglass,* 164–65.

"husband, and father!": Frederick Douglass to Lydia Dennett, April 17, 1857.

spirits were low: Chaffin, *Giant's Causeway,* loc. 3057.

186 *"barter in human flesh":* Ida B. Wells, *Crusade for Justice: The Autobiography of Ida B. Wells* (Chicago: University of Chicago Press, 1996), 162.

buying his freedom: Chaffin, *Giant's Causeway,* 214.

deal with his enslaver: Blight, *Frederick Douglass,* 171.

"personal safety": William Lloyd Garrison to Helen Garrison, September 17, 1846.

187 *"power over you":* Henry C. Wright to Frederick Douglass, December 12, 1846.

Douglass's answer to Wright: Frederick Douglass to Henry C. Wright, December 22, 1846.

188 *"sympathy of the community": The Liberator,* March 19, 1847.

thundered, in sum: The Liberator, January 8, 1847.

189 *"The Ransom of Douglass": The Liberator,* January 15, 1847.

Anti-Slavery Society in 1833: The Liberator, March 5, 1847.

"property in man": William Lloyd Garrison, "Declaration of Sentiments of the American Anti-Slavery Convention," Philadelphia, December 6, 1833.

191 *as his bodily independence:* Fought, *Women in the World of Frederick Douglass,* 93.

"aid to a great cause": Frederick Douglass to Mary Howitt, May 10, 1847, in Sarah Meer, *American Claimants: The Transatlantic Romance, c. 1820–1920* (Oxford: Oxford University Press, 2020), n. 124; *Howitt's Journal,* June 19, 1847, 50.

with fan mail: Mary Estlin to Maria Weston Chapman, October 18, 1847; Isabel Jennings to Maria Weston Chapman, August 2, 1847.

"interest in his welfare": Mary Brady to Maria Weston Chapman, ca. 1847.

192 *his new venture:* McFeely, *Frederick Douglass,* 148. McFeely offers no citation to support his explosive assertion. No such letter exists in the comprehensive collection in the Boston Public Library, nor has any other scholar ever cited one.

"teacher and a thinker": James McCune Smith, introduction to Douglass, *My Bondage,* 11.

193 Anti-Slavery Standard: Mayer, *All on Fire,* 373; Patsy Brewington Perry, "Before *The North Star:* Frederick Douglass' Early Journalistic Career," *Phylon* (1974): 98.

having his own paper: Frederick Douglass to William Lloyd Garrison, July 1, 1847, in *The Liberator,* July 23, 1847.

Boston movement unparalleled: The Liberator, July 23, 1847.

194 *"worth while to pay him":* Edmund Quincy to Caroline Weston, July 2, 1847.

"niggers in there": Frederick Douglass to William Lloyd Garrison, January 1, 1846, in

Foner, *The Life and Writings of Frederick Douglass*, 1:125. The Foner edition, published in 1950, uses dashes instead of printing out the full word. But the original letter, as it appears in *The Liberator* (July 23, 1847), uses the full word.

195   *"all the* wool": Edmund Quincy to Caroline Weston, July 30, 1847.

"their loving regards": William Lloyd Garrison to Richard D. Webb, July 1, 1847.

their western jaunt: William Lloyd Garrison to Helen Benson Garrison, August 9, 1847.

of the "rowdies": William Lloyd Garrison to Helen Benson Garrison, August 13, 1847.

stagecoach to Pittsburgh: William Lloyd Garrison to Helen Benson Garrison, August 13, 1847.

196   *"all parts of Great Britain!":* William Lloyd Garrison to Helen Benson Garrison, August 13, 1847.

"great energy and spirit": William Lloyd Garrison to Helen Benson Garrison, August 16, 1847.

abolitionist Pittsburgh: Brooks, *Liberty Power,* 81.

paper of Douglass's own: Blight, *Frederick Douglass,* 188.

Thomas Van Rensselaer: Frederick Douglass to Sydney H. Gay, August 13, 1847, in Foner, *The Life and Writings of Frederick Douglass*, vol. 5, *Supplemental Volume, 1844–1860* (New York: International Publishers, 1975), 277–78.

"strength and cheer": Frederick Douglass to Sydney H. Gay, August 20, 1847.

"anti-slavery revival": Frederick Douglass to Sydney H. Gay, August 31, 1847.

within a year: Frederick Douglass to Sydney H. Gay, September 17 and 26, 1847.

197   *heartland, the East:* William Lloyd Garrison to Helen Eliza Garrison, August 28, 1847.

graduation at Oberlin College: William Lloyd Garrison to Helen Eliza Garrison, August 28, 1847.

Black doctor, Dr. Peck: Benjamin Quarles, "Breach Between Douglass and Garrison," *Journal of Negro History* (April 1938): 144–54.

198   *might be typhoid:* Mayer, *All on Fire,* 371; William Lloyd Garrison to Helen Eliza Garrison, September 18, 1847.

"worn with our labours": Frederick Douglass to Sydney H. Gay, September 17, 1847.

to go to Buffalo: William Lloyd Garrison to Helen Eliza Garrison, September 18, 1847.

"leaving him at all": Frederick Douglass to Sydney H. Gay, September 26, 1847.

pay his doctors' bills: William Lloyd Garrison to Helen Eliza Garrison, October 19 and 20, 1847, in *Letters of William Lloyd Garrison,* 530–33.

"a bed of illness?": William Lloyd Garrison to Helen Eliza Garrison, October 20, 1847.

199   *two had arranged:* Samuel Joseph May to William Lloyd Garrison, October 4, 1847.

on September 17: Quarles, "Breach Between Douglass and Garrison," 147.

one of Douglass's sponsors: "Prospectus for an anti-slavery paper to be entitled North Star," ca. 1847, New York Public Library.

the stronger brand: William Lloyd Garrison to Helen Eliza Garrison, October 20, 1847.

"profitable one for himself": National *Anti-Slavery Standard,* September 30, 1847.

"decision in Boston": William Lloyd Garrison to Helen Eliza Garrison, October 20, 1847.

200   *British friends had sent him:* Frederick Douglass to Julia Griffiths, October 13, 1847.

cloaked in some shadow: Janet Douglas, "A Cherished Friendship: Julia Griffiths Crofts and Frederick Douglass," *Slavery & Abolition: A Journal of Slave and Post-Slave Studies* (2012): 265–66.

No one knows: Douglas, "Cherished Friendship," 266. Philip Foner describes Julia Griffiths as "a close friend of Wilberforce," though this seems unlikely. Foner, *Life and Writings of Frederick Douglass,* 1:87.

showed him around: Fought, *Women in the World of Frederick Douglass,* 93.

"camellia in your coat?": Julia Griffiths to Frederick Douglass, March 26, 1877.

into Douglass's enterprise: Frederick Douglass to Jonathan Carr, November 1, 1847.

201 *her Quaker friends:* Fought, *Women in the World of Frederick Douglass,* 78.

the Contessa: Fought, *Women in the World of Frederick Douglass,* 100.

"as it now does": Fought, *Women in the World of Frederick Douglass,* 94.

his newspaper there: Frederick Douglass to Amy Post, October 28, 1847.

the first issue: The North Star, December 3, 1847.

205 *on Douglass's radar:* John Stauffer, *The Black Hearts of Men: Radical Abolitionists and the Transformation of Race* (Cambridge: Harvard University Press, 2002), 140–43.

signed off, "Gerrit Smith": Gerrit Smith letter to Frederick Douglass, December 8, 1847.

produce the newspaper: McFeely, *Frederick Douglass,* 153.

206 *publish in their paper:* McFeely, *Frederick Douglass,* 152.

Douglass fretted: Frederick Douglass to Julia Griffiths, April 28, 1848.

the antislavery fairs: Fought, *Women in the World of Frederick Douglass,* 103–4.

"management of [his] affairs": Maria Weston Chapman to Frederick Douglass, September 22, 1848.

207 *what you say and write:* Anne Weston to Caroline Weston, November 12, 1848. Anne's letter to Caroline reports the fallout from Maria's sniping at Douglass to her English contacts again.

"an important enterprise": Joseph Lupton to Maria Weston Chapman, September 21, 1848. Weston Chapman's original letter to him is lost.

"[Charles L.] Remond": William Lloyd Garrison to Sydney H. Gay, April 27, 1848, in *Letters,* 552.

"opportunities to speak": William Lloyd Garrison to Sydney H. Gay, May 1, 1848.

member of the clique: William Lloyd Garrison to *The Liberator,* May 8, 1849, in *Letters,* 614.

20. Slave Power Rises and Abolition Power Rises

211 *national slavery: "disunion":* William Lloyd Garrison to Henry Wright, October 1, 1844.

remote and empty land: This Texas history is heavily drawn from Joel Sibley's foundational book about the centrality of Texas to abolition, *Storm over Texas: The Annexation Controversy and the Road to Civil War* (Oxford: Oxford University Press, 2005).

212 *evasive on the subject:* Brooks, *Liberty Power,* 96–98. Corey Brooks's history of the impact of the abolitionist third parties is foundational and the source of much of the insight in this section.

213 *of the "slave power":* Ohio senator Thomas Morris is often credited with coining the phrase "slave power." Jonathan H. Earle, *Jacksonian Antislavery and the Politics of Free Soil, 1824–1854* (Chapel Hill: University of North Carolina Press, 2004), 18.

the abolitionist cause: Brooks, *Liberty Power,* 96, n., 46, citing a letter from Lewis Tappan to his brother Benjamin.

in the two-party system: Corey Brooks, in *Liberty Power,* and Joel Sibley, in *Storm over Texas,* have led and exemplify this reexamination of the role of politics in sharpening the divide over slavery.

against annexing Texas: Brooks, *Liberty Power,* 98.

sponsoring Wilmot's Proviso: Brooks, *Liberty Power,* 106–10.

214 *spread of slavery:* Brooks, *Liberty Power,* 110–16.

the most extreme position: Bruce Ambacher, "The Pennsylvania Origins of Popular Sovereignty," *Pennsylvania Magazine of History and Biography* 98, no. 3 (July 1974): 341.

with helpless Mexico: Brooks, *Liberty Power,* 109.

abolitionist third party: Salmon P. Chase to Charles Cleveland, August 29, 1840.

215   *call themselves "abolitionists":* Brooks, *Liberty Power,* 85.
      Liberty standard-bearer: Brooks, *Liberty Power,* 95.
      emancipation and equality: Brooks, *Liberty Power,* 101.
      started to come loose: Brooks, *Liberty Power,* 135–40.
216   *dissidents to his third party:* Sewell, *Ballots for Freedom,* 135–36.
217   *"prefer Freedom to Slavery":* Brooks, *Liberty Power,* 140.
      "Freedom" in August: Sewell, *Ballots for Freedom,* 150.
      had equal say: Sewell, *Ballots for Freedom,* 156. Much of this discussion is from original
      sources in Sewell, *Ballots for Freedom,* 156–58.
218   *pursue the fugitives:* Calvin Schermerhorn, *Unrequited Toil: A History of United States*
      Slavery (Cambridge: Cambridge University Press, 2018), 175.
      cure for his health: According to Mayer, *All on Fire,* 385, "Garrison hoped to restore his
      health."
219   *"all the free States":* William Lloyd Garrison to Helen Eliza Benson Garrison, July 18,
      1848.
      Garrison's enthusiasm waned: William Lloyd Garrison to Edmund Quincy, August 10,
      1848
      "take great care": William Lloyd Garrison to Edmund Quincy, August 10, 1848.
      "present as delegates": The Liberator, August 18, 1848.
      the letter read: The Liberator, August 22, 1848.
      the Charleston Courier: *Charleston Courier,* February 1, 1849.
221   *less than a third: 1850 Census: The Seventh Census of the United States,* www.census.gov.
      resounding applause: The National Era, August 17, 1848.
      "this free soil *movement": The North Star,* August 21, 1848.
222   *"fiery furnace":* S. R. Ward, letter to *The North Star,* September 1, 1848.
      "Movement done?": The North Star, May 25, 1849.
      could not pick a leader: Corey Brooks, *Liberty Power,* 155.

21. The Private Lives of Public Activists

224   *Ohio state legislature:* Sewell, *Ballots for Freedom,* 205–7.
      mainstream politician to Washington: Sewell, *Ballots for Freedom,* 210.
225   *moved to Paris:* Chambers, *Weston Sisters,* 132.
      before, in 1842: Joan Goodwin, "Maria Weston Chapman and the Weston Sisters," *Uni-*
      tarian Universalist History & Heritage Society, April 27, 2001, uuhhs.org.
      "to the Cause": Clinton, "Maria Weston Chapman," 153.
      a family fortune: Chambers, *Weston Sisters,* 86.
      school in Weymouth: Chambers, *Weston Sisters,* 82–86.
      with the family: Maria Weston Chapman to Elizabeth Pease, January 15, 1848.
      precincts of European society: Maria Weston Chapman to Mary Estlin, January 24, 1852,
      describing abolitionists fearing social stigma, "and this in free England!"; Mayer, *All on*
      Fire, 353.
226   *he mourned:* William Lloyd Garrison to Elizabeth Pease Nichol, May 3, 1848.
      he acknowledged it was: William Lloyd Garrison to Maria Weston Chapman, July 19,
      1848.
      came to him instead: Historian Leigh Fought has done an amazing job reclaiming the
      story of Julia Griffiths and Frederick Douglass, as well as the other "women in the world
      of Frederick Douglass," which is the source of much material in this section.
      arrival in New York: Frederick Douglass to Isaac and Amy Post, April 22, 1849.

situation is palpable: Isaac Post to Amy Post, May 15, 1849.

227 *Douglass had written her:* Fee, "To No One"; Frederick Douglass to Julia Griffiths, April 28, 1848.

state of The North Star*:* Frederick Douglass to Julia Griffiths, April 28, 1848.

the paper afloat: Meaghan M. Fritz and Frank E. Fee Jr., "To Give the Gift of Freedom: Gift Books and the War on Slavery," *American Periodicals: A Journal of History, Criticism, and Bibliography* 23, no. 1 (2013): 61–62.

financial manager: Isaac Post to Amy Kirby Post, May 7, 1849.

Douglass was furious: Frederick Douglass to Amy Kirby Post, September 11, 1849.

the Liberty wing: Frank E. Fee Jr., "To No One More Indebted" *Journalism History* 37, no. 1 (Spring 2011): 12–26.

exquisitely discreet: Fought, *Women in the World of Frederick Douglass,* 104–5.

enslaver Hugh Auld: The Liberator, September 22, 1848.

"travelling in this country": Anne Warren Weston to Maria Weston Chapman, June 5, 1849.

228 *"politely as you can":* Debora Weston to Anne Warren Weston, April 21, 1850.

drum up interest: Fought, *Women in the World of Frederick Douglass,* 114–15.

on it for help: Fought, *Women in the World of Frederick Douglass,* 113.

sister on either arm: Fought, *Women in the World of Frederick Douglass,* 106–9.

shelter of the vessel: Fought, *Women in the World of Frederick Douglass,* 110–11.

old news to Douglass: Both Fought and Blight have discussed this well and at length; see Fought, *Women in the World of Frederick Douglass,* 111–12; and Blight, *Frederick Douglass,* 204–5.

229 *was their equal: The North Star,* June 18, 1850; *The Times* (London), June 29, 1850, in Foner, *The Life and Writings of Frederick Douglass.* 2:131.

"still more so": Selected Journals of Caroline Healey Dall, ed. Helen Deese (Charlottesville: University of Virginia Press, 2006), 472.

Nell wondered: William Cooper Nell to Amy Kirby Post, July 15, 1850.

Eliza was married: Betsey Cowles to Amy Kirby Post, December 1, 1850.

all over Rochester: Frederick Douglass to Samuel D. Porter. January 12, 1852, in Blassingame et al., *Frederick Douglass Papers,* 512–13.

230 *a terrible loss:* Mayer, *All on Fire,* 386–87.

Garrison's personal support: Mayer, *All on Fire,* 386–87.

22. Compromise Makes Conflict Worse

231 *Radical Abolition Party:* Stacey M. Robertson, *Parker Pillsbury: Radical Abolitionist, Male Feminist* (Ithaca: Cornell University Press, 2000).

"bloody system of slavery": Frederick Douglass, "The Union, Slavery, and Abolitionist Petitions: Addresses Delivered in Hingham, Massachusetts," November 4, 1841.

232 *"republican form of government":* Robert Pierce Forbes, *The Missouri Compromise and Its Aftermath* (Chapel Hill: University of North Carolina Press, 2007), loc. 495. Much of this paragraph is drawn from Forbes's masterly revisionist history.

slavery in the territories: Forbes, *Missouri Compromise,* loc. 575.

233 *returning the runaways:* Brooks, *Liberty Power,* 162–65.

234 *speed of electricity:* Freeman, *Field of Blood,* 169–70. Joanne Freeman first called this to my attention. It is additive to the impact of steam printing and cheap paper, described earlier.

235 *"authority over the domain":* William H. Seward, "Speech on the Admission of Califor-

nia Delivered in the Senate of the United States, March 11, 1850" (Washington, D.C., 1850). See also *The Works of William Henry Seward*, ed. George E. Baker, vol. 1 (New York: Redfield, 1853), 51–93.

"and therefore perpetual": Seward, *Works*, 1:108.

throughout the country: Sinha, *Slave's Cause*, 491.

reproducing Seward's text: The Liberator, July 19, 1850.

"what they have done?": Green-Mountain Freeman, August 1, 1850.

236 *a thousand dollars:* "The Fugitive Slave Law of 1850," *Bill of Rights in Action* (Winter 2019).

novel Uncle Tom's Cabin: "Today in History: June 5—Uncle Tom's Cabin," Library of Congress.

across the North: John Frick, *Uncle Tom's Cabin on the American Stage and Screen* (New York: Palgrave Macmillan, 2012), xii and passim.

sent back to Baltimore: Hamlet's story is related in Paul Finkelman, ed., *Fugitive Slaves and the American Courts: The Pamphlet Literature* (New York: Garland, 1988). The story of the impact of the Fugitive Slave Law is well told in DelBanco, *The War Before the War*, 264–85.

238 *refusal to convict:* Gary Collison, "'This Flagitious Offense': Daniel Webster and the Shadrach Rescue Cases, 1851–1852," *New England Quarterly* 68, no. 4 (December 1995): 609–25.

streets of Boston: Mayer, *All on Fire*, 405.

sovereign's positive law: DelBanco, *The War Before the War*, 278.

sidesteps all these issues: James W. Stone, *Trial of Thomas Sims* (Boston: Wm. S. Damrell & Co, 1851).

during the Civil War: "'The Whole Land Is Full of Blood': The Thomas Sims Case," Boston African American National Historic Site, National Park Service.

239 Prigg v. Pennsylvania *in 1842:* Ronald Osborn, "William Lloyd Garrison and the United States Constitution: The Political Evolution of an American Radical," *Journal of Law and Religion* (2008): 80.

"friends of freedom": The Liberator, June 6, 1851.

23. Douglass Recruits the Constitution

240 *political activist position:* The historian Paul Finkelman has very thoroughly laid out an intellectual road map of Douglass's thinking beyond the context of the fraught relationships in which the change was embedded. In "Frederick Douglas's Constitution: From Garrisonian Abolitionist to Lincoln Republican," *Missouri Law Review* (2016): 1. His article alerted me to the January 1850 debate and reinforced my understanding of the relationship between nonvoting and nonresistance.

all of its provisions: C. H. Chase to Frederick Douglass, January 23, 1849.

241 *"pro-slavery instrument":* The North Star, February 9, 1849.

"than has been done": Gerrit Smith to Frederick Douglass, February 19, 1849.

"print it," he said: Gerrit Smith to Frederick Douglass, March 16, 1849.

essay on the subject: The North Star, March 16, 1849.

242 *subject with Gerrit Smith:* Frederick Douglass, "Is the Constitution Pro-Slavery? A Debate Between Frederick Douglass, Charles C. Burleigh, Gerrit Smith, Parker Pillsbury, Samuel Ringgold Ward, and Stephen S. Foster in Syracuse, New York," January 17, 1850, in Finkelman, "Frederick Douglass's Constitution."

Smith was undeterred: Gerrit Smith to Frederick Douglass, March 30, 1849.

"not yet seen them": Foner, *The Life and Writings of Frederick Douglass,* 1:377.

turning Douglass's head: Blight, *Frederick Douglass,* 214; William Powell in the *National Anti-Slavery Standard,* August 14, 1851.

243   *shared love of gardening:* Stauffer, *Black Hearts,* 162.

"hate the colored race": Gerrit Smith to Frederick Douglass, June 1, 1850.

was "well supported": Frederick Douglass to Gerrit Smith, March 30, 1849.

"all are wrong": Frederick Douglass, "Oath to Support the Constitution," *The North Star,* April 5, 1850.

outside the South: After Free Soil, Chase called himself an "independent Democrat," part of his campaign to build an antislavery coalition from existing parties.

244   *and South America:* Salmon P. Chase to Frederick Douglass, May 4, 1850.

"moral," not climatological: Frederick Douglass to Salmon P. Chase, May 30, 1850.

Cazenovia, New York: The story of the Cazenovia Convention was memorialized by a local history buff in a pamphlet published by the local historical society, Hugh Humphreys, "'Agitate! Agitate! Agitate': The Great Fugitive Slave Law Convention and Its Rare Daguerreotype," 1994, Madison County, N.Y., Historical Society.

"plunder, burn and kill": "Letter to American Slaves," *The Anti-Slavery Bugle,* September 28, 1850.

245   *appears in Douglass's paper:* Frederick Douglass, "A Letter to the American Slaves from Those Who Have Fled from American Slavery," *The North Star,* September 5, 1850.

"held in perfect contempt": *The North Star,* September 5, 1850.

246   *themselves as at risk:* Christopher J. Beshara, "The Hidden History of Black Militant Abolitionism in Antebellum Boston," October 9, 2009, Social Science Research Network, ssrn.com.

"with innocent blood": *The Liberator,* October 18, 1850.

terms of resistance: Frederick Douglass, "Resistance to Blood-Houndism: Address Delivered In Syracuse, New York," January 7–8, 1851.

his vulnerable brethren: *The Liberator,* October 11, 1850.

"bosom of the patriarchs!": E.Q., "The Faneuil Hall Riot," *National Anti-Slavery Standard,* reprinted in *The Liberator,* January 10, 1851.

247   *nasty letter from Ireland:* We have only Douglass's reply. Frederick Douglass to Richard Davis Webb, September 12, 1850.

Liberty Party faction: Richard Davis Webb to Anne Warren Weston, November 14, 1848.

248   *"the Constitution are concerned":* Frederick Douglass to Gerrit Smith, May 21, 1851.

no-voting theory: William H. Pease and Jane H. Pease, "Boston Garrisonians and the Problem of Frederick Douglass," *Canadian Journal of History* (Fall 2016): 43.

Constitution as proslavery: Pease and Pease, "Boston Garrisonians," 42.

"cease to be grateful": *The Liberator,* May 23, 1851.

249   *1852 annual meeting:* Blight, *Frederick Douglass,* 217–18.

cause that mattered: Frederick Douglass to Gerrit Smith, May 1, 1851.

"incapable of legalization": Gerrit Smith to Frederick Douglass, June 9, 1851.

change of mind: Henry O. Wagoner to Frederick Douglass, July 31, 1851; George W. F. Mellen to Frederick Douglass, August 11, 1851.

with Garrison's faction: The history of the contretemps appears in Richard Davis Webb to Frederick Douglass, November 17, 1851.

Anti-Slavery Standard: *National Anti-Slavery Standard,* October 2, 1851.

250   *in his own outlet:* *Frederick Douglass' Paper,* October 16, 1851.

intolerance of criticism: *Frederick Douglass' Paper,* November 6, 1851.

"stung to the quick": Emma Mitchell to Maria Weston Chapman, January 1852.

"*better than an enemy*": *Frederick Douglass' Paper*, May 20, 1852.
secretary of the convention: Sewell, *Ballots for Freedom*, 246.
251 *gave up his radicalism:* Blight, *Frederick Douglass*, 252.

24. The Political Divorce

255 *have a proper name: The Liberator*, November 14, 1851.
criticism at fault?: Blight, *Frederick Douglass*, 222.
its heretical views: Mayer, *All on Fire*, 429.
256 *criticizing* The Liberator: *The Liberator*, April 22, 1853.
"*both sides of the Atlantic*": Abby Foster Kelley to William Lloyd Garrison, March 30, 1852.
"*disgrace upon himself*": Maria Weston Chapman to John Bishop Estlin, March 9, 1852.
web of correspondents: Anne Warren Weston to Mary Anne Estlin, April 4, 1852.
"*for business purposes*": Frederick Douglass to Samuel Porter, January 12, 1852.
thrown Julia Griffiths out: Fought, *Women in the World of Frederick Douglass*, 124; Blight, *Frederick Douglass*, 221.
257 *opponent Stephen Foster: Frederick Douglass' Paper*, May 27, 1853.
"*people of this country*": *Frederick Douglass' Paper*, August 19, 1853.
for the May article: Frederick Douglass' Paper, August 19, 1853.
258 "*no special circular*": *Frederick Douglass' Paper*, August 19, 1853.
"*Refuge of Oppression column*": *The Liberator*, September 9, 1853.
"*but it is unavoidable*": William Lloyd Garrison to Samuel Joseph May, September 23, 1853.
join them in Syracuse: Samuel Joseph May to William Lloyd Garrison, September 11, 1853.
the Constitution protected slavery: "The Jerry Rescue and Its Aftermath," Syracuse and the Underground Railroad, Special Collections Research Center, Syracuse University Library.
259 "*apostle of American abolition*": *The Liberator*, November 11, 1853.

25. The Personal Divorce

260 *attacked Douglass personally: National Anti-Slavery Standard*, September 24, 1853.
261 *father was sometimes in:* Fought, *Women in the World of Frederick Douglass*, 115.
ten dollars each: Fought, *Women in the World of Frederick Douglass*, 114–15, 117.
example of the form: Fee, "To No One," 17.
compromises it involved: Julia Griffiths to William Seward, October 11, 1853.
Boston's radical abolition movement: Anne Warren Weston to Maria Weston Chapman, June 5, 1849.
receiving his paper: Julia Griffiths to William Seward, April 8, 1851.
"*on my behalf*": Frederick Douglass to Gerrit Smith, July 14, 1852.
state of its "treasury": Julia Griffiths to Gerrit Smith, October 26, 1852.
262 *fan of Griffiths either:* Fought, *Women in the World of Frederick Douglass*, 118. On several occasions, Griffiths asserted that her advocacy was not to be confused with the nascent women's rights movement going on around her in upstate New York. "I am no 'women's rights,'" she told Gerrit Smith in a report on an antislavery meeting. Julia Griffiths to Gerrit Smith, October 26, 185[?]. The letter probably was written in 1853, because in it

she asked Smith to contribute to the second edition of her *Autographs for Freedom*, which was published later that year.

start a "festival": Fee, "To No One," 16.

"unhappiness in his household": The Liberator, November 23, 1853.

"a whine of persecution": Blight, *Frederick Douglass*, 225.

have the argument: Frederick Douglass to Samuel D. Porter, January 12, 1852.

263   *did not believe her:* The Liberator, December 16, 1853.

"the law of the land": The Liberator, December 16, 1853.

264   *"imply any thing immoral":* The Liberator, December 16, 1853.

"witnesses in Rochester": The Liberator, December 16, 1853.

265   *"the Nigger of it":* Fought, *Women in the World of Frederick Douglass*, 141.

"Miss Jezebel Griffiths": Robertson, *Parker Pillsbury*, 110.

always fragile alliance: Stauffer, *Black Hearts*, 153–54. Stauffer provides an invaluable history of McCune Smith describing the white paternalism he called "Garrisonism." James McCune Smith, editorial, in Ripley, *Black Abolitionist Papers*, 4:261–62; "From Our New York Correspondent," *Frederick Douglass' Paper*, February 16, 1855.

266   *white speakers over Black: Frederick Douglass' Paper*, December 15, 1854.

McCune Smith himself: National Anti-Slavery Standard, December 23, 1854, reprinted in *Frederick Douglass' Paper*, January 19, 1855.

extraordinary editorial in response: Frederick Douglass' Paper, January 26, 1855.

Rochester Ladies' Anti-Slavery Society: Blight, *Frederick Douglass*, 224.

267   *content of the book:* Contemporary collections reveal, however, that "most of the signatures are in facsimile." openlibrary.org/books/OL24367569M/Autographs_for_freedom #editions-list.

before the war: Narrative of the Life of Frederick Douglass, an American Slave, Written by Himself (Cambridge: Harvard University Press. 2009).

knew Abraham Lincoln: Henry Louis Gates Jr. and John Stauffer, "Five Myths About Frederick Douglass," *Washington Post*, February 10, 2017.

(1863–1865): Epilogue: Three Meetings and a Funeral

269   *met the president:* Douglass, *Life and Times* (1892), 421.

270   *"how to defend them":* Frederick Douglass, "Another Word to the Black Man," *Douglass' Monthly*, April 1863.

what whites earned: Beshara, "The Hidden History of Black Militant Abolitionism in Antebellum Boston."

Confederate prisoners of war: Frederick Douglass to George L. Stearns, August 1, 1863.

old Boston Brahmin: John Stauffer, *Giants: The Parallel Lives of Frederick Douglass and Abraham Lincoln* (New York: Twelve, 2008), 12.

Boston sponsor would: Douglass, *Life and Times* (1892), 421.

"a civil reception": Douglass, *Life and Times* (1892), 421.

take him around: Stauffer, *Giants*, 12.

271   *relayed during a speech:* Douglass, "Our Work Is Not Done," speech delivered at the American Anti-Slavery Society in Philadelphia, December 3, 1863.

what they were paid: Douglass, *Life and Times* (1892), 423.

272   *since the war began:* S. C. Gwynne, *Hymns of the Republic: The Story of the Final Year of the American Civil War* (New York: Scribner, 2019), 119.

radical convention: Blight, *Frederick Douglass*, 430.

"and on the battlefield": Frederick Douglass to E. Gilbert, May 23, 1864.

273   *"affect its outcome":* Gwynne, *Hymns of the Republic,* 36.

"come what will": "Interview with Alexander W. Randall and Joseph T. Mills, August 9, 1864," in *The Collected Works of Abraham Lincoln,* vol. 7 (Cabin John, Md.: Wildside Press, 2008), 507.

in refugee camps: Blight, *Frederick Douglass,* 435.

274   *becoming "American citizens":* Douglass, *Life and Times* (1892), 434–35.

faltering northern armies: Blight, *Frederick Douglass,* 437–38.

finally took Atlanta: Jesse Greenspan, "Union Troops Capture Atlanta," *History.com.*

the president's invitation: Blight, *Frederick Douglass,* 438.

275   *witness the occasion:* Blight tells a very moving version of this event in *Frederick Douglass,* 457–60. Much of the rest of this story comes from Douglass, *Life and Times* (1892), 439–42; Stauffer, *Giants,* 276–79.

"and righteous altogether": Abraham Lincoln, "Second Inaugural Address," March 4, 1865.

276   *a "man among men":* Blight, *Frederick Douglass,* 444.

would have been honored: Blight, *Frederick Douglass,* 445.

INDEX

Page numbers in italics refer images.